THE LANGUAGE OF
AFRICAN LITERATURE

THE LANGUAGE OF AFRICAN LITERATURE

Edited by Edmund L. Epstein and Robert Kole
With an Introduction by Edmund L. Epstein

Africa World Press, Inc.

P.O. Box 1892
Trenton, NJ 08607

P.O. Box 48
Asmara, ERITREA

Africa World Press, Inc.

P.O. Box 1892　　　　　　　　P.O. Box 48
Trenton, NJ 08607　　　　　　Asmara, ERITREA

Copyright © 1998 Edmund L. Epstein and Robert Kole

First Printing 1998

All rights reserved. No part of this publication may be reproduced, stored in a retrieval system or transmitted in any form or by any means electronic, mechanical, photocopying, recording or otherwise without the prior written permission of the publisher.

Cover and Book design: Jonathan Gullery

This book is set in New Baskerville and Syntax

Library of Congress Cataloging-in-Publication Data

The Language of African Literature/edited by Edmund L. Epstein & Robert Kole
　　p. cm.
　　Includes bibliographical references.
　　ISBN 0-86543-534-0. – ISBN 0-86543-535-9 (paper: alk. paper)
　　1. African literature–20th century–History and criticism.
　　2. African literature (English)–20th century–History and criticism. 3. Narration (Rhetoric) I. Epstein, Edmund L.
　　II. Kole, Robert.
　　PL8010.L36　　1996.
　　809'.8896' 0904–dc20　　　　　　　　　　　　96-43316
　　　　　　　　　　　　　　　　　　　　　　　　　　CIP

PRINTED IN CANADA

Contents

Introduction ix
Edmund L. Epstein

Literature of the General Area

Language as Sensation: The Use of Poetic and
Evocative Language in Five African Autobiographies 3
Tony E. Afejuku

Translation: a Distinctive Feature of
African Literature in English 19
Oluwole Adejare

West African Literature

Toward a Speech-Act Approach to
Nigerian Literature in English 41
Efurosibina Adegbija

Code-Switching in Soyinka's *The Interpreters* 57
James O. Omole

The Language of Passion in Soyinka's
The Interpreters: A Stylistic Analysis 73
James O. Omole

The Styles of Abiku: Two Related
Diatypes of English..81
Mabel Osakwe

Densely Speaking: To Do Or Not To Do:
A Comparative Stylistic Analysis of Soyinka's
and Clark's Poems 89
Mabel Osakwe

The Syntax and Semantics of "Idanre"
Noun Phrases: A Linguistic Spectacle 103
Mabel Osakwe

The Development of Code in
Soyinka's *The Road:* A Stylistic Analysis 113
Michael Cosser

Rhetorical and Linguistic Games in
Comic Aesthetics 153
Taiwo Oloruntoba-Oju

Indirectness in Discourse: A Study in Paradoxical
Communication Among the Igbos 169
Bertram A. Okolo

D.O. Fagunwa's Narratives:
A Rhetorical Analysis 185
Gabriel A. Ajadi

East African Literature

Lexical Cohesion in Okot p'Bitek's
A Song of Prisoner 205
Ogo A. Ofuani

The Stylistic Significance of the Graphological
Structure of Taban lo Liyong's *Another Nigger Dead* 229
Ogo A. Ofuani

Taban lo Liyong's *The Uniformed Man:* A Reconstructivist
and Metafictional Parody of Modernism 251
F. Odun Balogun

South African Literature
Register as a Function of Contextualization:
A Survey of the Southern African Variety of English 265
Benjamin J. Magura

Contributors 289

Index 291

Permissions

Issues of *Language and Style:an International Journal* in which articles have appeared or are scheduled to appear:

A. Literature of the General Area

Afejuku, Tony E. *Language as Sensation: The Use of Poetic and Evocative Language in Five African Autobiographies.* Vol. 23, No. 2 (Spring 1990):217-226.

Adejare, Oluwole. *Translation: a Distinctive Feature of African Literature in English.* Vol. 20, No. 2 (Spring 1987):145-160.

B. West African Literature

Adegbija, Efurosibina. Toward a Speech-Act Approach to Nigerian Literature in English. Vol. 21, No. 3 (Summer 1988):259-270.

Omole, James O. Code-Switching in Soyinka's *The Interpreters.* Vol 20, No. 4 (Fall 1987): 385-395.

Omole, James O. *The Language of Passion in Soyinka's The Interpreters: A Stylistic Analysis.* Vol. 23, No.1 (Winter 1990): 39-44.

Osakwe, Mabel. *The Styles of Abiku: Two Related Diatypes of English.* Vol. 21, No. 1 (Winter 1988): 98-103.

Osakwe, Mabel. *Densely Speaking: To Do Or Not To Do: A Comparative Stylistic Analysis of Soyinka's and Clark's Poems.* Vol. 25, No.1 (Winter 1992): 3–12.

Osakwe, Mabel. *The Syntax and Semantics of "Idanre" Noun Phrases: A Linguistic Spectacle.* Vol. 24, No. 3 (Summer 1991):255-261.

Cosser, Michael. *The Development of Code in Soyinka's The Road: A Stylistic Analysis.* Vol. 24, No. 1 (Winter 1991): 49-76.

Oloruntoba, Taiwo. *Rhetorical and Linguistic Games in Comic Aesthetics.* Vol. 25, No. 3 (Summer 1992):259–269.

Okolo, Bertram A. *Indirectness in Discourse: A Study in Paradoxical Communication Among the Igbos.* Vol. 23, No. 4 (Fall 1990): 495-505.

Ajadi, Gabriel A. *D.O. Fagunwa's Narratives: A Rhetorical Analysis.* Vol. 25, No. 2 (Spring 1992):131-146.

C. East African Literature

Ofuani, Ogo A. *Lexical Cohesion in Okot p'Bitek's A Song of Prisoner.* Vol. 24, No. 2 (Spring 1991):221-238.

Ofuani, Ogo A. *The Stylistic Significance of the Graphological Structure of Taban lo Liyona's Another Nigger Dead.* Vol. 21, No. 3 (Summer 1988): 301-314.

Balogun, F. Odun. *Taban lo Liyong's The Uniformed Man: A Reconstructivist and Metafictional Parody of Modernism.* Vol. 24, No.3 (Summer 1991):263–271.

D. South African Literature

Magura, Benjamin J. Register as a Function of Contextualization: A Survey of the Southern African Variety of English. Vol. 25, No. 1 (Winter 1992):13–30.

INTRODUCTION

Edmund L. Epstein

The journal in which all of the articles in this volume were originally published, *Language and Style: An International Journal,* will shortly be in its thirtieth year. In the course of its career it has welcomed articles on all aspects of style and all traditions of literature and linguistics. Especially rich has been the harvest of articles on African writers in English. The sixteen articles in the present collection represent only a handful of recent and current issues of the journal; new articles on the subject are constantly arriving and will be published in their turn.

The articles in this book deal with the language structures and narrative conventions of sub-Saharan African authors writing in English. The nature and characteristics of literature in English by African writers are described in two ways. One way employs the most sophisticated means of linguistic and cultural analysis on the works of African writers. The other way analyzes the rich influence of indigenous African languages on African writers in English.

Africa is incredibly rich in languages—over 3,000 indigenous languages by some counts, and many creoles, pidgins, and lingua francas. In addition, many other non-indigenous languages are spoken in Africa, with English as the most prominent. The literature in English from African writers is extremely rich and varied. The main reason for this fertility is the excellent educational system in much of sub-Saharan Africa. English is widely taught and spoken in sub-Saharan Africa: more than 54,000,000 sub-Saharan Africans speak English as their first language, and more than 23,000,000 speak English as their second language.[1] In addition, pidgins and creoles based on English are spoken by millions of sub-Saharan Africans. The major pidgins and creoles include Krio, Gambian Creole, Liberian Creole, and varieties of Pidgin English in Ghana, Togo, Nigeria, Cameroon, and Fernando Po.

English is or has been the official language in many African countries. In West Africa, it is at present (1995) the official language in all six states—Sierra Leone, Ghana, Gambia, Nigeria, Cameroon (with French), and Liberia. In East Africa, English is the official language in four of the six countries—Uganda, Malawi, Zambia, and Zimbabwe. It also plays a prominent part in the other East African states; English was established as the official language of Kenya in 1963, a status it lost in 1974 to Swahili, and it was a joint official language with Swahili in Tanzania until 1967.

Many of the articles in this book describe the effect of indigenous African languages on the varieties of English spoken in sub-Saharan Africa. There are three language families of indigenous languages in Africa—the Afro-Asiatic languages, the Nilo-Kordofanian languages, and the Khoisan languages. The writers of the articles in this book treat only writers from sub-Saharan Africa and linguistic features from the language family to which almost all the sub-Saharan languages belong—the Nilo-Kordofanian.[2] The languages of the other sub-Saharan language family—the Khoisan languages—are not treated.[3] Only one people speaking an Afro-Asiatic language is mentioned—the Hausa, who speak a Chadic language.

Eight of the indigenous sub-Saharan languages provide substratum languages for the varieties of English presented in the literature in English of sub-Saharan Africa. These include four West African Kwa languages—Yoruba, Igbo, Ijo, and Ewe—of the Niger-Congo branch of the Nilo-Kordofanian language family, and four from the Niger-Congo group—the Bantu languages Swahili, Shona, Sotho, and Zulu, spoken mainly in South Africa.[4]

The linguistics faculties of African universities contain some of the most advanced linguists practicing in the fields of literature and linguistics. The authors of articles in this collection are associated with linguistics and literature faculties in many universities, among them the Universities of Ibadan, Benin, Ife, Ilorin, Bendel State University-Abraka, the University of Witwatersrand in South Africa, and Botswana-Garbarone.

The first article in the collection treats writers from all over sub-Saharan Africa and is quite broad in scope: it treats five African novelists from West, East, and Southern Africa—Camara Laye, from Guinea, Wole Soyinka from Nigeria, R. Mugo Gatheru from Kenya, and Ezekiel Mphahlele and Peter Abrahams from South Africa. The use of poetic and evocative language in the works of these five novelists is analyzed, mainly in terms of speech rhythms, incantations, and "musical" intonations.

West African literature is the subject of eleven articles, all of which contain close linguistic and cultural analysis of the literature of the region. While it is the work of Wole Soyinka that occupies center stage in these articles, the linguistic practices of other West African writers such as Chinua Achebe, James P. Clark, D.O. Fagunwa, and Amos Tutuola are extensively described and analyzed.

East African literature is the subject of three articles, which analyze the works of Okot p'Bitek and Taban lo Liyong.

Finally, the function of register in Southern Africa is the subject of a long article by Benjamin Magura.

Together these articles present a varied and rich picture of African literature in English, a literature of great richness and power, a literature of world importance, and one which is entitled to the most closely detailed and advanced linguistic and stylistic analysis. The editors hope that this volume provides a major contribution to the study of literature in this area.

Notes

1. (Statistics from Crystal: 1995, 109.) There are probably many other English-speakers in sub-Saharan Africa, but only approximate figures are available for Botswana, Cameroon, Gambia, Ghana, Kenya, Lesotho, Liberia, Malawi, Namibia, Nigeria, Sierra Leone, South Africa, Swaziland, Tanzania, Uganda, Zambia, and Zimbabwe.

2. Some linguists regard the Nilo-Kordofanian family as really two families—Congo-Kordofanian (its major branches Niger-Congo and Kordofanian) and Nilo-Saharan (including Songhai, Saharan, Maban, Fur, and the many Chari-Nile languages).
3. The Khoisan language family includes 30 to 50 languages, among them Bushman and Hottentot, with about 120,000 speakers.
4. There is also mention in passing of Acholi, a Chari-Nile language (Nilo-Saharan).

Works Cited

Comrie, Bernard, ed. *The World's Major Languages.* New York: Oxford University Press, 1987.

Crystal, David. *An Encyclopedia Dictionary of Language and Languages.* Oxford: Blackwell, 1970.

Crystal, David. *The Cambridge Encyclopedia of the English Language.* Cambridge: Cambridge University Press, 1995.

Greenberg, J. H. *The Languages of Africa.* 3d ed. Bloomington, Indiana: Indiana University Press, 1970.

LITERATURE OF THE GENERAL AREA

✵

LANGUAGE AS SENSATION:
THE USE OF POETIC AND EVOCATIVE LANGUAGE IN FIVE AFRICAN AUTOBIOGRAPHIES

Tony E. Afejuku

Five African autobiographies are remarkable for their aesthetic appeal: the Guinean Camara Laye's *The African Child*, the Nigerian Wole Soyinka's *Ake: The Years of Childhood*, the Kenyan R. Mugo Gatheru's *Child of Two Worlds*, the South African Ezekiel Mphahlele's *Down Second Avenue*, and Peter Abrahams's *Tell Freedom*.[1] Although these autobiographies are realistic accounts, there is a deliberate attempt on the part of the writers to turn them into "interesting studies in the art of autobiographical recreation."[2] These writers, without exception, do this by using language that is often poetic and evocative.

All the autobiographers here use language that can arouse strong emotions to show their own feelings toward the objects or persons described. They use words with poetic and evocative connotations; words that are affective, metaphoric, imagistic, rhythmic, and symbolic. In *The African Child*, for instance, Laye describes landscapes to reflect his state of mind:

> The next day, I continued my train journey. But a complete change had taken place in me. Was I getting used to it already? I do not know; but my feelings about mountains were suddenly modified, so much so that, from Mamou to Kindia, I did not leave the window for a moment. I was watching, with enchantment now, a succession of peaks and precipices, torrents and cascades of water, wooded slopes

> and deep valleys. Water sprang and flowed every where, and gave a kind of animation to every thing.It was a wonderful spectacle; a little terrifying, too, whenever the train seemed to go too close to the edge of the precipice. And because the air was of extraordinary purity, every thing could be seen in the minutest detail. It was a happy land, or at least it seemed happy. There were innumerable flocks of grazing sheep, and the shepherds would wave to us as we passed....
>
> The train went on and on; just as it had seemed to puff painfully up the mountains, now it seemed to be rolling joyfully down. (121)

Before this time, Laye felt the plain on which he had lived had a "familiar, friendly face" (120). But the train's journey into the mountains as it glides towards Mamou is an emblem for his spiritual state as he leaves a familiar land. By the second day of the journey his feelings are changing, and now he can sit at the window and watch with "enchantment" the landscape with its "succession of peaks" and animating "cascades of water."[3]

Laye carefully chooses his words and constructs his sentences to reflect his feeling of joy. One is struck by the almost sing-song effect of the sentences, an effect that makes it easy for the passage as a whole to be set in lilting music. One cannot miss the music produced by the almost chanting tone in

> I did not leave the window for a moment. I was watching with enchantment now a succession of peaks and precipices, torrents and cascades of water, wooded slopes and deep valleys. Water sprang and flowed every where, and gave a kind of animation to every thing.

The musical effect is enhanced by the following: 1) the alliteration in the words "*w*as *w*atching *w*ith;" "*p*eaks and *p*recipices;" 2) the pleasant "s" sound in "succe*ss*ion . . . peak*s* . . . pre*c*ipi*c*es;" "torrent*s* . . . ca*s*cades" and "*s*lope*s* . . .;" 3) the repetition of the conjunction "and" in strategic places in the sentences, whose significant use of parallelism in phrase and clause equally enhances the rhythmical development of the passage. The alliteration and consonance discussed here is also quite evident in the original version in French:

Je regardais et cette fois avec ravissement, se succéder cimes et précipices, torrents et chutes d'eau, pentes boisées et vallées profondes.[4]

Laye also uses contrast to stress the fact that although the spectacle was "wonderful," yet this feeling was occasionally punctuated by the fact that he knew some worry, something that was a "little terrifying," "whenever the train seemed to go too close to the edge of the precipices." But the general feeling is one of elation which the three poetic elements identified above reflect.

Another instance of poetic elation occurs when Laye catches sight of the peninsula of Conakry:

> As night was falling the peninsula of Conakry came in sight, brightly illuminated. I caught sight of it from far off, like a huge shining flower laid on the sea; it was joined to the mainland by its stalk. The water all round it was shining softly, shining like the heavens; but the sky does not possess that quivering animation. Almost at once, the flower began to expand, and the water receded: for a few moments more, it lay on each side of the stalk, then it disappeared. We were now getting rapidly nearer. When we had entered the lights themselves of the peninsula, the heart of the flower, the train came to a stop. (122)

Likening a peninsula to a flower lying on the sea may not be original or striking, yet it conveys Laye's elation in such a way that the reader accepts it without hesitation. This passage provides a good example of Laye's ability to build up a rhetorical and climactic scene by a deliberate and strategic use of parallelism and pauses that reflect his excitement on this night of nights when the "peninsula of Conakry came in sight, brightly illuminated" and "when the water all round" "was shining softly, shining like the heavens." We can note from such parallelisms and pauses that Laye's style is very expressive; it explicitly shows the writer's feelings toward his subject.

Generally speaking, since Laye's style depends on poetic and effective devices such as alliteration, consonance, imagery, repetition, and parallelism, his language may be described as poetic prose.

Mphahlele, like Laye, also writes poetically, although his style is more abstract. The following passage from *Down Second*

Avenue, taken from the first "Interlude" where Mphahlele is roused from sleep by the snoring of his uncles in the dead of night, is a useful illustration of the point:

> Saturday night. Darkness. Sounds of snoring from my uncle at the corner. Like the muted lowing of a cow [. . . .] My younger brother doesn't stir beside me. Nor the younger uncle the other side of him under the same blanket as we [. . . .] I know the cold air coming through the hole in the flooring boards will whip us out of sleep as it plays upon bare flesh, else one's legs will rest on my neck and then I shall jump up with a scream. My sister also on the floor is kicking the legs of the table she's sleeping under. Grandmother and three of Aunt Dora's children are lying quiet on the old double bed. The only door and the only window are shut. Hot. With two frayed blankets on us it's good to feel hot. I can't sleep I can't get up to walk about in the yard because my bones are aching because I was cleaning the house and turning every thing up and choking in the dust I was making [. . . .] Tins of beer dug into the floor behind the stack [. . . .] No policemen will find it easily. Policeman? Saturday night [. . . .] a police whistle, the barking of dogs [. . .] I hear heavy booted footsteps, it's sure to be a person running away from the law [. . . .] Saturday night and it's ten to ten, I can hear the big curfew bell at the police station peal "ten to ten, ten to ten" for the Black man to be out of the streets to be at home to be out of the Policeman's reach. Year after year every night the sound of the bell floats in the air at ten minutes to ten and the Black man must run home [. . . .] The whistle is very near now and the hunted man must be in Second Avenue [. . . .] (44-45)

Here the fast rhythm of the prose, made effective by the intermittent abandonment of punctuation, reflects the constant tension and restlessness of life in a South African ghetto. It lends the passage a lyrical (and hence poetic) touch and makes verbal brevity a way of life that a writer like Mphahlele, who knows that life so well, cannot ignore. The effectiveness of the passage is further enhanced by the gradual extension of consciousness from the sleeping boy (Mphahlele) to his younger brother and to the other sleepers as well as to the "night beyond the walls and to those who suffer in it, whose suffering or danger obtrude so strongly into the consciousness of the boy."[5]

Despite this preceding remark, there is the tendency to see the passage as an abstract one. It may seem contradictory to say this, but what we have is more of Mphahlele's comprehension of the recreated reality through his own intellectual reflection than anything else. What redeems the passage is the emotional, evocative appeal and the poetic attempt to convey meaning by suggestion and implication. This commentary is interesting to us because the misery and poverty of the reflecting boy's household are indirectly hinted at or reflected in the crowded room with its poor ventilation. In fact, sentences that suggest this poverty and misery include the following: "I know the cold air coming through the hole in the flooring boards will whip us out of sleep as it plays upon bare flesh"; "Grandmother and three of Aunt Dora's children are lying quiet on the old double bed"; "The only door and the only window are shut. Hot. With two frayed blankets on us it's good to feel hot." This attempt to convey meaning by suggestion is a feature of the "Interludes," which, apart from acting as artistic summations of past events, contain the most poetic elements in *Down Second Avenue.*

Another instance of the poetic quality of Mphahlele's language can be found in the final "Interlude," where we see Mphahlele wanting to possess what the whites in South Africa enjoy, but is denied to blacks:

> Pictures, fantasies, strivings, wishes, desires, memories and all other creatures of the intellect come to torment your being. Then you think how sordid life is; how ludicrous the very idea of life is; what a fruitless, petty, endless game it may be and mustn't be. Things close in upon you; you find yourself in a tightly closed-up room [....] The strivings and desires in you continue to torment you, to tease you out of yourself. But there was no exit from that prison. You knew it was your soul that was imprisoned.
>
> Of course, the easiest way out would be to leave the soul in this cage, and start a new life, resolve to fling ambition to the winds, and just become a thoroughly sensuous animal; leave inspirations, ambition, ideals, planning and aesthetics to the elect.

Furthermore:
> Those electric lights in the distance continue to blink and tease the spirit of night; little sparkling fires, so unearthly, so inorganic. (202)

Unlike the earlier passage of the supposed reflection of the boy, here we see the mature Mphahlele talking and dealing with a state of emotion, with psychological reality, in a very abstract, intellectual sort of way. Expressions like "creatures of the intellect," "very idea of life," "leave inspirations, ambition, ideals, planning and aesthetics to the elect," "so unearthly, so inorganic" reflect Mphahlele's intellectual concern. But they are not devoid of emotional overtones that help to underscore the poetic quality of the passage.

It is necessary to note here that the electric lights Mphahlele sees as symbols of knowledge and his intellectual longings are unfortunately out of his reach; "they assume . . . the unattainable" (201). Although beautiful, they paradoxically mirror the confusion in his mind and his longings. Furthermore, their "sparkling fires," although real, are yet "so unearthly" and "so inorganic" that he cannot discern anything meaningful or worthwhile in them. But through them, and this is paradoxical, he perceives his material deprivation. In the electric lights he sees the socially forbidden things and the white man's magnificence and splendor, which are forever denied him and his fellow blacks. This perhaps explains why they are "so unearthly, so inorganic." Thus, through this image of light Mphahlele enables us to see the darkness in his mind and the disillusionment that leads to the bitterness that forces him to leave South Africa and go into exile.

It is needless to stress that by means of such images and symbols, Mphahlele imbues his narrative with life, and sustains the reader's interest. And if it is true, according to Longinus, that the "stimulus of powerful and inspired emotion"[6] constitutes a significant element of sublimity, which is part of what poetry is, then there is no doubt about it that the above passages enhance the poetic quality of Mphahlele's narrative.

In Soyinka's *Ake* we find a poet employing rhetorical devices to achieve great narrative beauty and vividness. Soyinka is so masterly, so poetic, and so evocative in his tone and style that his narrative never lacks sustained beauty, both expressional and musical. According to Egudu, "The first is realized by means of the special use of language, particularly imagery, and the second is effected through sound and rhythm."[7] The following extract might be seen to lack imagery, but it graphically reveals how Soyinka tries to achieve expressional and musical beauty by a special use of language:

> A trio emerge with an outsize radio-cassette player in full blast [. . . .] They move on to the trinket-and-cosmetic shop, their jaws implacably churning through the gummed-up troughs of a synthesized feed in every conceivable idiom, pause at McDonald's, bury corpses of sausage-rolls in their mouths and drown the mash in cocacola. (157)

The above passage is from chapter ten, in which Soyinka laments, among other things, the changes that have taken place in Ake, including new and Western (European and American) food items like sausages, which have dethroned indigenous food items like *guguru-and-epa* (roasted corn and groundnuts) and *robo* ("hard-fried balls of crushed melon seeds") (156). Soyinka underscores his displeasure for the "sausage king" by means of dislocation, by associating it with an idea that is strange to and unconventional for it. By saying that the trio in the passage "bury corpses of sausage-rolls in their mouths" (here, in a symbolic sense, we can interpret "mouths" as cemeteries), Soyinka is telling us that sausage-rolls, which are supposed to be "finely minced meat," are revolting to the taste buds. He is telling us that sausages are not proper for human consumption. Furthermore, the phrase "synthesized feed" suggests a food item that has lost all its nutritional value due to the process of chemical reactions it underwent in the course of its production. Thus we can draw the inference that Soyinka does not want us to eat sausages. The idea Soyinka presents jolts our common sense, and his use of language is characteristic of 'poetic language [which] organizes . . . the resources of every day language and sometimes does even violence to them, in an effort to force us into awareness and attention."[8]

Aside from the above dislocation of language, which gives

the extract expressional beauty, there is also poetic rhythm, which gives it musical beauty. The tone and diction of the sentences suggest that it is composed by a craftsman of a high order who keeps tight control on his material in order to achieve poetic rhythm. The point I am making here will be better appreciated if we attempt to rewrite or rearrange the two sentences that compose the extract along the lines of verse, thus:

> A trio emerge with an outsize radio-cassette player
> in full blast,
> They move on to the trinket-and-cosmetic shop,
> Their jaws implacably churning through the
> gummed-up troughs
> Of synthesized feed in every conceivable idiom,
> Pause at McDonald's,
> Bury corpses of sausage-rolls in their mouths
> And drown the mash in coca-cola

This re-arrangement, which places line-endings where pauses occur, and where pertinent information is added to a preceding one in each longer clause of the second sentence, gives the impression that Soyinka's sentences can be seen in terms of verse lines whose drift and gravity compel us to see the language of recreation as a sacred and careful exercise in musical beauty—despite the revolting idea it suggests.

Anyone familiar with Soyinka's writing knows that he reveres the Word. His interest in words, in language, which he always uses in his own special sense, has always been a source of study for the wary critic.[9] In the following passage Soyinka shows that he has enriched his autobiographical art not only through his use of words, but also through his experiences with them and his speculation on these experiences:

> Along Dayisi's Promenade I also sang, but only on those occasional late evenings when I was on an errand [. . . .]
> I sang to buoy up my spirits against the dangers of the dark, against figures who drifted past in the dark and who, for all I knew might be spirits or kidnappers. There had accrued to me a formidable weapon in my armoury of incantations against the unknown, after my role as The Magician on prize-giving day at St. Peter's in Standard III.

Even if most dangerous spirits did not converse in English, there was no way that they could mistake the ferocious will of the counter-force marching along Dayisi's promenade and singing at the top of his voice:

> For I'm a magician
> You all must know
> You'll hear about me wherever you go
> You can see my name in letters large
> For Anthony Peter Zachary White
> Is a man who always gives delight . . .

[. . .] Why poultry? It was one of the baffling details of that children's opera. (150-51)

Words are used as means of communication and as poetry, as incantations, as songs and sounds, which the young Soyinka uses as "weapon(s)," in a symbolic sense, to "buoy up" his "spirits against the danger of the dark." The sounds of words used in this way fascinate the boy and breed in him emotions before he even understands their full import and meanings. "Why poultry?" he asks in an endeavor to understand why that word should be used in the above song he repeatedly sings as a counterforce "against the figures who drifted past in the dark" any time he goes on errands. "These undecipherable lyrics led to strange interpretations, and I was engaged in belting out some of these when I bumped into Mr. Orija the organist" (152). Soyinka plays on words as on the strings of Dayisi's guitar; he listens intently to Dayisi's guitar for all its nuances, and lives almost exclusively in a world of word sensations in which language is employed as a means of transporting reality into something else.

From all that has been said above, it is clear that Soyinka brings his poetic gift to bear on his choice of images and language generally.

In *Tell Freedom* Abrahams underscores the poetic quality of his work in the way he chooses and arranges words to convey specific meanings, pictures, and emotions. He uses language in a way suited to the experience he wishes to convey. Abrahams's prose — his metaphors, similes, and the rhythm of words, which are carefully chosen and arranged to achieve sensuous overtones — all enhance the reader's interest. Of particular interest is the way Abrahams employs his metaphors and other figures of speech to give concreteness to even the most abstract notions. For example, in the last lines of the book, Abrahams tells us:

> I walked briskly down to the docks.
> And all my dreams walked with me. (311)

Here dream is personified into a companion; but more important, it also symbolizes Abrahams's ambition to escape from the oppressive atmosphere of South Africa into freedom to become the writer who would "tell Freedom," that is, tell about the free world outside South Africa, about happenings there.

Abrahams's tendency to render even the most abstract notions as physical realities is a distinguishing feature of his narrative and allows us to refer to him as a materialist. He repeatedly conveys personal wishes, aspirations, actions, feelings, or sensations through material or physical realities. Perhaps the best example of this is the passage where Abrahams's elder brother Harry, who is serving a fourteen-day jail-term at a reformatory for a gambling offense, is "breaking rock under the hot sun." The young Abrahams, who accompanies his elder sister Maggie and Enna, his brother's fiancée, on the visit to Harry, is the center of consciousness:

> The afternoon sun slanted westward, but only slightly. A lone eagle circled overhead. Once, it spread its great wing and swooped down low. No doubt to see what manner of men these striped beings were. Then, with movements of great power and grace, it climbed. It made an almost straight line up. I watched it grow smaller, hazy, and then merge into the blue sky that had suddenly grown infinitely far removed from the world of men. I longed, suddenly, to be like that eagle, able to fly right out of the range of this place so that I would not have to watch my brother breaking rock under the hot sun. (135-36)

Abrahams's intention is clear. His brother's imprisonment demonstrates that life in a penal institution is not essentially different from that lived in the wider South African society; prison, in fact, is a replica of the parent society. It is a symbol of universal social oppression in the same way Harry stands for many anonymous fellow prisoners as well as many colored South Africans outside prison. The picture of Harry "breaking rock under the hot sun" conveys Abrahams's convictions about the raw and subtle modes of exploitation, cruelty, and injustice in the prisoner's world as well as in the world outside prison.

The prison with its disturbing emotions contrasts with the splendid picture of the bird, of the graceful and powerful eagle, which is said to be a symbol of freedom and release from the world of men itself. This majestic and lovely eagle that stands for the wish of the oppressed human spirit to regain freedom and all its rights creates in Abrahams a feeling of envy, for he wants to be like it, free and far away from the cruelty of the here and now. Moreover, the bird's geographical setting ("the blue sky that had suddenly grown infinitely far removed from the world of men") is alluring because of the peace and security there, a place where Harry or any colored or Black South African will not suffer the ordeal of "breaking rock under the hot sun." If a critic like Obiechina were asked to comment on this tendency in Abrahams to render abstract notions as physical realities, he would perhaps call it "reification," a term he applied to Okara's similar tendency in *The Voice* because it (the tendency) gives "the quality of 'thingness' to mental and abstract constructs."[10]

The poetic quality of *Tell Freedom* is also sustained by its various sound effects. At times this takes the form of a mere repetition built into the sentence structure of a passage to give a balanced, pleasing rhythm:

> To this street and this house came the Ethiopian. There, he wooed my mother. There, he won her. They married from that house. They found a house of their own further down the street. They made of it a home of love and laughter. (11)

Repetition is a device familiar from poetry, for example, a ballad. It is used here to enhance the artistic pleasure of the narrative.

Abrahams equally tries to achieve pleasing rhythm through onomatopoeic sound effects, as witnessed, for example, when he and Aunt Liza are travelling to Elsburg in a train.

He tries to reflect the sounds of the moving train through:

> At Fordsburg station our train was on the point of departure. We scrambled on. The train moved off. The engine puffed and screamed a shrill warning. We found a place near the window. I stood with my nose pressed against the dirty windowpane, watching the world go by.
>
> The engine puffed and snorted. Every now and then, when the train curved round a bend, it screamed its shrill warning. And the wheels, under me, whispered: "O-n a-w-a-y. O-n a-w-a-y. O-n a-w-a-y." Then they said: "On away. On away. On away." (16)

For the boy, who is travelling on a train for the first time, it was an exciting experience. Hence its vivid description is rendered in brief sentences to achieve a fast tempo that fits the onward movement of the train.

Such poetic use of language as seen in the above instances makes *Tell Freedom* a captivating autobiography to read.

In *Child of Two Worlds*, Gatheru's utterance is tuned for the reader by the power of nostalgic evocation made noteworthy by his understanding of the virtues of clarity and simplicity. Unlike the other autobiographers, he exhibits a sparseness of figurative language. But this, poetically speaking, does not have an adverse effect on the narrative in any way:

> But the link has now been broken and I Mugo — son of Catheru, will start a new chain with new links. My people, the Kikuyu, were great workers in iron, and they discovered many centuries ago how to make the finest chains. I have long know that the iron must be good if a chain is to be strong. And so I went to America to be smelted and hammered and beaten and drawn, even as our smiths forge useful and ornamental objects from their iron. I have been laid on the anvil!
>
> My people, the Kikuyu, are being smelted, hammered, beaten and drawn, too, by the great forces that I have now learned, after my college education, to call urbanization and industrialization and acculturation. I have learned,

too, that I am what the sociologists call a marginal man — a child of two worlds. (2)

In this passage we see Mugo Gatheru's nostalgia and the expression of the bitterness and pain for the culture of his people that has been broken by Western influence. In spite of this influence, however, he still retains some aspects of his culture. That is why he is "a marginal man — a child of two worlds," and by remembering his past he renews his affiliation with his community. Gatheru appropriately uses the metaphor of the iron and the chain that is laid on the anvil to signify the transformation he and his people have undergone as a result of European "urbanization and industrialization and acculturation." Despite the use of this metaphor, however, the passage, like most others in the narrative, is not rich in powerful and compelling imagery. Its hallmark is passion. This, coupled with its clarity and simplicity of diction, enhances its poetic quality.

Generally speaking, Gatheru's style, his use of language, matches that of a writer whose narrative is a mixture of praise and lament, as *Child of Two Worlds* partly is; his use of language matches that of a communal poet or communal prose writer, a "recounter of communal history, treasurer of communal memory"[11] (and Gatheru somewhat sees himself in this light) who must recreate things past through unvarnished descriptions.

In conclusion, if we agree that part of the poetic writer's role is to employ figurative language to heighten meaning and to recreate remembered scenes, sensations, emotions, and psychological states, then these five writers do this adequately. Or to put it differently: it follows from the above analysis that the eloquent literacy of the autobiographers derives from their use of poetic and evocative language, which underscores the profundities of the autobiographies.

UNIVERSITY OF BENIN—NIGERIA

Notes

1. Camara Laye, *The African Child*, trans. James Kirkup (London: Fontana, 1955); Wole Soyinka, *Ake: The Years of Childhood* (London: Rex Collings, 1981); R. Mugo Gatheru, *Child of Two Worlds* (1964; rpt. London: Heinemann, 1975); Ezekiel Mphahlele, *Down Second Avenue* (1959; rpt. London: Faber

and Faber, 1973); Peter Abrahams, *Tell Freedom* (1954; rpt. London: Faber and Faber, 1981). All page references to these texts refer to these editions.
2. I made this remark in a forthcoming essay in *The Literary Griot*.
3. For a similar view on this, see Adele King, *The Writings of Camara Laye* (London: Heinemann, n.d.), 35.
4. Camara Laye, *L'Enfant Noir* (Paris: Plon, 1972), 145.
5. See Gerald Moore, *Twelve African Writers* (London: Hutchinson, 1980), 47.
6. Longinus, "On the Sublime" in *Classical Literary Criticism*, trans. T.S. Dorsch (1969; rpt. Harmondsworth: Penguin,1975), 108.
7. Romanus Egudu, *The Study of Poetry* (Oxford: Oxford University Press, 1977), 11-12.
8. René Wellek and Austin Warren, *Theory of Literature* (1942; rpt. Harmondsworth: Penguin, 1980), 24.
9. See, for instance, Niyi Osundare, "Words of Iron, Sentences of Thunder: Soyinka's Prose Style," *African Literature Today* 13 (1983): 24-37; also see Ossie Onuora Enekwe, "Wole Soyinka as a Novelist," *Okike* 9 (1975): 72-86.
10. Emmanuel Obiechina, *Culture, Tradition and Society in the West African Novel* (1975; rpt. Cambridge University Press, 1980), 174.
11. These words and the idea they express are borrowed from Chinweizu, Onwuchekwa Jemie and Ihechukwu Madubuike who applied them to Senghor. See their *Toward the Decolonization of African Literature: African Fiction and Poetry and Their Critics*, Vol. I (Enugu: Fourth Dimension, 1980), 282.

Works Cited

Abrahams, Peter. *Tell Freedom* London: Faber and Faber, 1954; rpt.1981.
Chinweizu, Onwuchekwa Jemie, and Ihechukwu Madubuike. *Toward the Decolonization of African Literature: African Fiction and Poetry and Their Critics*, Vol. I, Enugu: Fourth Dimension, 1980.
Egudu, Romanus. *The Study of Poetry*. Oxford: Oxford University Press, 1977.
Enekwe, Ossie Onuora. "Wole Soyinka as a Novelist," *Okike*, 9

(1975): 72-86.
Gatheru, R. Mugo. *Child of Two Worlds*. London: Heinemann, 1964; rpt. 1975.3.
King, Adele. *The Writings of Camara Laye*. London: Heinemann,[n.d.]
Laye, Camara. *L'Enfant Noir*. Paris: Plon, 1972..
——. *The African Child*, trans. James Kirkup (London: Fontana, 1955).
Longinus, "On the Sublime" in *Classical Literary Criticism*, trans. T.S. Dorsch. Harmondsworth: Penguin,1969; rpt. 1975.
Moore,Gerald. *Twelve African Writers*. London: Hutchinson, 1980.
Mphahlele, Ezekiel. *Down Second Avenue* (1959; rpt. London: Faber and Faber, 1973). 10.
Obiechina, Emmanuel. *Culture, Tradition and Society in the West African Novel*. Cambridge, England: Cambridge. 1975; rpt. 1980.
'Osundare, Niyi.' "Words of Iron, Sentences of Thunder: Soyinka's Prose Style," *African Literature Today*, 13 (1983): 24-37.
Wellek, René, and Austin Warren, *Theory of Literature* Harmondsworth: Penguin, 1942; rpt. 1980.

TRANSLATION:
A DISTINCTIVE FEATURE OF AFRICAN LITERATURE IN ENGLISH

Oluwole Adejare

That translation is used by some by authors of African Literature in English (ALE) is not a new discovery. Lindfors (1968) and Afolayan (1971) have identified it in the works of Achebe and Tutuola, respectively. Though these publications are well known, the debate on the status of translation in ALE has continued. Doubts concerning its use as an aesthetic feature are frequently expressed. Young, one of the early researchers into the language of ALE, expresses such doubts in concrete terms:

> ...as a general route to literary liberation, it [translation] is precarious, for whereas the "African vernacular" he [Achebe] has compounded for himself shows a flexibility in his hands, it remains a solution to immediate artistic problems rather than a prognosis of a new African medium in English. (40)

This statement raises three important questions that have not received adequate answers: Is literary liberation involved in the production of ALE texts? Is translation a precarious route to literary liberation? What is the role of translation in the development of a distinct style of ALE? We shall try to provide answers to these questions in this article and, in the process, provide a comprehensive view of the diversity entailed in the use of translation in ALE.

The data analyzed are selected from *The Palm-Wine Drinkard* (PWD), *The Voice* (Voice), *Arrow of God* (AOG), *The Combat*

(Combat), *The Interpreters* (Interpreters), *The Lion and the Jewel* (LJ), *Kongi's Harvest* (KH), *This Earth, My Brother* (Earth), *The Gods Are Not To Blame* (Gods), *Labyrinths* (Labyrinths), *One Man, One Wife* (MW), *Death and the King's Horseman* (DKH), and *The Trials of Brother Jero* (Trials). Page references are to the editions cited at the end of the article.

Types of Translation in ALE

Before we proceed to answer the questions raised above, a preliminary discussion of the term translation is essential. This would enable us to know clearly what we are talking about and how it is manifested in the variety of English under discussion.

Translation is a linguistic concept, and it cannot be meaningfully discussed outside that discipline. Unfortunately, translation is a problem area in modern linguistics. Translation theories are uniformly weak in one aspect: they, like the sentence grammars from which they are derived, can only account fully for formal meanings. But formal meanings in isolation are radically different from text meaning (see Adejare 1982). Indeed, as argued elsewhere (Adejare forthcoming), translation is not simply the transfer of textual material from a source language into a target language as Catford (1965) suggests. Rather, it is the transfer of the message of a text or text unit of a source language into the same message in a target language. This implies that there are three types of translation, one each for the three potential levels of meaning that can be identified in a text. Thus, the three levels of text meaning — primitive, prime order, and second order — have corresponding translation types: primitive-level translation, prime-order-level translation, and second-order-level translation.

The three types of translation are found in ALE texts. Examples shall be given to show the features of each type of translation and the scope of its use.

Primitive-Level Translation

Primitive-level translation is the first step in text translation. Here, only formal equivalents are accounted for, without any regard for the message transmitted by the text. This can be illustrated at the levels of lexis and grammar.

Lexis

The last item in the sentence " Dzenawo's son is to be outdoored" (Earth: 11) is outstanding. *Outdoor* is not a normal English verb. Thus, *outdoored* needs explanation. The item is the primitive equivalent of *christened* in Ewe, Awoonor's mother tongue. At this point, the writer selects the primitive equivalent rather than the prime-order equivalent to reflect the fact that another language is involved in the fictionalized situation and that the ceremony is different in some aspects from its English equivalent.

Outdoored may be used by West African writers whose mother tongues belong to the Kwa group of languages. For instance, Yoruba, another language of the Kwa family, uses the word *ikomojade (outdooring* the child) for what in an English text would be *christening*.

It should be noted that it is only in the choice of the lexical item *outdoored* that Awoonor uses a primitive-level equivalent. The other elements of the structure of the clause conform to English form rules. Examples of this type of translation are numerous in ALE texts. The following are a random selection: "I want one of my sons to join this people and be my *eye* [representative] there" (AOG: 55). "Pray for us *who spoil things*" [sinners] (SL: 119). "My father's father [grandfather] owned it" (MW: 84).

Grammar

The translation of the elements of the grammatical unit at the primitive level in ALE can be illustrated from texts at the group and clause levels.

Group

The clause in English has four possible elements of structure — (S), (P), (C), and (A) — each of which constitutes a group. We shall illustrate translation at this point with a passage that reveals something interesting about Tutuola's language, the influence of the editor on the final version of a text.

In narrating the episode, "THE LADY WAS NOT TO BE BLAMED FOR FOLLOWING THE SKULL AS A COMPLETE GENTLEMAN" (PWD: 25), the following conditional clauses occur, among others:

if the bombers saw him in a town . . .
if they did throw it . . .

As presented, nothing suggests that any type of translation is involved in either of these clauses; polysemy makes inconclusive the evidence of the only doubtful item, bombers (aircraft or soldiers trained for bombing).

However, those are not the clauses Tutuola wrote. Thanks to the reproduction of a page of the original manuscript on page 24, we know that the clauses he wrote are:

if the bombers see him in a town . . .
if they throw it . . .

The editor has, through his attempt to make the text comprehensible, distorted Tutuola's language. The fact that a similar clause on the same page, "if this gentleman go to the battle field," is written the same way as those cited above, shows the writer's consistency in the use of present-tense form where the past is required.

Each of the three italicized items in the above clauses is a predicator functioning as a verbal group. Primitive-level translation is responsible for Tutuola's consistent use of the present for the past. The use of *see* for *saw* and *throw* for *threw* reflects the absence of morphological markers for tense in Yoruba where the pairs, *see* and *saw*, and *throw* and *threw*, each has one form, *rí* (see) and *ju* (throw), respectively. Thus, the cited verbal groups are primitive-level equivalents for their corresponding Yoruba verbal groups, and they illustrate the fact that translation at the primitive level may be confined only to the group.

Clause

Primitive-level translation may also cover an entire clause. In order to show that Tutuola is not the only user of this type of translation and that the type can be aesthetically motivated, we shall illustrate translation at this level with an example from the works of a writer well known for his linguistic sophistication. Okara's "His chest was not strong" (Voice: 23) is a clause that appears to conform to English form rules and therefore could pass for a textual equivalent. But it is a primitive-level translation of the Ijo clause *Owo agbobu be krua a.* The fact that it is a primitive-level translation of the entire clause emerges when it is compared with the prime-order-level equivalent that conveys the message *he is not brave.* The lack of correspondence between the meaning of the primitive equivalent and the message of the prime-order equivalent shows the distinction between primitive- and prime-order-level translation.

African writers, with varying degrees of linguistic attainment, use primitive-level translation as shown above. This means that translation is not peculiar to Achebe, as Young seems to suggest, and that it has further implications that shall be dealt with below.

Prime-Order Level Translation

In systemic textlinguistics, the prime-order-level is the level at which the message is derived from a language event through a combination of formal primitive meanings with the components of the simple situation. Situation, though divided into simple and complex in systemic textlinguistics, has three components as in orthodox systemic grammar. These are thesis, immediate situation, and wider situation (see Ellis 1966; Berry 1975). The clause, "I hate flying planes," traditionally used to illustrate syntactic ambiguity, can be used equally to illustrate the function of situation in the realization of prime-order-level meanings. The ambiguous unit in the clause is the nominal group, flying planes, which occupies the complement position and has different primitive meanings. Flying planes may mean (a) planes that can fly, (b) being a plane's pilot, and (c) being a passenger on a plane. This ambiguity will disappear when the components of the simple situation are combined with the formal meanings of flying planes. Using thesis alone, only one of the three possible meanings of the expression would be the message in a specific text. For instance, the thesis for the text in which (a) would be acceptable would be *toy planes,* that for

(b) *choice between flying planes or helicopters,* and that for (c) *mode of traveling.* Thus, situation enables a specific message to be derived from several primitive meanings of a single formal unit. Such messages are directly transmitted from the encoder to the decoder.

African writers in English translate mother-tongue texts at this level. The type of source-language text normally involved in prime-order-level translation is either common speech or metaphors left undecoded by the writer. Let us illustrate briefly with texts.

Common Speech

Drama is a genre in which the translation of mother-tongue texts of common choice between speech is virtually inevitable in the variety under examination. A scene in which monolingual Africans are involved would be a disaster if no attempt is made to indicate the difference between the medium used among the characters and the medium the writer uses to communicate this to an audience. Though the conflation of two linguistic systems that this involves is difficult, translation at the prime-order level provides a fairly easy way out of the difficulty.

Trader in Soyinka's *Trials* is an example of an African monolingual character. Her reply to Amope's unsavory remark that her fish is rotten is an example of prime-order-level translation: "It is early in the morning. I am not going to let you infect my luck with your foul tongue by answering you back" (Trials: 51). The two sentences are translated from the Yoruba source: "*O s'aaro. Emi ko ni je ki o ko ori buruku re ran mi nipa dida e lohun.*"

To turn the Yoruba source into the English prime-order-level equivalent, the author made adjustments to the primitive-level equivalents of the sentences). He, for instance, added "early in the" to "It is morning" (the primitive equivalent of the first sentence. He also edited the second sentence: *ori buruku* is rendered as "ill-luck" rather than "head-bad" (its unadjusted primitive meaning), or "bad head" (its adjusted primitive meaning). Further, "with your foul tongue," which is absent in the source, is added to disambiguate the primitive equivalent of the source language's text unit.

Without using prime-order-level translation, it is hard to imagine how Soyinka would have reflected the true Yoruba sales experience as effectively as he does here. Prime-order-level translation enables him to reflect the Yoruba semiotics of the source in the English equivalent. The belief that the first customer of the day sets the pattern for others throughout the rest of the day is obvious in the statement of Trader. The Yoruba belief in the potency of the spoken word is also portrayed by her refusal to answer Amope back. Thus, the equivalent translation reflects both the form and the simple situational component of the source text.

Rotimi's Gods provides an example of a different kind:

Aderopo: Your highness.
King's Bodyguard: The king greets you. (Gods: 18)

This exchange is a prime-order-level translation that reflects the way discourse between an *oba* and an ordinary citizen is conducted in the days when *obas* ruled. The Yoruba source of the translation is:

Visitor: Alaye [owner of the world]
King's Proxy: Oba n'ki e [The-one-who-hides is greeting you]

This prime-order-level translation provides an economical way of reflecting an aspect of the ancient Yoruba culture. The choice before the author is either to translate the discussion as done in the text or to describe it in the stage direction without indicating the actual words used in the event.

From translation of common speech, let us move to the use of prime-order-level translation of undecoded metaphors.

Undecoded Metaphors

Translation of undecoded metaphors at the prime-order-level can be found in all genres in ALE. Such metaphors are appropriated from the mother tongue and used for different aesthetic purposes. They may be ordinary metaphors or proverbs.

An ordinary metaphor translated at the prime-order level can be exemplified by "Father of bats" (Interpreters: 118). The metaphor is translated from Yoruba, *Baba oobe*. *Oobe* (house bat) is a metaphor that means *thief* in Yoruba. It derives this meaning from the fact that house bats are notorious for eating soup ingredients kept in the rafters of the traditional huts. That they do it at night and are never caught in the act provides a further analogy between the bats and thieves. Thus, "Father of bats" is a metaphorical way of telling Lazarus that he is a leader of the underworld at the point where the prophet saves Noah from being lynched. Had Soyinka not intended to reflect the fact that the dialogue in which the expression occurs is conducted in Yoruba, he would have selected some other metaphors from his vast resources of the English language.

Proverbs, the palm oil with which complex African thoughts are coated for ease of understanding (apologies to Achebe), are probably the most common form manifesting the use of translated mother-tongue metaphors in ALE. They have been so much studied that we could just stop at mentioning them without citing any examples. But the scope of their use has never been fully realized; they are usually discussed as if they are limited to plays and novels. To provide the balance, we shall cite our first example of this aspect of translation from the least likely source, poetry, and the least likely poet, Okigbo:

> The child in me trembles before the high shelf
> on the wall,
> The man in me shrinks before the narrow neck
> of a calabash; (Labyrinths: 65)

These lines from "Elegy of the Wind" are translated from the Yoruba proverb *Owo omode ko to pepe, t'agbalagba ko wo keregbe.*

The use of a Yoruba proverb by an Igbo-English bilingual may surprise some readers, but it is not difficult to explain: the time spent at Ibadan as an undergraduate, manager of the local branch of Cambridge University Press, member of the Mbari Club (whose membership includes artists working in the Yoruba medium), as well as the years spent teaching at Fiditi Grammar School, a town close to Oyo city, provided ample opportunity for Okigbo to familiarze himself with Yoruba.

In translating the proverb at the prime-order level, Okigbo makes some additions to the source text. He adds "in me trembles" and "in me shrinks" to the proverb. These help to embed the proverb into the message of the poem— the agonizing decision that cooperation within the framework of a politically bankrupt and genocidally oriented Nigeria is no longer feasible for members of the cannibalized unit of that entity. The proverb shows, however, that the poet is equally aware of the grave implications of lack of cooperation between units of the same entity. Like the elder and the child who would not cooperate, both sides would lose in the end; the child would not get what is on the high shelf, while the man would not get what is in the calabash.

One more example will do: "When the head of the household dies, the house becomes an empty shell" (Gods: 9). This is the author's prime-order-level translation of part of a proverb, *Baale ile ku, ile d'ahoro* (Father of house die, house become ruin). In the context of the play, the use of any other equivalent would have defeated Rotimi's purpose of adapting a Greek play, in English translation, for an African situation.

Prime-order-level translation is therefore widely used in ALE texts. It indicates linguistic and cultural differences between the medium and the experience.

Second-Order-Level Translation

The second-order level is complex. Here, in addition to primitive meanings and the simple situation that generate a prime-order text message, a complex situation is involved. The complex situation handles fictionalization, distorted situations used for achieving literary aesthetics. The interesting aspect of this level is that fictionalization affects not only the situational components of the text, but also the form in which the text is coded. Thus, more often than not, a fusion of form-meaning and message is the norm here. For translation, this means that the options from which equivalents in the target language can be selected are considerably narrowed. The search for equivalent forms that structurally and semantically duplicate the message of a second-order text can be daunting.

The need to reuse literary texts existing in the mother tongues of different writers, however, compels them to use this type of translation in ALE. But few writers achieve the feat of reflecting the aesthetics of the source language in the translated versions. Most merely translate a second-order text into the prime-order level with the resultant loss of the essential aesthetic ingredients of the source. However, a few writers achieve this almost unattainable feat. One of them is Soyinka. DKH, because of the nature of its fictionalized situations, contains a large number of Yoruba second-order texts, particularly *ofo* (incantations). Below is an example:

> The river is not so high that the eyes of a fish are covered.
> The night is not so dark that the albino fails to find his way. (DKH: 43)

The source text is:

> *Omi ki i kún, ko b'oju eja.*
> *Ookun ki i kùn, ka mo m'afin.*

Though Soyinka fails to find phonological equivalents for *kún* (high) and *kùn* (dark), he succeeds in finding equivalents for many other structures of the original. This becomes obvious when the two versions of the text are divided into parallel structures. For instance,

> The river is not so high. . . .
> The night is not so dark. . . .

compares favorably in form and meaning with:

> *Omi ki i kún*
> *Ookun ki i kùn.*

Similarly,

> . . .that the eyes of a fish are covered
> . . .that the albino fails to find his way

is a satisfactory equivalent for

> *ko b'oju eja*
> *ka mo m'afin.*

This translation fairly accurately conveys the message of the original. The only divergence is found in the last unit of the translation, "That the albino fails to find his way" instead of "that we fail to know the albino" (a more accurate equivalent for *ka mo m'afin*). This type of variation is a common feature in Soyinka's translation of Yoruba second-order texts, and his reason for adopting that strategy is aesthetic. The source-language text is reshaped, where necessary, so that the translated version would fit into the semantic and semiotic framework of the text that he is using the mother-tongue material to create. This is what happens in the example cited above. Soyinka slightly modifies the original, which stresses the albino's distinctiveness, into his own version, which stresses the albino's ability to see in the dark, because of the contextual imperatives of the fictionalized situation. The intention is to stress that Elesin must see his way to glory through the darkness of temptations, rather than that he is a distinguished individual.

Thus, this and other examples from Soyinka satisfactorily provide hard-to-come-by second-order illustrative texts.

In sum, three kinds of translation are extensively used in the texts of ALE. In the process of establishing them, we have provided the evidence with which to answer the questions raised at the beginning of this article. Let us now turn to them.

Is Literary Liberation Involved in the Production of ALE?

The most important words in the above question are "literary liberation." In this nominal group, the modifier "literary" contrasts with "political" in "political liberation." This suggests that "literary bondage" is manifested in the texts of ALE and immediately raises further questions: What is the nature of the literary bondage? Who is being liberated?

Literary bondage in this context can only mean linguistic bondage. From one perspective, the use of the language of ex-colonial overlords in literary-text production can be seen as a form of literary bondage for, if nothing else, it is a reminder of the ugly experience of colonialism and all its attendant deprivations. However, from another perspective, it could be argued that whether or not the language of the former imperial power is used for literary-text production, the colonial experience remains a scar that no cosmetic surgery can hide. Perhaps, then, the associative relationship between "political liberation" and "literary liberation" transfers the dreaded substance of the former to the shadow of the latter. This becomes clearer when we consider who is being liberated.

Who, in our second question, can refer only to the society or the individual writer. To suggest that precolonial, colonial, and postcolonial African societies need literary liberation in any form is to resurrect the ghost of the spurious belief that Africans have neither languages nor cultures, and, by implication, no literatures. This belief has long been proved wrong and needs no further examination. We shall only restate that African societies need no literary liberation because there was never a time when traditional literary forms were not in active existence.

It could then be that the individual writer is the one who needs literary liberation. There is a sense in which the African writer in English may be said to need literary liberation. A writer resident in the metropolis of the former imperial power and who writes for an audience of that society may need literary liberation. His works would be evaluated against the background of the mother tongue's linguistic and cultural norms. We must concede that a few texts produced by African writers fall into this category. Emecheta's *Second Class Citizen*, a plea for acceptance addressed to the British, is an example. A cry of pain by one in the diaspora, its concern is only marginally relevant to the day-to-day experience of the inhabitants of Accra, Nairobi, and Lagos. However, when writers in this category address the home audience, the shackles of alienation break, as evident in *Double Yoke*, Emecheta's fictional account of her experience in a Nigerian university.

But writers in this category are few and the texts involved even fewer. Restricting our examples to Nigeria, for every Emecheta there are scores of Soyinkas, Achebes, and Okigbos, and for every *Second Class Citizen* there are hundreds of books like *Kongi's Harvest, Arrow of God*, and *Labyrinths*. The true writer of ALE is home-based. He co-exists with literary artists working in the mother tongue and, more often than not, makes use of materials from the mother tongue. Such a writer does not need literary liberation. He is liberated by the existence of languages and literatures in the societies that nurture him and from which his immediate audience is drawn.

The question of whether literary liberation is involved in the production of ALE is, therefore, irrelevant. The answer to the next question reinforces this fact.

Is Translation a Precarious Route to Literary Liberation?

The answer to this question (from the answer given to the first question) is obviously negative. But for the fact that it offers us the opportunity to identify the root of the problem of literary liberation, we would have left it at this point.

Literary liberation refers to the mock epics fought between two groups of intellectuals who became prisoners of a literary war (of words) and continued to imagine that the war was still being fought when they broke from forgotten POW camps. On the one hand are the intellectual Mungo Parks, who saw in the first blurred glimpse provided by the linguistic cataracts of Tutuola's PWD the source of the literary Niger and would not be persuaded that the cataracts have since given way to Kainji Lake and the source of power represented by the Achebes, Awoonors, and Ngugis. On the other hand are intellectual nationalists who keep the opposing side engaged with the old song of nothing-but-protest. Here is not the proper place to go into details about this issue. We shall only observe, for now, that though the intentions of both sides are noble, the literary liberation war, as in all wars, has developed to a stage where the adversaries have forgotten the issue that led to a resort to arms.

In retrospect, in place of a discussion of the real issue, what we have is an arsenal of potent verbal weapons: "Negritudism," "Tarzanism," and the complex of "Racism," "anti-Racism," and "anti-Racist-Racism." Most of these are only emotionally injurious, but some, like "Larsony," coined by the novelist A. K. Armah from the name of the critic Charles Larson, to mean "using fiction as criticism of fiction," can draw real intellectual blood. In the spirit of that war, few tigers were restrained enough from baring their fangs. The battles, well documented on the pages of the first journals on ALE, have now subsided, though the type of challenge posed by Young's statement encourages the formation of guerrilla units of African Aesthetics who are planning fresh intellectual ambushes.

But what is the real issue? Simply that languages that are colonial heritages are being used to create literature; that

Caliban, while keeping the secrets of his mother tongue, has learnt to read the magic books of Prospero and turned his knowledge to cast new and occasionally unfamiliar spells. The time wasted on this issue would have been more productively spent on other important activities, if the historical development of English in Africa had always been taken into account. English was an alien—and an alien's—language when Africans started to venture into its creative use. The struggle for literary liberation at that uncertain stage can be understood, particularly as the main audience was the foreign owners of the language themselves. But with the development of English, by default or design, from a "foreign" into a "second" language, literary liberation becomes irrelevant, for, in spite of the linguistic fiction that enthrones the native speaker as the final arbiter in matters of usage of his language, it has to be conceded that a language belongs to anybody who uses it. The native speaker of any language who is afraid of corruption of his language, would have to wipe out all dialect users of the language before having any justification for attacking the heretics of the second-language environment. What we are saying in no uncertain terms is that a native speaker has no special ability for determining all the acceptable texts of his language. Indeed, no native speaker knows all the varieties of his language. The second-language user in fact has an advantage over a monolingual mother-tongue user, in that the former has available to him an alternative system of communication. Of course, as a bilingual, his language use will always differ in some respects from that of native speakers, but that is natural. Native speakers' dialects differ too. But for the bilingual it is not a matter of minimal difference. He has two linguistic systems and two world structures which can be brought together through translation. This is not limited only to everyday language use but also extended, by the imperatives of reality, into literary text creation.

Thus, the question of whether translation is a precarious route to literary liberation is again irrelevant. The contrast between Moses Olaiya's (Baba Sala) irresistible Yoruba comedies and Soyinka's English satires on the one hand, and the parallels between Fagunwa and Tutuola on the other, are all aspects of the literature of a people, which in concert with the complementary texts from the Achebes, reflect a shared experience. Though how they articulate such experience is important, why they choose any of the media available to them, or even fuse such media through translation, is irrelevant.

When the literary wars have waned and the warriors are weary, the literary texts will remain bilingual and monolingual. The relevant question from the perspective of this article is whether translation has any role to play in the development of a distinct style of *ALE*.

Translation as a Distinctive Feature of ALE

The question of what role translation should have in the development of a distinct style of ALE cannot be answered without understanding the role translation plays in existing ALE texts. One major role for translation in this variety of ESL is the aesthetic role. We shall supply additional data to show the extensive use of this feature.

As the above analysis shows, the chances of an ALE text containing pockets of translation are high, even when the text is written primarily in standard English. With the few exceptions of writers such as Tutuola, for whom translation is an idiolect, translation generally functions as an aesthetic motivator. Humor, satire, characterization, and the derivation of new idioms can be motivated by translation. Let us briefly explain.

Humor

Translation can be used to induce humor, particularly when primitive translation is used in a context suitable for standard English or prime- and second-order level translation. The following is an example:

> *I have come to report that* it *come* to my information that one prominent Chief, namely, the Elesin Oba, is *to commit death* tonight *as a result of native custom.* (DKH: 26)

In this passage, Soyinka uses primitive-level translation for Amusa's report to provide some humor. The italicized expressions are primitive-level translations from Yoruba. But Pilkings, the District cum Police Officer who is being addressed, speaks only standard English and thus could not make much sense of the intelligence report. Indeed, he wrongly concludes that Elesin would commit ritual murder. This near-Babel situation cannot but be humorous.

Satire

There is no better example of the use of translation for satire than a passage that is a satire on translation:

> *Samson:* Be comforted they plead, and she is comforted. As the reverend preacher said to his congregation, Comfort ye my people and the half illiterate interpreter said, comfort ye this comfort; my people - is my people. This comfort is my people.
>
> *Together:* Comfort yi enia mi ni. (Road: 197)

This is double-edged satire. The anecdote quoted by Samson is a confusion created by a translator of a sermon operating at the primitive level. Confused by the fact that comfort can function both as a common and proper noun and the fact that the words *ye* (English) and *yi* (Yoruba) sound alike, he thought that the preacher is laying claims to a married member of the congregation named Konfoti and translated the English sentence into the Yoruba primitive level. Konfoti's husband, also present in church, is alleged to have stood up to make a counter-claim during the sermon and the service ended in confusion. The anecdote is a satire on the use of a foreign language for worship when the congregation is made up of monolinguals who speak a different language. But the satire equally refers to the character and his friends. As leader, they have a half-illiterate, half-mad Professor, who utilizes his imperfect knowledge to sustain the superstitious beliefs of the touts and, by issuing them forged driving licenses, to promote death on the roads.

Characterization

Translation can also be used as an economical way of presenting character types. The following passage, whose main feature is primitive-level translation from Yoruba, is an example:

Teacher, I thank you greatly. You have always said good words to me. You are my brother from heaven. From now on I know that. So whatever you tell me, I shall do . . . No. No let me finish the words of my mouth. You were born many years after I was born. But you are older than I . . .
(MW: 34-35)

The passage reveals first of all that the character is a Yoruba monolingual through the use of primitive-level translation: "good words" (*oro rere*), that is, "sensible words"; and "finish the words of my mouth" (*pari oro enu mi*), that is, "land" or "conclude."

Our main interest, however, is in the way the translation is used to indicate the type of character the speaker is. The passage shows the speaker as the appreciative type. Joshua, after being convinced that education could make his son become like Teacher, shows his appreciation through sincere praise. "You are my brother from heaven" is an example of praise showing deep gratitude, particularly as "brother" in this context means "born of the same mother," a primitive-level translation of *omo iya*.

Aluko probably might have been able to achieve the same effect through other means. But the use of translation makes the passage outstanding and culturally relevant.

Derivation of New Idioms

Translation is also a means of deriving fresh idioms. Soyinka is the most notable writer who does this. Having used several examples from his works, however, we shall turn elsewhere for a passage to illustrate this feature. The example comes from Kole Omotoso's *Combat*.

In this sentence, "Their faces seemed to burst into smiles" (Combat: 34), *burst into smiles* is a prime-order-level translation of Yoruba, *bu si erin*. In mother-tongue English (EMT), this idiom has equivalents such as *wide grins, broad smiles*, or, if *burst* must be used, *burst into laughter*. By turning to Yoruba, Omotoso has added one more idiom to the English language.

New idioms derived from translation bring along with them a vivid perspective of the world, which enriches the source language. There is no more effective way of describing bursting into smiles then "burst into smiles." Further, such idioms convey semiotic meanings. For instance, to burst into a smile is more African than European. Translation, from what has been shown in this section, plays several important aesthetic roles in the existing texts of ALE and, as far as the future is concerned, it should continue to play such roles. No alternative is imaginable. Indeed, more than any other feature, it is "the prognosis of a new African medium in English," contrary to Young's view. Its extensive scope of use, its variations, and the fact that it is unavoidable in certain circumstances, show that things cannot be otherwise.

Conclusion

What is said of translation in ALE applies to all true ESL situations. Translation is, and should remain, the dominant linguistic feature of the ESL literary variety. The linguistic soil that nurtures ESL ensures that. The bilingual or multilingual situations in which ESL literary texts are produced compel the interaction between the mother tongues of creative writers and English, the medium in which they write. For fictionalization, writers have to use either mother-tongue monolingual or bilingual/multilingual situations existing in their societies. This sociolinguistic reality can be neglected only at great peril to authenticity, even creativity. A fictional situation must, after all, be firmly rooted in an identifiable sociocultural milieu if its decoder is to have a point of reference in reality, and the text an immediate audience.

Language is a social phenomenon, serving to transmit the totality of experience of its users, usually called culture. Literature, a variety of language use, cannot therefore exist in a cultural or linguistic vacuum. For the ESL writer, the operational background is bilingual/bicultural. The fact that the seminal thoughts and social inspirations of such writers must sprout from the soil of the mother tongue, with or without a sprinkling of imported cultural fertilizer, further compels interlingual interaction and, consequently, translation.

The only alternative to the use of translation in ESL literary texts has been identified by Soyinka, through Kongi's

Reformed Aworis. After rejecting "verse" (English) and "proverbs" (the mother tongue), they are left with a dialect to be characterized by "ideograms in algebraic quantums" (KH:72). Certainly, nobody would recommend such a dialect for the literary variety of ESL.

UNIVERSITY OF IFE—NIGERIA

Works Cited

Achebe. C. *Arrow of God*. London: Heinemann African Writers Series (AWS), 1965
Adejare, O. "Towards a Systemic Textlinguistic." Paper read at Ninth International Systemic Workshop; Current Applications of Systemic Theory, Winters College, University of Toronto, Canada. Aug. 25-28, 1982.
———. "Theory of Text Translation." In A. Afolayan, *What Is ESL?* London: Longmans (forthcoming).
Afolayan, A. "Language and Sources of Amos Tutuola." In C. Heywood, ed., *Perspectives on African Lirerature*. London: Heinemann, 1971.
Aluko, T.M. *One Man, One Wife*. Lagos: Nigerian Printing & Publishing Co. 1959 ; republished in *AWS*. London: Heinemann, 1967; rpt. 1970.
Armah, A.K. "Larsony or Fiction as Criticism of Fiction." *Positive Review* 2 (1978).
Awoonor, K. *This Earth, My Brother*. London: Heinemann, 1971.
Berry, M. *Introduction to Systemic Linguistics*. London: Batsford, 1975.
Catford, J.C. A *Linguistic Theory of Translation*. London: Oxford Univ. Press, 1965.
Ellis, J. "On Contextual Meaning." In C.F. Bazell et al., eds., *In Memory of Firth*. London: Longmans, 1966.
Firth, J.R. *Papers In Linguistics 1934–1951*. London: Oxford Univ. Press, 1957.
Lindfors, B. "The Palm Oil with which Achebe's Words are Eaten." *African Literature Today*. I-4. Nairobi: Heinemann, 1966.
Okara, G. *The Voice*. London: Heinemann with Andre Deutsch (*AWS 1970*), 1964.
Okigbo. C. *Labyrinths*. London: Heinemann, 1971.
Omotoso, K. *The Combat*. London: Heinemann, 1972.
p'Bitek, O. *Song of Lawino*. Nairobi: East African Publishing House,

1966.

Rotimi, O. *The Gods Are Not To Blame.* London: Oxford Univ. Press, 1971.

Soyinka, W. *The Lion and the Jewel.* London: Oxford Univ. Press, 1963.

────── *The Trials of Brother Jero.* London: Oxford Univ. Press, 1964.

────── *The Interpreters.* London: Andre Deutsch, 1965; reissued, Glasgow: Fontana, 1972.

────── *Kongi's Harvest.* London: Oxford Univ. Press, 1967.

────── *Death and the King's Horseman.* London: Methuen, 1975.

Tutuola, A. *The Palm-Wine Drinkard.* London: Faber & Faber, 1952.

Young, P. "Tradition, Language and the Reintegration of Identity of West African Literature in English." In E. Wright, ed., *The Critical Evaluation of African Literature.* London: Heinemann, 1972.

WEST AFRICAN LITERATURE

TOWARD A SPEECH-ACT APPROACH TO NIGERIAN LITERATURE IN ENGLISH

⋆

Efurosibina Adegbija

Contemporary appraisal of Nigerian Literature in English tends to be generally either structuralist and formalist or Marxist and sociologically oriented. This paper highlights the main traits of these approaches and argues that both tend to becloud the context of most texts. It is proposed that a speech-act approach to the criticism of Nigerian literature in English will fill this important gap. Soyinka's *Madmen and Specialists* is used to briefly illustrate the intended direction of the approach.

Structural/Formalist Approach

Three essays in a recent book on the use of English for communication in Nigeria (Unoh 1986) illustrate the typical structuralist tendency. Adewoye (1986:97-106) examines "The Beauty of Language in Selected Novels of Chinua Achebe." The tenor of Adewoye's appraisal is demonstrated by the following quotation:

> Therefore, since each novel considers different societies and different epochs in Nigeria, there is of necessity going to be significant difference in diction, imagery, syntax and idioms employed to deal with the author's preoccupation in the novels. (98)

Adewoye then goes on to examine, for instance, the simple language used by Obi and the satiric viewpoint of the author. He also provides examples of the different kinds of diction used by Achebe, how they portray the social setting, and the use of proverbs, simile, satiric humour, flashbacks, rhetorical devices, and prophetic symbols (such as the struggling python in *Arrow of God*, the new yam as a symbol of continuity of life and regeneration, and the moon as an illustration of the impermanent nature of human achievements). Essentially, Adewoye extols isolated instances of the beauty of Achebe's use of language. Each item is broken down and examined with a view to demonstrating its function in the overall cosmos of the entire novel: such an approach focuses on form.

The structuralist and formalist orientation of Emenyonu's 1986 article, "Buchi Emecheta's Voice: Language Usage in *The Bride Price* and *The Joys of Motherhood*," can be seen in this quotation:

> African writing has become uniquely identified for its subtle language through the artistic use of African proverbs, sayings, aphorisms, and the incorporation of humorous anecdotes within the mainstream of the narrative. (1986:122)

He goes on to present an interesting account of Emecheta's literal translation of Igbo words, her use of similes and proverbs, of dialogue in narration, of the use of the art of suspense, of figurative expressions, and so on. Once again, a literary text is seen as a magnificent artistic edifice, akin to an architectural wonder. The critic's role, this approach tends to imply, is to dismantle this magnificent textual edifice piece by piece and thus illustrate to the reader of what stuff it is made.

In a similar vein, though different in focus, is Olapade Ajeigbe's "The Language of Nigerian Literature in English." He suggests that there is a traditional class of Nigerian writers who transliterate, such as Soyinka, Clark, Achebe, and Rotimi. In the words of Achebe:

> I feel the English language will be able to carry the weight of my African experience. But it will have to be a new English, still in full communion with its ancestral home but altered to suit its new surroundings. (1965:30)

Another class, into which Amos Tutuola is put, translates directly from the mother tongue. In an attempt to discover the patterns of language or the "features which reveal the essence of some of the writers," Ajeigbe does something very much in the structuralist mode. He, like the scholars discussed earlier, examines metaphors, similes, and the like from the viewpoint of whether the author transliterates, or translates.

We can go on and on. However, these three articles demonstrate beyond doubt the essential structuralist and formalist spirit: "the investigation of the specific properties of literary material, of the properties that distinguish such material from material of any kind" (Pratt 1977:3, quoting Ejxenbaum, 1926:9). That is, structuralists break down a text into its component parts in an attempt to recover its core, its gem, its overall essence. While it is arguable that the articles discussed above deal specifically with language, other literary appraisals in the structuralist mode are possessed of the same spirit of piece-by-piece analytical decomposition of particular qualities (see, for example, Lindfors 1972 and Dathorne 1972).

The creed of this type of structuralist/formalist criticism is that form is supreme over content. Consequently, content is mentioned mainly in respect to its contribution to the style or the language, to the dramatic techniques of irony, satire, the use of content for dramatic purposes and its dramaturgical effects, and so forth. Often there is a subtle implication that content is dispensable while emphasis is placed, instead, on an author's idiosyncratic use of language. Even when an attempt is made to create a balance between form and content, there often tends to be a surreptitious inkling that form is still supreme; this is preached loud and clear in the critic's bias.

Marxist and Sociological Approaches

The Marxist and sociological approaches have been lumped together because they are fathered by the same set of ideas: the functionality of content. Literature should be functional in helping society. The distinguishing hallmark of Nigerian Marxist criticism is its almost obsessive concern for the masses. For the strict Marxist critic, any literary text that is not so oriented is not worth its salt. Motivated by this overriding concern, these critics are disposed to aggressiveness and they implicitly or explicitly hurl attacks at formalists and structuralists. Content is placed high above form, though occasionally there is a concession to a dialectical relationship between form and content. As the emphasis is on the message of a text, these critics often write in the vernacular or in pidgin so they can reach the masses. Odun Balogun's "Populist Fiction: Omotosho's Novels" (1983:98-121) is typical of this approach. We are told that Omotosho is concerned with

> the common people, and among the common people he singles out the "dejected, rejected and neglected." Invariably, his characters consist of people for whom suffering has become so much routine that they no longer seem to realize that there could be any happiness. (98)

Verbal art is seen principally as a medium for social change. Even while discussing style, these critics tend to link it with appeal to the masses. Says Omotosho:

> simplicity of language and of technique is one of the most important characteristics of any literature whose appeal must be to the masses of the people. Other characteristics are that such a literature must be brief and that it must be cheap. (1976:7)

Discussion of style in this mode often serves more or less as an appendix or a footnote to the decrying of the miserable, despicable lot of the rejected, the oppressed, the neglected, and the downtrodden masses.

Speech-Act Theory: What Is It?

The core principle of speech-act theory is that in uttering a sentence a speaker, besides making a proposition about a state of affairs in the world — about the truth or falsity of a proposition, committing himself to a future course of action, or making somebody else do something — also performs an action such as requesting, stating, commanding, or informing. To use John L. Austin's phrase, words are intended to "do things" (1962), to perform particular functions. Every utterance performs a speech act, which may be direct or indirect. While the main point or purpose ("illocutionary force") of a direct speech act may be easily identifiable, that of an indirect speech act—in which we say something and convey another, or convey both what we have said and something else—may not be. To arrive at the illocutionary force of an indirect speech act, a hearer will have to base his inference on the speaker's illocutionary force and on the nonliteralness of the particular locution(s) uttered. No speech act can be fully understood without the requisite Mutual Contextual Beliefs (Bach and Harnish 1979) shared by both the speaker and the hearer or, in our case, the writer and his audience. Hence, depending on the Mutual Contextual Beliefs that a hearer brings to bear, a particular speech act may convey an illocution different from that intended by the speaker. Similarly, one locution is capable of several illocutionary forces (see Adegbija 1987). Pratt (1977:86) nicely sums up the advantages of speech-act theory that are relevant to literary works:

> Speech act theory provides a way of talking about utterances not only in terms of their surface grammatical properties but also in terms of the context in which they are made, the intentions, attitudes, and expectations of the participants, the relationships existing between participants, and generally, the unspoken rules and conventions that are understood to be in play when an utterance is made and received.

A speech-act approach would most likely possess greater explanatory power than current approaches. It would also illuminate literary texts from the perspective of actual language use and "increase attention to interpersonal and discursive, rather than merely formal, aspects of literature" (Fowler 1981:18).

Applications of Speech-Act Theory to Nigerian Literature in English

A speech-act approach to Nigerian Literature in English would be both fruitful and intellectually productive in that it would fill a gap in the more fashionable approaches to literary appraisal discussed earlier. This viewpoint can be corroborated by an examination of some of its promising potentials.

In the first place, a speech-act approach does not aim at throwing away completely formalist and Marxist/sociological ideas. Rather, it would build on their advantages and insights: the importance of style in conveying a message in the former, and the value of a message for the society for which it is intended in the latter. Proceeding from the whole to the part would be a major hallmark and point of departure of a speech-act approach. As argued in Adegbija (1982), many extended bodies of discourse contain one or more master speech acts that can be identified as their chief *raison d'être*. That is, writers tend to have an overriding goal, a predominant message, or a particular speech act that the sequences of utterances in their entire body of works are intended to perform. It is reasonable, therefore, that literary appraisal should seek to identify the superordinate status of this dominant speech act whose illocutionary force(s) rules over an entire literary corpus. Literary appraisal should, first and foremost, seek to know what this master speech act is, what its illocutionary force is, what aspects of the contextual structure of an entire text or series of texts forcefully help to convey it, and how the remaining sequences of speech acts in the text have been related to it.

Within the purview of the type of inquiry that a speech-act approach would engage in, the functions of the master speech act and other individual speech acts performed will become supreme, thereby allowing language use to receive its proper credit rather than its being considered merely incidental. Says Fowler (1981:28): "linguistic structure is not arbitrary but is determined, or motivated, by the functions it performs." Halliday (1970), in a similar vein, observes: "The particular form taken by the grammatical system of language is closely related to the social and personal needs that language is required to serve." The plain truth, then, is that no literary text can exist outside of language. Nevertheless, whereas it cannot be claimed *in toto* that language is the text, nor that the text is language, the role of language in a literary text should be seen as not only paramount, but also as ineluctable and ineradicable.

Moreover, the contextual underpinning of a text could,

within the speech-act appraisal orientation, be seen as part and parcel of a work of art. Consequently, it would be unnecessary to invoke it extraneously, nor would its use in the explicating of literary phenomena require being apologetic or regretful. As Labov (1972) clearly points out, no use of language can be divorced from its social context since social meaning is "parasitic upon language" (297). By the same token, the explication of a literary text cannot be divorced from the pragmatic, social, and linguistic milieu (what Adegbija [1982] referred to as pragma-sociolinguistic context) that gave birth to it. As Fowler rightly observes, the inclusion of such dimensions of language in stylistics shifts attention from merely formal or structuralist perspectives to a view of literature as "social discourse" (18). He further observes that

> it is a mistake to regard literary texts as autonomous patterns of linguistic form cut off from social forces.... From this perspective, literature is, like language, interaction between people and between institutions and people. To regard it as social discourse is to stress its interpersonal and institutional dimensions, concentrating on those parts of textual structure which reflect and influence relations with society. (18)

The most dynamic and fascinating aspect of the speech-act approach—and one which, in my view, has greater potential for literary explication than anything the present approaches offer—is the scholarship on indirect speech acts defined above (see also Adegbija 1982:34, Searle 1972, and Davison 1975). Thus, apparently inexplicable aspects of literary texts that often defy the critical powers of expert critics could be elucidated by the concept of indirect speech acts, usually understood on the basis of inference springing from mutually shared factual background information. Typically, the surface structure of an indirect speech act is not necessarily semantically or illocutionarily coterminous with the intended illocutionary force. Consequently, a text that appears to be merely making a statement about a state of affairs in society could, when we burrow deeper into it via a speech-act approach in which mutual contextual beliefs are taken into account, contain the most withering of attacks, the most devastating of rebukes, and the most piercing of satires. From this perspective of indirect speech acts, therefore, every literary work could be a potential mine into which scholars can dig for literary gold. In this regard, Searle (1979) writes:

> In indirect speech acts, the speaker communicates to the hearer more than he actually says by way of relying on their mutually shared background information, both linguistic and non-linguistic, together with the general powers of rationality and inference on the part of the hearer. To be more specific, the apparatus necessary to explain the indirect part of indirect speech acts includes a theory of speech acts, certain general principles of cooperative conversation (some of which have been discussed in Grice [1975]), and mutually shared factual background information of the speaker and hearer, together with an ability on the part of the hearer to make inferences. (32)

In an indirect speech act, the mutual contextual beliefs help determine that the direct illocutionary act cannot reasonably be taken to be the sole act being performed by a speaker in a particular utterance. This realization inevitably leads the hearer to seek an alternative explanation for the speaker's utterance (see Bach and Harnish 1979:72). This perspective makes natural rather than gratuitous a critic's attempt to explain what a writer means by the use of, for instance, a particular symbol to convey a particular out-of-the-ordinary, extraneous, or unconventional meaning in a literary text. In doing this, it would provide ready explanation for cohesion at the word, sentence, and speech-act levels.

By virtue of its sensitivity to the global and historical *context* of a text, a speech-act approach would fuse both synchronic and diachronic perspectives to provide richer insights into contemporary Nigerian literature in English. While a synchronic perspective would be principally concerned with the text *per se*, with its present life, context, and contemporary meaning, a diachronic perspective would introduce dimensions of meaning relating to the historical, global context enveloping a text. Such access to diachronic contexts is particularly relevant for a full explication of indirect speech acts. In fact, diachronic contexts typically constitute central aspects of the mutually shared beliefs that are crucial for the understanding of the full illocutionary force of an indirect speech act.

Before concluding, I want to illustrate the direction that a speech-act approach to Nigerian literature in English could follow by a brief exposition of aspects of Wole Soyinka's *Madmen and Specialists*. This exposition should not be misconstrued for a full-blown speech-act analysis of the play, which I hope to present in a future work.

An Illustration of Speech-Act Analysis

The speaker-hearer or writer-reader relationship is of paramount importance in a speech-act approach. Four kinds of audiences can be postulated for Soyinka's *Madmen and Specialists*. The first would be the make-believe, intratext audience. This concept refers to the characters within the play as partakers in social discourse and interpersonal relations. They live within a world of their own as created by the author, and the meaning one character attributes to a particular speech can be unique in its potential to contribute to the total meaning of the entire text. When, for instance, Dr. Bero tells the priest that "human flesh is delicious" and pulls the priest's cheeks to emphasize his point, the mutually shared background knowledge of the intratext audience leads to different reactions and interpretations. The priest is, at first, convinced that Dr. Bero must be joking because of his belief that the eating of human flesh is universally regarded as repugnant and barbaric. The priest, with his religious background, is not only astounded by Dr. Bero's claims, but almost sickened in a fashion that could be expressed as "God have mercy upon this poor sinner." His hypocrisy is, however, foregrounded by his selfish, lighthearted, patronizing jokes, a demonstration of his inability to empathize at a moment when Bero is obviously deranged, and oppressed by war-thoughts.

The second type of audience, the *immediate-context, extratext* audience, brings to bear upon the interpretation of the play the general background possessed by the *make-believe, intratext* audience as well as their individual cultural experiences within the immediate sociocultural context with which the text deals. The *immediate-context, extratext* audience in *Madmen and*

Specialists—the Yorubas— share the same cultural experience with the author. For them, the eating of human flesh is traditionally associated with witchcraft, wickedness, and the possession of devilish spiritual powers. This dimension, undoubtedly, comes to bear on Dr. Bero's assertion that "human flesh is delicious." It would also contribute to their interpretation of the total speech-act functions of the text.

The *nonimmediate, extratext* audience is very much similar to the *immediate-context, extratext* audience in shared values and beliefs. However, there could occasionally be certain culturally specific assumptions that the second type of audience has but the third does not. The entire Nigerian audience, with its awareness of the Nigerian civil war and its ravages, of the wanton destruction of human life that accompanied it, of the military politicians who claim they have come to clean up the mess created by the civilians while creating an even greater mess, are part of this audience's mutual contextual background shared with the writer. Consider the following speech by AAFAA:

AAFAA (posing).

In a way you may call us vultures. We clean up the mess made by others. The populace should be grateful for our presence. (He turns slowly round.) If there is anyone here who does not approve us, just say so and we quit. (His hand makes the motion of half-drawing out a gun.) I mean, we are not here because we like it. We stay at immense sacrifice to ourselves, our leisure, our desires, vocation, specialization, etcetera, etcetera. The moment you say, Go, we . . . (He gives another inspection all round, smiles broadly and turns to the others.) They insist we stay.

The rich political and cultural loading and depth of this speech contributes much to the meaning of the text; however, its satirical commentary on military politics in the Nigerian context can be fully appreciated only by the immediate context, extratext audience of the author (the Yorubas in this case) as well as the nonimmediate context, extratext audience of Nigerian literature in English—Nigerian society as a whole.

The final class in our taxonomy is the *global context, extra-*

text audience, which would include any non-Nigerian audience that reads or watches the play. Except for very exceptional situations in which a member of this type of audience has had the opportunity to share in the experiences and cultural life of the first three kinds of audience identified, a literary text may be given a shallow interpretation bereft of crucial sociocultural knowledge of the context of the play.

Besides the background information and the speaker-audience mutual contextual beliefs that constitute crucial aspects of the decoding of meaning in Nigerian literature in English, there is also the issue of felicity or appropriateness-conditions for the performing of speech acts, which many speech-act theoreticians emphasize. The speech acts in *Madmen and Specialists* can only be fully understood within the felicity conditions involving the existence of man's inhumanity to man during the Nigerian civil war and the power lust or power-crazy tendency of both the high and the low within the Nigerian context. It is only when we assume these felicity conditions in the context of the play that we can understand the full and incisive nature of its indictment of man's complacency in barbarism.

Besides the kinds of insight that a speech-act approach would provide into Nigerian literature in English, the issue of what master speech-act the play aims at performing would also be paramount. To answer this, one would need to have read the play thoroughly, examined the different sequences of speech-acts in it, and discerned what linguistic-pragmatic, and social aspects of the context make the various speech acts cohere and thus help us in identifying the main message of the play.

On the surface level, it would seem that the play makes a statement about man's inhumanity to man, and comments on a general human propensity towards wickedness and "eating up" each other — that is, toward cannibalism. Human wickedness is perpetrated from place to place, profession to profession, and class to class in a "timeless parade" (8). A human being, the play seems to state, cringes for "more power to his swagger-stick" (10). Even the vultures who purportedly "clean up the mess made by others" luxuriate in power drunkenness as is manifested by their constant harsh tortures of Goyi (14) and the cripple (76-77). Dr. Bero, just returned from the war front, appears to have been entirely sapped dry of his humanity. His cannibalistic tendency is manifested in his despicable treatment of Old Man, upon whom he wields his power as a specialist. Old Man, in turn, wields power over the mendicants, who also exercise power over each other by treating each other cruelly. Si Bero, "whose mouth runs like a gutter" (22), equally wields power over the mendicants; we thus have a recurrent cycle of inhumanity.

Soyinka's master speech-act, therefore, is a bold, incisive statement, couched in the "As" philosophy, namely, that human suffering and wickedness is, was, and shall be; there is a recurrent cycle of human barbarity, enacted in the war, which has robbed Old Man, Bero, and the mendicants of their abilities to be human, creating an apparently iinevitable cycle of cannibalism: "As was the Beginning, As is, Now, As Ever shall be . . . world without" (36). Thus, wickedness and oppression have become "the first step to power . . . power in its purest sense. The end of inhibitions. The conquest of the weakness of your too human flesh with its sentiment" (37), so much so that Blindman advises: "Remember, even if you have nothing left but your vermin, discriminate between one bug and the next" (38). "As is everywhere" (39); that is, human cruelty, man's inhumanity to man is endemic and constitutes a wretched cycle from which not even the priest, the "mitred hypocrite" (33), can claim to be free.

Further emphasizing the statement about man's cannibalism, Soyinka indicates that exploitation of human infirmities eventually comes to be accepted as the norm, adjusted to as the status quo: "As, was, Is." There is a longing to perpetuate this status quo. Such a desire reechoes in the cripple's words: "I wish I had the power. Gives a man a sense of power to watch others twitch like so many broken worms" (42). All the above interpretations spring from the writer-audience context sketched out earlier. From the foregoing, therefore, it would seem that the predominant illocutionary force of the play is that of a Constative: a bold, daring, and striking statement about man's inhumanity to man.

We would be mistaken, however, if we construe the master speech act of *Madmen and Specialists* as merely "a powerful dramatic statement." Indeed, it is this and, like every indirect speech act, much more. Its depth can be burrowed into if we consider the contextual beliefs sketched out earlier, especially those possessed by the make-believe, intratext audience, the immediate context, extratext audience, and the nonimmediate context, extratext audience. Within the framework of an inhuman, power-thirsty, and overambitious populace, almost everybody becomes a madman who craves for power, no matter the cost. It is from this contextual background that *Madmen and Specialists* can be seen as an indirect speech act with a directive illocutionary force. In effect, it constitutes a satiric, caustic, and incisive rebuke of a cracked-up society with its collective and exalted cannibalism. Given the mutually shared contextual background between the playwright and his audience, the play functions more as a rebuke and a stern warning to turn from evil. In effect, it functions as a call to the altar of repentance. This subtle, powerful message is conveyed through an indirect speech act, vividly, incisively, and forcefully. Readers with the appropriate contextual background will know or make the inference that the play has a directive illocutionary force in which they are being called to turn away from evil to good. This interpretation is conversationally implied (see Grice 1975) in the entire text. It is also this conversational implicature that gives the play its universal appeal.

Conclusion

Essentially, then, this study has drawn upon the findings of speech-act theoreticians and sociologists to suggest that a radically different approach to literary appraisal in Nigeria is desirable. Such an approach would possess more explanatory power and would help us see literary texts as just another context of language in use. We would thus focus on literature as a register of language use that must be seen along with other verbal activities (see my speech-act analysis of consumer advertisements, Adegbija 1982; of Ogoni proverbs, Adegbija 1986; and of several instances of the use of language in day-to-day communication in Nigeria, Adegbija 1987). From the speech-act perspective, therefore, a *literary text* is not seen merely in formalist terms as something that possesses features or properties to be highlighted, but, instead, as a *dynamic social occasion in which acts are being performed with words in a social context*. This observation is, of course, without prejudice to Fowler's point that literature works with "pretend speech acts or imaginary speech acts or representations of speech acts" (1981:184) within a particular pragma-sociolinguistic milieu or context that may potentially have applications for other contexts.

Overall, then, a speech-act approach focuses on macrostructures rather than microstructures. While admittedly both perspectives must go side-by-side for a fuller and more thorough literary explication, our focus has been on macrostructure, the neglected cornerstone in linguistic literary criticism that is normally superordinate in discourse. For this reason, we suggest, it demands a superordinate posture in our analyses.

The approach outlined here also has the prospect of yielding a natural, more explanatory, deeper, and all-encompassing understanding of Nigerian literature in English and of texts in general than the more fashionable approaches. It also offers a ready explanation for cohesion—linguistic, social, cultural, and global—within a text. It also provides insight into the sociocultural milieu and context-dependent way in which a particular text has its being and allows linguistic literary critics to examine the possible range of meanings conveyed by a literary artist.

UNIVERSITY OF ILORIN—NIGERIA

Works Cited

Achebe, C. "English and the African Writer." *Transition* 4.18 (1965):27-50.

Adegbija, Efurosibina. *A Speech Act Analysis of Consumer Advertisements*. University Microfilms International, No. 8307973. Bloomington: Indiana University Ph.D. Dissertation, 1982.

———. "A Speech Act Analysis of Ogoni Proverbs." Unpublished manuscript, 1986.

———. "Speech Act Functions: Dimensions of Communication and Meaning in the English Language in Nigeria." *ITL Review*

of Applied Linguistics 76 (1987): 43-62. Leuven, Belgium.
Adewoye, Sam. "The Beauty of Language in Selected Novels of Chinua Achebe." In Unoh: 97-106.
Ajeigbe, Olapade. "The Language of Nigerian Literature in English." In Unoh: 107-18.
Austin, John. *How to Do Things with Words.* 2nd ed. Ed. Jo Urmson and Marina Sbisa. Cambridge, Mass: Harvard University Press, 1962.
Bach, Kent and Robert M. Harnish. *Linguistic Communication and Speech Acts.* Cambridge, Mass: The MIT Press, 1979.
Balogun, Odun. "Populist Fiction: Omotosho's Novels." *African Literature Today: Recent Trends in the Novel* 13 (1983): 98-121.
Cole, Peter, and Jerry Lee Morgan (eds.). *Syntax and Semantics, 3: Speech Acts.* New York: Academic Press, 1975.
Dathorne, O . R . "Okigbo Understood: A Study of Two Poems." *African Literature Today: A Journal of Explanatory Criticism* 1.1 (1972):19-23.
Davison, Alice. "Indirect Speech Acts and What to Do with Them." In Cole and Morgan: 143-86.
Emenyonu, Ernest. "Buchi Emecheta's Voice: Language Usage in *The Bride Price* and *The Joys of Motherhood.*" In Unoh: 119-34.
Fowler, Roger. *Literature as Social Discourse: The Practice of Linguistic Criticism.* Bloomington: Indiana University Press, 1981.
Grice, H P. "Logic and Conversation." In Cole and Morgan: 41-58.
Halliday, M.A.K. "Language Structure and Language Function." In *New Horizons* in *Linguistics.* Ed. J. Lyons, Harmondsworth: Penguin, 1970, 140-65.
Heringer, J. *Some Grammatical Correlates of Felicity Condition and Presuppositions.* Bloomington: Indiana University Press, 1972.
Jeyifo, Biodun. *The Truthful Lie: Essays in a Sociology of African Drama.* London: New Bacon Books, 1985.
Labov, William. "The Study of Language in Its Social Context." In *Language and Social Context.* Ed. Pier Paolo Giglioli. Harmondsworth: Penguin, 1972: 283-307.
Lindfors, Bernth. "The Palm Oil with which Achebe's Words Are Eaten." *African Literature Today: A Journal of Explanatory Criticism* 1.1 (1972):2-18.
Omotosho, Kola. "Producing Literature for the Masses in a Developing Nation: The Nigerian Experience." Paper presented at the Independent Papua New Guinea Writers'

Conference, July 1–4, 1976.
Pratt, Mary Louise. *Toward a Speech Act Theory of Literary Discourse.* Bloomington: Indiana University Press, 1977.
Searle, John. *Expression and Meaning: Studies in the Theory of Speech Acts.* Cambridge: Cambridge University Press, 1979.
Soyinka, Wole. *Madmen and Specialists.* Ibadan: Oxford University Press, 1971.
Unoh, S.O., ed. *Use of English in Communication: The Nigerian Experience.* Ibadan: Spectrum Books, 1986.

CODE-SWITCHING IN SOYINKA'S *THE INTERPRETERS*

※

James O. Omole

As a consequence of the need to universalize their works in terms of the range of their readership, African writers face the artistic dilemma of relating their world views in a language other than their own, the language of their colonial masters. Therefore, one characteristic feature of their writing is the presence of bits and pieces (if not chunks) of their own native languages. This is particularly so with plays and novels, where both narrators and characters freely mix English with expressions from the native language. Even those writers who are variously denounced or praised by critics for their "pretense" to master English as if it were their mother tongue are not free from such artistic code-switching. One such work is Wole Soyinka's *The Interpreters*.

The interpreters of the title are five young middle-class men. Their search for identity in their society provides the plot and most of the themes of the novel. In their search, they meet both politicians who expose them to corruption and other problems and a religious cult that does not satisfy their expectation of salvation. Their story is narrated in multiple flashbacks. This technique enables Soyinka to develop his characters in different times and places, as well as with various figures, ranging from politicians to messengers.

Given the variety of people from all classes with whom they interact and the different geographical locations in which they do so, their different languages become a focus of interest. Soyinka uses a spectrum of linguistic varieties such as English, Yoruba, West African pidgin English, nonstandard English, and even a phony American accent. Occasionally, two or more of these are used in a single speech situation by the narrator as well as by some of his characters. This is known as code-switching in sociolinguistics, and it is used with great skill by Soyinka in *The Interpreters*.

Code-switching, according to Einar Haugen, refers to "the alternate use of two languages, including everything from the introduction of a single unassimilated word up to a complete sentence or more, into the context of another language" (21). It presupposes a degree of proficiency in two or more languages from which a speaker or writer can switch back and forth.

Lance (1969) associated switching with relaxation and an informal atmosphere and suggested that it is not due to inadequacy of linguistic competence. In the same year, Gumperz and Hernandez concluded that switching conveyed a secondary meaning of formality or solidarity. In 1970, Gumperz went further to assert that switching serves definite communicative ends and is, therefore, more or less a metaphoric process (129-48).

Hasselmo (1970) did research into the linguistic circumstances of switching as recorded from Swedish speakers who cannot maintain consistent discourse in their native language. He distinguished between *clean* and *ragged* switching. The former has little or no interference, while the latter is characterized by phonetic interference from the first language (179-210).

Rayfield's important study (1970) noted the instance of switching among Yiddish speakers of English in California. She offered two sets of explanation for switching:

    a) As a response to the speech situation, such as:
       (1) entry of an outsider
       (2) quotation of utterances known only in one language (e.g., proverbs)
       (3) the carry over effect of a single loan-word

b) As a rhetorical device, such as:
  (1) emphasis by repetition in another language.
  (2) pointing up an unexpected aspect
  (3) bringing out a contrast
  (4) making a parenthetical remark, etc. (Rayfield 119)

Rayfield's findings are significant for their empirical status and their capacity for universal application either in sociolinguistic or literary studies.

Code-switching is not an exclusively linguistic concern; it is also a fairly common literary issue. In literature, it can be described as a device some writers employ (as Soyinka did) to make "the fictional worlds of literature correspond to the empirical historical world" (Traugott and Pratt 376). It is a type of "linguistic realism" whose source can be traced back to the advent of literary realism in the nineteenth century when writers could no longer overlook the reality of language differences. Consequently (using Traugott and Pratt's examples), writers such as Joseph Conrad and D. H. Lawrence started manipulating the plots of their novels for the sake of linguistic realism. For example, in *Under Western Eyes*, Conrad created a linguistic intermediary by presenting the text as a reconstruction, in English, of events contained in the diary of a Russian. The purpose of this device is to explain why the text is in English rather than Russian, especially since the novel is about Russia and the Russian exile community in Switzerland at the end of the czarist period.

However, the principle of linguistic realism now goes well beyond plot manipulation. Other techniques include the use of a metalanguage to specify what language is being spoken and how, as in Lawrence's *The Plumed Serpent*:

> Her thin, eager figure had something English about it, but her strange, wide brown eyes were not English. She spoke only Spanish or French. But her Spanish was so slow and distinct and slightly plaintive, that Kate understood her at once. (166)

Another technique is the use of expressions from the other language, sometimes with accompanying translation, as in many African novels.

The most interesting technique (but one some English purists decry as bizarre) is the attempt to make English somehow look or sound like another language. Amos Tutuola, the first Nigerian novelist to render the Yoruba oral tradition in English, offers in *The Palmwine Drinkard* an almost literal translation of Yoruba into English:

> But the old man who had promised me that if I could go to Death's house and bring him, he would tell me whereabouts my palmwine tapster was, could not wait and fulfill his promise because he himself and his wife were narrowly escaped from the town. (16)

The important expression to note here is "whereabouts my palmwine tapster was," which should have been "the whereabouts of my palmwine tapster." But instead, we have

whereabouts   my palmwine tapster   was

which in Yoruba is

Ibiti   mi   elemu   wa

Sentences or expressions like this sporadically occur throughout the novel.

Code-switching as a manifestation of linguistic realism is more prevalent in multilingual societies, where the need to reach the widest possible readership conflicts with the wish to present the exact experience and create the same linguistic effect as in the other language. For instance, the poetic effect of Yoruba cannot be adequately appreciated in English translation. Besides this constraint, there is also the problem created by cultural relativity, which has always impeded an accurate presentation of thoughts and feelings in a language other than one's own. Of course, human institutions, cultures, and experiences are not always identical. This is why many African novels written in English often feature words, phrases, and occasional sentences from their native languages.

The Interpreters features not only words and sentences from Yoruba (Soyinka's mother tongue), but also expressions in West African pidgin English, affected standard English, American English, and nonstandard English. To a great extent, these linguistic codes are a microscopic representation of the multilingual Nigerian society, which has about 400 languages and dialects. English, the language bequeathed to Nigeria by the British colonial administration, is not just the country's official language, it is also the only language common to the various language groups and the educated elite. Pidgin ranks second in that it is the language of uneducated businessmen, messengers, and many unskilled workers. It is spoken throughout the nation but with a greater frequency in the south. Nonstandard English cuts across the length and breadth of Nigeria, and it is usually an indicator of the level of education of its speakers. It does not command respect, nor is it used for any serious social purpose. It may be said that the various linguistic codes represent not just the sociolinguistic complexity of Nigeria, but also reflect the social involvements of the novel.

The Interpreters criticizes three groups in Nigerian society: the intelligentsia (the central characters), the politicians with whom they are in conflict, and a religious cult to whom they turn without success. With the exception of Sekoni and one female student who briefly appear in the novel, all the characters are bound together "by a common lack of positive, articulated, and humane values" (Jones 161).

If most of the characters are bound together by their deficiency in positive values, they are different in the language with which they communicate whatever values they have. For instance, standard English is spoken by the intelligentsia and, to some extent, by the politician, but with some phonetic interference and occasional substandard grammar. Pidgin English is spoken by Mathias (who sometimes speaks nonstandard English) and Greenbottle, the waiter. Nonstandard English is spoken mainly by the assistant to the religious leader, while Yoruba is spoken by one unnamed young waiter.

In spite of this analysis, it is difficult to make a neat dichotomy of the various linguistic codes used because the individual characters within their respective groups engage in switching from one code to another. For instance, the narrator, for reasons we shall soon highlight, sometimes switches to Yoruba from his sophisticated English. So also does Chief Winsala, the politician whose pronunciation is characterized by interference by Yoruba sound patterns, and who occasionally uses nonstandard grammar. We also have Peter, the German

journalist, whose pretentious American English is betrayed by his mixture of German with English sounds. Finally we have the professor, whose pronunciation is too perfect to be standard and whose phoniness is betrayed by his interchanging pronunciations of "Ceroline" and "Caroline."
In view of the interwoven nature of the linguistic codes, it is best to study the codes on two general levels. The first is the narrative level, by which we refer to the author's general design in including all the codes present in the novel (it also includes the narrator's fairly constant switching from English to Yoruba). The second level is the dialogic level, which refers to the switching from one form of language to another (including linguistic interference) by the various characters.

Narrative Code-Switching

On the narrative level, Soyinka uses the five major codes as a foregrounding device, an iconic element in the sense that they help him to capture the complexity of Nigerian society. The codes illustrate the variety of people and the networks of their interaction. Thus, when the elite are confronted with the commoners, the language of each side (either in quality or type) quickly indicates the relationship between them.

Second, much of the setting of the novel or the shifting scenes of incidents are identifiable by the numerous Yoruba expressions. Most of the scenes take place either in Lagos, Ibadan, or Osa. However, Lagos and Ibadan are by far more prominent, not so much because they are directly mentioned in the novel, but because of the Yoruba expressions used. For instance, *se wa s'omo fun wa* is from a Lagos dialect of Yoruba, as *Aladura* and *apala* also refer to a very common feature of life in Lagos and Ibadan, respectively.

Furthermore, Yoruba expressions, especially when used by the narrator, refer to concepts that cannot be expressed in English, as Rayfield noted in her study. Examples include *amala, apala, iyun, ikori, dansiki, agbada, igunuko, abetiaja,* and the Yoruba deities in Kola's pantheon. These cultural references, mostly terms for food, dress, and traditional religion, are difficult to translate into English. Even if a form of translation could be forged, it would inevitably mutilate the writer's meaning. Thus, some of the expressions are products of cultural relativity.

But then there are some Yoruba expressions used by the narrator that can easily be translated into English. Examples are *oyinbo's* (white men's), *ibeji* (twins), and a host of others. Generally, when the narrator uses a Yoruba expression in place of its possible English equivalent, he does so either for reasons of contempt or contrast. For instance, he refers to the intelligentsia or the elite in the society as "the new oyinbos." He also talks of *ibeji*, which are wood figurines carved in the form of twins in contradistinction to baby twins. However, most expressions that can be replaced by their English equivalents are found in the speech of some of the characters in the novel.

Soyinka uses so many linguistic codes, especially American English, to give the novel more than local appeal. The diversity of codes adds an international dimension, although this is achieved by other factors such as the roles played by Joe Golder, the black American lecturer, and the British wife of Ayo Faseyi.

Finally, in the words of Traugott and Pratt regarding code-switching in literature, the numerous codes can be said to be "highly systematic and based upon particular appropriateness conditions" (374). The codes are instrumental in that they confirm the characters' status in society. Besides, code-switching often reveals attitudes, dispositions, and feelings, just as the occasions and circumstances warranting the switching often illuminate a personality. In short, Soyinka tries to capture societal reality (including mob mentality) and personality profiles by means of language, as will be seen in our discussion of code-switching by some of the characters.

Dialogic Code-Switching

The intelligentsia in *The Interpreters* rarely code-switch, except when they refer to Yoruba cultural objects and institutions (such as food) and the Yoruba deities in Kola's pantheon. As a matter of fact, there are only four instances of such switching. The first is Kola's mention of *ewedu* (a slimy vegetable soup). The second is the reference to Egbo by some of his colleagues as *omo alufa* (the son of a reverend), which points out Egbo's moral contradiction as the son of a spiritual leader and a compulsive womanizer. The third instance is an externalized thought of Egbo's when he refers to Simi as *ayaba Osa omo Yemoja*, a form of chant of family names, meaning queen of the sea, daughter of Yemoja (a water deity) (Soyinka 57). The fourth instance is when Sagoe jokes in pidgin English with Mathias about the toilet at the "Independence Viewpoint." The near-religious devotion to English by the intelligentsia— even in their most relaxed moments or when they are conversing with illiterate messengers and waiters— presents English as a language of power or authority and suggests some sort of maladjustment on their part in society.

On the other hand, pidgin is presented as a language of solidarity among the less educated. Hence it is spoken by the messenger Mathias, the waiter Greenbottle, and the taxi driver whom Sagoe exploits. The following exchange shows Soyinka realistically depicting how the use of codes distinguishes the classes in Nigerian society:

> Trying not to be obvious, he felt his pockets one after the other. No money anywhere. Not a penny.
> "Where you wan go for Obalende?"
> "To the police station."
> He knew these individualist taxi-drivers. They preferred personal settlement to stopping at the first policeman and laying a charge. The taxi-driver looked round sharply, made a wrong assumption. His manner became instantly servile, ingratiating.
> "Oga mi, hm, so even Nigeria Police no fit arrest this foolish rain."
> For a moment Sagoe nearly betrayed himself. Then he understood and ceased to worry. "What," with just the edge of menace in his voice "is the matter with your windscreen wiper?"
> That confirmed it. "Sah? You mean the wiper, sah?"
> Sagoe did not condescend to repeat his question.
> "Oga, na dese foolish firm o. Na today today I take car commot for service, then rain begin and look my trouble. De thing no gree work."
> "You have no speedometer either."
> "Enh, oga mi, you see wetin man dey suffer. Sixteen

pound ten na in den charge me for service. Unless we Africans drive all dis foreign firm . . . "
"Stop!"
"Oga, enh, you say make a stop?"
"I said stop. Stop!"
"Ha, oga, make you no vex now . . . I beg you, oga, I still get case for court for driving wit no light."
"Are you deaf? Stop right here!"
The man stopped, a jelly now, and convinced also that he had lost hope of a pardon by his delay in obeying the officer. He prostrated right inside the car, wringing his hands for pity.

This passage clearly illustrates the status (and one of the abuses) of the English language in Nigeria. English represents power and authority. Hence Sagoe, who can speak pidgin English as fluently as he does standard English, never condescends to speak it with the taxi driver. Instead, he uses English to terrorize the man into unquestioning submission.

The word *oga* is very important in this respect for it means 'boss' or 'master.' Consequently, the taxi driver who offhandedly asked Sagoe initially, "Where you wan go for Obalende?" (Where do you want to go at Obalende?), quickly changes to a conciliatory and obsequious "Oga mi, hm, so even Nigeria police no fit arrest this foolish rain" (My master, hm, even the Nigeria police cannot stop this foolish rain).

The important thing here is not just the insinuation that Sagoe is a policeman or his halfhearted threat, but the language. The taxi driver knows too well that those in the Nigerian police force who speak the type of English Sagoe speaks must not be crossed. English, therefore, is the language of authority, if not oppression, in the novel.

Unlike the intelligentsia, the politicians (represented by the board members, including Chief Winsala and Sir Derinola) often switch from English to Yoruba, even in situations where conformity to an official language is expected. An instance of this occurs during a board meeting in which Sekoni refuses to be a party to professional sinecurism by asserting that, as an engineer, he cannot continue with signing vouchers, letters, and bicycle allowances. His idealistic stance shocks the board members so much that, in the attendant pandemonium, one of the members asks *"Omo tani?"* (Whose son is he?) (27). Another instance occurs during Sagoe's meeting with Chief Winsala at the Hotel Excelsior. During their discussion, Winsala refers to white men as all the oyinbo and later asks Sagoe for a bribe with the euphemistic expression *"Se wa s'omo fun wa?"* (Will you behave like a son to us?) (84). Winsala's code-switching in this circumstance is an attempt to assume a sort of solidarity with Sagoe, whom he had earlier derided at an interview. Because of the shameful demand he is making, Winsala resorts to a characteristic Yoruba euphemism that an elderly person uses for such a demand as a means of neutralizing a possible belligerent reaction from Sagoe, thus building in the question an escape valve should Sagoe react negatively. Later, when he discovers that Sagoe clearly understood and was ready to cooperate, he becomes more direct. When Sagoe becomes impatient with him and pretends he is going into his room to look for more money, Winsala is happy, saying "When the sanitary inspector looks under the bed he's looking for *kola*, not *tanwiji*" (85). *Kola* is another Nigerian euphemism (more or less direct) for bribe, while *tanwiji* is a mosquito larva sometimes found in water pots.

The second time Chief Winsala code-switches from English to Yoruba is during his disgraceful encounter with Greenbottle, the waiter, when the chief cannot pay for the extra drinks he orders. On realizing that Greenbottle is ready to engage him in physical combat, Winsala mutters:

> *"Agba n't'ara*... it is no matter for rejoicing when a child sees his father naked, *l'ogolonto. Agba n't ara.* The wise eunuch keeps from women; the hungry clerk dons coat over his narrow belt and who will say his belly is flat? But when *elegungun* is unmasked in the market, can he then ask egbe to snatch him into the safety of *igbale*? Won't they tell him the grove is meant only for keepers of mystery? *Agba n't'ara.* When the Bale borrows a horse-tail he sends a menial; so when the servant comes back empty-handed he can say, Did I send you? The adulterer who makes assignations in a room with one exit, is he not asking to feed his scrotum to the fishes of Ogun? *Agba n't'ara."* (91)

Ironically, before this showdown, Winsala has been addressing and threatening the waiter in English, pronouncing cheeky as "*sh*eeky" (a characteristic feature of Yoruba interference with English). "You are sheeky. If you sheek me I will get you sacked. Now get away," he says (90).

However, the moment he perceives imminent disgrace, he talks quietly to himself in his humble native language, abandoning the language of authority. Two things are of interest in the Yoruba expressions he uses. One is the emphasis he places on *Agba n't'ara*, which is repeated four times in a paragraph of twelve lines. The expression implies a full consciousness of one's old age and its deserved respectability. By this utterance, Winsala realizes the indignity with which he has been conducting himself. The second is the metaphoric nature of the switching. He realizes he will soon be naked *(l'ogolonto)*, not only physically but also morally, and that his masquerade *(elegungun)* will soon be unmasked in public and will not have any protection, even in his cult *(igbale)* of corruption. This is indeed a good example of what Traugott and Pratt call situational codeswitching, a switching motivated by embarrassment and belated self-consciousness.

In an almost similar type of clash of values between Dehinwa and her relatives from home (who typically represent the traditional people in the novel), we see another use of code-switching. Earlier, Dehinwa and her mother together with her aunt, who had arrived at night, unannounced, had had an argument on the question of marriage and the type of man Dehinwa could and could not marry. The argument started when the aunt informed Dehinwa of the vision an *Aladura* (Christian sect noted for visionary capability) had concerning her: that she had a son. This point led to the issue of the paternity of the child, which was actually the whole point of the parents' visit — they resented the possibility of Dehinwa getting married to a northerner whom they refer to as *Gambari* (a contemptuous Yoruba reference to the Hausas in northern Nigeria). They therefore came over not only to discuss it with her, but also to warn her against moving with certain types of men. Dehinwa advised her parents against such a visit in the future in case she has a man with her in the house. The mother's reaction was firm: she would shout *ibosi* (a shout of shame) on such a man and humiliate him in public. The words *Aladura, Gambari,* and *ibosi* indicate the traditional values and beliefs of many Yorubas. The *Aladuras* are seen as a special religious sect whose visionary ability should be reckoned with in matters of significance, such as the choice of a marriage partner. *Gambari* reflects the tribalistic and parochial tendency of some Yorubas who regard their Hausa neighbors as less human than themselves. Finally, *ibosi* signals the revulsion Dehinwa's mother has at the idea of a man staying the night with her working-class daughter — a matter of traditional morality. When viewed in their total significance, those words do not merely portray the traditional values and character of Dehinwa's people or even of some Yoruba traditional ideas and beliefs; they also represent a clash of modern values with the old ones. In spite of all the traditionally persuasive expressions used to convince her, Dehinwa never uses any Yoruba words in her discussion with her mother. Informal and familiar as the situation ought to be, she spoke to her mother in the language of her class throughout.

Another character who switches from English to Yoruba is Lazarus, the leader of the religious cult. Although his switching is not so frequent, it is important because Soyinka uses it to ridicule the idea of Christ's victory over death. To understand this better, a brief idea of Soyinka's attitude toward death is necessary. He believes that death is one of the basic realities of life, and that human beings must learn to accept it. Lazarus' sermon emphasizes the powerlessness of death over human beings since Jesus has conquered death. By using distinct graphological characters to highlight various biblical quotations in support of this doctrine, Soyinka draws our attention to the fallacy of this view. He reintorces this irony by having Lazarus use such contextually funny Yoruba expressions as *gidigbo, Ologomugomu* and *fun-fun-fun* in his sermon. Soyinka is clearly being satirical at this point.

For the purpose of illustration, *gidigbo* has an English equivalent, 'head butt' or 'wrestling,' which would have been equally appropriate, but because Soyinka (not Lazarus) wants to ridicule the idea of Christ's victory over death, he says:

"He wrestled with death and he knocked him down. Death said, let us try gidigbo and Christ held him by the neck, he squeezed that neck until Death bleated for mercy." (165)

Soyinka advances the ridicule when Lazarus compares Death to *Ologomugomu* (a spectral figure). The satire ends when Lazarus says that

"even Martha the sister of the dead man held her nose with a scarf when the son of man [Jesus] asked her to remove the stone [of the cave]. She made *fun-fun-fun* with her nose." (167)

Fun-fun-fun is the sound a person makes on encountering a putrid odor. The statement is intended to deride the biblical passage that quotes Jesus as saying "Our friend, Lazarus, sleepeth." We cannot but ask ourselves if a man asleep could become so revoltingly odious. The code-switching here is remarkably appropriate. It is used as an instrument of satire and as a means of puncturing a doctrine that is repugnant to Soyinka.

The scene in which a mob is chasing the thief, Noah, is another episode of code-switching. Because of the anonymity of the mob, it is not possible to identify those doing the switching. This is as it ought to be. Nevertheless, there are at least five instances of switching in the mob scene, representing a true characteristic of mob identity. Languages of denunciation can be as many as the people who constitute the mob. Also, all forms of linguistic vulgarity, curses, and derision are possible, as shown by the following examples: *"Ole! Ole-e-e-e-e"* (thief! thie-e-e-e-ef); *"Omo Ole"* (son of a thief), *"Ole! E fi 'gbati fun yeye!"* (Thief! Give the bastard a slap), "Just lend me your stick, Alakori" (no English equivalent, but it is a term of abuse greatly resented by the Yoruba tribe); "Are you shy? Remove your dark gaga [contemptuous reference to sun glasses] so that we can recognize your face" (117). The code-switching paints a realistic picture of a mob and portrays the typical attitude to hoodlums in Nigeria.

So far, we have discussed code-switching from English to Yoruba. Another form of code-switching is the one described by Hasselmo (1970) as ragged. It involves not just the use of linguistic features of a different language or dialect, but also features of interference from the first language. This is the sort of codeswitching that Peter, the German journalist, does. Peter is portrayed as a clumsy and disreputable character. He uses American pronunciation with ridiculous interference from his German language. Consequently, he pronounces the voiced interdental fricative (ð) as (z), the voiced alveolar fricative. He has neither a sense of direction nor a perceivable value system. This is revealed in his abortive attempt to be American in speech, even though his German background will not allow him:

> "Yeah. Wall, not really. I'm German but I use 'merican passport. Just gonna get m'self a zrink. So soree couldn't come down wi'ze others to Lagos, burra had a date wiz a Minister. I'm a journalist, you know, reckon Bandili told you. Did you paint ze town red last night? Fabulous guy your Minister, real feller of a guy. Invired me to spend a weekend at his country residence." (136)

Peter represents those foreigners who are also struggling with their value system. He is not only "unbearable," he is, to use Hasselmo's term, "ragged" in character. Peter wants to be what he is not, just as Joe Golder, the black American lecturer in history, whose complexion is more white than black, wants to be ebony black by continually torturing himself in the hot sun.

They are not the only phony characters in the novel. Professor Oguazor is the personification of pretense and false values. He lives in a "plastic" world, not the world of reality. His living room, his language, and his conduct all suggest hypocrisy and contempt. But here we will concern ourselves not with the plastic fruits and flowers in his house, nor with his illegitimate daughter, but with his linguistic affectation.

It is a sociolinguistic fact that, in a bilingual situation, if a person's performance in a second language is as perfect as or very close to that of the native speakers of the second language, such a person becomes culturally suspect in his society. This seems to be the case with Professor Oguazor, whose idea of "meral terpitude" clashes with his own actions as well as with his language, which portrays him as pretentious and snobbish. Soyinka makes his hypocrisy obvious by placing him side by side with his wife, whose pronunciation is no different from that of other members of the intelligentsia. But here we have the professor whose pronunciation is patently above the received pronunciation (RP). Worse still, the pronunciation is inconsistent. Sometimes he pronounces his wife's name as "Caroline"; at another point he calls her "Ceroline." He succeeds in making himself despicable, corrupting a language he pretends to know so well. Below are some of the features of his pronunciation:

come—cem
musn't—mesn't
ladies—ledies
fond—fend
moral—meral

It should be mentioned that these are not features of linguistic interference; they are a product of affectation. It is no wonder that Eldred Jones describes him as "the novel's main satirical butt of the Ibadan establishment" (161). If nothing else shows this, the way in which he expresses himself does. Code-switching is again used here as an instrument of satire. The speech below distinguishes the professor among other members of his class:

> "The whole centry is senk in meral terpitude. We are just wetting to discover the responsible student, then we will know what to do with him." (249)

Because the Professor is placed among equally knowledgeable members of his class, the satire becomes more pungent and obvious. With him, Soyinka completes his satirical intent in *The Interpreters*.

Whatever amount of success *The Interpreters* enjoys as a work of art is partly dependent on code-switching. Both the linguistic varieties and the more specific switching from one code to the other contribute immensely to the aesthetic quality of the novel. First, it gives the novel a great measure of realism both in setting and content. More important, it reflects the author's craft at building characters and situations. It is used not only as an instrument of satire, but also as a means of depicting the themes of the novel, such as the clash of values between the old and the new, and intellectual hypocrisy.

UNIVERSITY OF WISCONSIN—MILWAUKEE

Works Cited

Ackley, Donald. "Wole Soyinka's *The Interpreters.*" *Black Orpheus* II, nos. 5 and 6 (1970):50-57
Gumperz, John. "Verbal Strategies in Multilingual Communication." *Monograph Series on Language and Linguistics.* Washington, D.C.: Georgetown University, 1970.
———and Edward Hernandez. "Cognitive Aspects of Bilingual Communication." *Working Papers* 28. Berkeley: University of Califomia, 1969.
Hasselmo, Nils. "Code-Switching and Modes of Speaking." *Texas Study in Bilingualism: Spanish, French, German, Czech, Polish, Serbian and Norwegian in the South-West,* ed. G. Gilbert. Berlin: Walter de Gruyter, 1970.
Haugen, Einar. "Bilingualism, Language Contact, and Immigrant Languages in the United States." In *Advances in the Study of Societal Multilingualism,* ed. Fishman. The Hague: Mouton, 1978.
Jones, Eldred D. *The Writings of Wole Soyinka.* London: Heinemann, 1973.
Lance, Donald M. *A Brief Study of Spanish-English Bilingualism: Final Report.* Texas: College Station, 1969.
Lawrence, D. H. *The Plumed Serpent.* London: Heinemann, 1955.
Leech, G. N. and M. H. Short. *Style in Fiction.* New York: Longman, 1981.
Rayfield, Joan R. "The Languages of a Bilingual Community." In *Janua Linguarum Series.* The Hague: Mouton, 1970.
Soyinka, Wole. *The Interpreters.* New York: Africana Publishing, 1965.
Traugott, E. C. and M. L. Pratt. *Linguistics for Students of Literature.* New York: Harcourt Brace Jovanovich, 1980.
Tutuola, Amos. *The Palmwine Drinkard.* New York: Grove Press, 1953.

THE LANGUAGE OF PASSION IN SOYINKA'S *THE INTERPRETERS*:
A STYLISTIC ANALYSIS

James O. Omole

A novel such as *The Interpreters* is composed of many situations and events. These are commonly described in different registers, that is, varieties of language suitable to the varying situations. In this sense, a novel may draw upon a wide range of registers, ranging from the conversational and philosophical to the professional, technical, and religious. A close examination of such linguistically distinct situations can help reveal their aesthetic functions in the larger context of the novel as a whole.

Such linguistically distinct situations in *The Interpreters* include the lovemaking scenes. These scenes, among others, demonstrate Wole Soyinka's experience as a poet since they are characterized by a poetic use of language. This poetry in his prose is one of the problems in understanding Soyinka's style, which Niyi Osundare (1983) describes as "words of Iron, sentences of Thunder" (24). This poetic style consists of metaphors, syntactic reductions, ambiguity, grammatical foregrounding, and referential inexplicitness that jar the expectations of readers. Such a poetic style within a prose narrative is disruptive and hence difficult, especially if one fails to appreciate its possible artistic motives. This paper will look at the language used in the love-making scenes in which Soyinka's prose is elevated to the level of esoteric poetry. In doing so, it explicates Soyinka's artistic device for describing an otherwise indecorous subject. There are two love-making scenes in *The Interpreters*. The first is Egbo's initial sexual encounter with Simi; the second is his deflowering of a student. In these scenes there is a deliberate avoidance of sexually explicit words and expressions. The words employed are euphemistic in reference while the syntax is poetic in structure. One possible reason for this is that Soyinka may be using poetic language to depict scenes of high emotion. These claims are substantiated at various points. First, Egbo's encounter with Simi is described in terms that are neither direct nor specific.

> As the taxi stopped his hand flew towards his pocket, but Simi stopped him, placing her hand on the bulge beneath his pocket and Egbo winced, "Save it," she said. In the house she locked the door and turned to him, "Don't be too anxious. You are not very experienced at all." (Soyinka 1972:59)

Although there is no direct mention of love-making, the word *bulge* suggests "erection," which Egbo is trying to cover up by putting his hand in his pocket. Simi placing her hand on it also hints at what is about to happen. We are informed that Egbo "winces" and that Simi advises him to "save it." They "lock the door," and again Simi warns him not to "be too anxious." Later, we are let into Egbo's inner thoughts:

> [I]f I talk, I shall surely burst. If I speak this rising boast will surely go down again. And are all women like this, that they know men on sight? That they can tell them inside out . . . ? She had gone into an inner room . . . (59)

The expression *this rising boast* is inexplicit and ambiguous in the sense that it could refer literally to Egbo's maddening desire to make love to Simi, or it could refer metaphorically to Egbo's "bulge." The stage of erection is sometimes figuratively referred to as a *boast* in Yoruba. The Yoruba saying *oko n leri; obo n leri; ipade dori bedi*, (the penis is boasting; the vagina is boasting; the place of duel is in the bed) supports this interpretation. Other words and expressions used to describe this stage of Egbo's sexual adventure include *Jaws . . . clamped in a vice, standing above her, heart . . . pounding, touched him about* and *Egbo felt himself lifted* (59). This euphemistic language describes the sexual foreplay; the sex act is described in a highly poetic register characterized by metaphors and phrasal repetitions. The description partly comprises Egbo's thoughts and his inaudible mumblings at the different stages of intercourse. The mumblings consist of his personal or private metaphors, and suggestive lexical items. The passage below marks the beginning of the act, the stage of coitus.

> I am that filled bag in a stiff breeze riding high grass on Warri airfield, when it lay fallow... "My dear, what are you saying?"... filled bag in a stiff breeze, high on the airfield, when it lay fallow... "What is it, my dear?" (60)

This metaphoric passage recalls Egbo's youthful experience at the Warri airfield. Egbo is the bag filled with desire, and he is being blown by the stiff breeze of emotion. Simi is the airfield on which he is riding (there is a play on the word "airfield" here), and her pubic hair, the grass. The words *filled bag, stiff, lay,* and *high* suggest sexual objects, positions, and acts.

The intensity of the act is described in equally intense language, marked by blatantly confusing syntax and ambiguous diction: "through hidden floods a sheath canoe parts tall reeds, not dies, God not dies a rotten hulk... " *Hidden floods* and *tall reeds* may be taken to refer to Simi's private parts and pubic hair, while a *sheath canoe* refers to Egbo's penis penetrating through Simi's pubic hair (he is probably wearing a sheath). *Not dies, God, not dies a rotten hulk...* is confusing in syntax and ambiguous in diction. *Not dies,* repeated twice, is plainly ungrammatical; but when considered along with the complement *a rotten hulk, dies* seems to function as a verb. But its position suggests it could also be a noun. We are then left with the interpretation of *dies* as objects. "Dies" are tools or devices for imparting a desired shape, form, or finish to a material or for impressing an object or material. Again, this interpretation will not stand because of the phrase *a rotten hulk*, which could mean 1) "a heavy clumsy ship," 2) "a bulky or unwieldy person or thing," 3) "the body of an old ship unfit for service," or 4) "an abandoned wreck or shell of a ship used as a prison." But because of the overall navigation imagery, we may say that Egbo, albeit ungrammatically, internally rejoices that his "Sheath Canoe" (his penis) does not die "a rotten hulk." In other words, his penis which on page 58 he fears may be "limp" or become a "raw cotton plug," is not after all useless. In short, the lexical and syntactic ambiguity and confusion here may be seen as a foregrounding device representing the uncontrollable ecstasy Egbo is experiencing. This seems to be supported by the following passage: "And a lone pod strode the baobab on the tapering thigh, leaf shorn, and high mists swirl him, haze-splitting storms, but the stalk stayed him" (60). This passage describes the climax of the whole act of orgasmic fulfillment. The "lone pod," suggestively used because of its shape and reinforced by its loneliness, refers to Egbo's penis, and the "baobab" is Simi, whose thigh is described as "tapering" (referring to its shape). "Leaf-shorn" in this context connotes that Simi is naked: the baobab without its leaf is Simi without her clothes. So involved in the whole ecstatic experience, Egbo feels swirled along by "high mists" and feels as if he is experiencing a storm. The words *haze* and *mists* are important yardsticks for measuring Egbo's experience. The two words are more or less synonymous. Since in this context they "swirl" Egbo, mists can be taken as Egbo's sperm (liquid or water droplets) that swirl around, dimming his vision. Figuratively, *haze* suggests vagueness of mind. Here Egbo is at the stage of orgasm; he is psychologically and visually unconscious, so much so that only "the stalk stayed him." Only "a slender upright object" or "connecting part", his penis, holds him in position. This is the climax of Egbo's sexual initiation. The completion of the act is described below:

> When it lay flooded when it lay flooded. There were tassels for the man, sweet roots for the child, and above cloud curds waited for the chosen one of God . . . Parting low mists in a dark canoe . . . in darkness let me lie, in darkness cry.... (60)

When it lay flooded, repeated for poetic effect, suggests that Simi's vagina lay flooded with Egbo's sperm. Egbo's penis now assumes a "tassel" shape, a drooping bunch of sinews ("tassels for the man"). Egbo, the child, has now been initiated: he now has "sweet roots." However, the referent of "the chosen one of God" is not clear. It may refer to Simi, that is, as the one chosen by God to initiate Egbo. At this stage of the act, the high mists (sperm) that swirl Egbo now become "...parting low mists" in Simi's "dark canoe" (vagina). Thus what is high is now low; what has gathered is now parting, and the "rising boast" has finally gone "down again." The emotional "storm" on the lovemaking seas is now calm, giving a momentary rest to Egbo and Simi's sheath and dark canoe. We must note the rhyming of the last two clauses, one full, the other elliptical. It gives the passage a tone of conclusiveness.

Although comparatively much shorter, the description of Egbo's second sexual encounter, this time with a female student, is stylistically similar. However, Egbo is now the initiator while the girl is the initiated. The action is described in only three sentences:

> Egbo drew her to him. The hardness was only an outside crust, only the stubborn skin on her self-preservation and it gave in his eager hands. The centre pure ran raw red blood, spilling on the toes of the god, and afterwards he washed this for her protesting shamefacedly in the river. (134).

There are some important poetic devices to note in this short passage. First is the ambiguous use of the word *hardness*. It may refer to the hitherto inscrutable toughness of the lady's character or to her hymen. This is evident in the appositive relationship between *the hardness*, and . . . *the stubborn skin on her self-preservation*. Whichever sense we choose becomes "an outside crust" because the girl easily gave in to Egbo's touch. The phrase *outside crust* serves to emphasize the ease with which she gave in. The second sentence is also a good example of syntactic compression that characterizes poetry. In that sentence alone lie the details of Egbo's action. He uses his finger to rip open the lady's hymen, that is "the stubborn skin on her self-preservation," consequently, the "centre pure ran raw red blood." "The centre pure" is an instance of poetic inversion that euphemistically refers to the lady's private parts. Besides this, the sentence is significant for its sound effect. *Ran, raw,* and *red* alliterate. *Pure raw* and *blood,* all monosyllables, dominate the sentence, emphasizing the harshness and abruptness that attend the experience. The middle stress on *red* clogs the otherwise regular rhythm of the sentence. This makes the clause entirely appropriate to the sense of the passage: the clogging of the vagina, first by her hymen, then by blood. The "toes of the god" is an allusion (another poetic device) to the foot of the Olumo rock. We notice a sort of grammatical fusion in the word *this* in the third sentence. It refers either to the blood or the centre, making them one and the same thing. The non-finite clause, *protesting shamefacedly in the river*, seems to be semantically illogical, for it suggests that Egbo, the subject of the clause, was "protesting shamefacedly" while washing the blood. Given the contrasting personalities of Egbo and the girl, it is the girl who should be protesting, more so when she has just surrendered something so dear to her to a man she hardly knows.

These poetic devices serve important aesthetic functions. The anaphoric nominal *the hardness* unites the girl's previous reputation of toughness with her implied resistance to Egbo's desire. So also does the appositive construction *The hardness . . . the stubborn skin on her self-preservation* makes the girl's resistance identical with her virginal virtue. *This* also unites vagina and blood. These instances of co-referentiality emphasize the sexual unity between Egbo and the girl.

Overall, Soyinka's style or register in the passages analyzed is appropriate to their emotional significance. First, it is a means of freely discussing a taboo subject such as sex. An open discussion of such topics usually takes the form of euphemism, characterized by suggestiveness and indirectess. In this case, the poetic register is also used as a foregrounding device for indicating emotional intensity and its attendant loosening of control. Through the use of confusing register (ambiguous expressions) and grammatical deviance, Soyinka depicts Egbo's incoherence during his emotional ecstasy. Such language also artistically distinguishes the sexual scenes from other less emotional scenes in the text.

UNIVERSITY OF ILORIN—NIGERIA

Works Cited

Omole, James O. "A Sociolinguistic Analysis of Wole Soyinka's *The Interpreters.*" Diss. University of Wisconsin at Milwaukee, 1985.

Osundare, Niyi. "Words of Iron, Sentences of Thunder: Soyinka's Prose Style," *African Literature Today*, Vol. 13, ed. Eldred D. Jones, New York: Africana Publishing, 1983.

Soyinka, Wole. *The Interpreters.* New York: Africana Publishing, 1972.

THE STYLES OF ABIKU:
TWO RELATED DIATYPES OF ENGLISH

Mabel Osakwe

Distinct varieties of English have evolved depending on the user and the uses to which the language is being put. So prominent is this feature that the term "dialect" has been extended to include "register," "diatype," and "field." In this paper we shall focus our attention on the use of English as a vehicle for expressing an African concept — an experience that is quite foreign to the English language.

The socio-situational features that have constrained the language of the two poems considered here are quite peculiar and interesting. Particularly interesting is the regional and field situation. In addition to these, however, we shall also consider other socio-situational or contextual features like "mode" and "tenor" of discourse.[1]

J.P. Clark published his "Abiku" in 1965 and Wole Soyinka published his version two years later. Both texts are similar because, apart from belonging to the same genre they are drawn from the same African myth: Abiku, the wandering child who dies and returns repeatedly to plague the mother. Both poems are also written to be read, not necessarily to be spoken. Apparently, then, they are similar in field and mode of discourse.

They differ, however, in terms of graphological lineation. Clark's is written in free-verse paragraphs and Soyinka's in eight quatrain stanzas. This difference in form can be accounted for by the addresser-addressee relationship (tenor). Clark's extended discourse reflects the adult speaking voice, while its simple language shows that it is addressed to a child:

Coming and going these several seasons,
Do stay out on the baobab tree,
Follow where you please . . .

ABIKU

Coming and going these several seasons,
Do stay out on the baobab tree,
Follow where you please your kindred spirits
If indoors is not enough for you.
True, it leaks through the thatch
When floods brim the banks,
And the bats and owls
Often tear in at night through the eaves,
And at harmattan, the bamboo walls
Are ready tinder for the fire
That dries the fresh fish up on the rack.
Still, it's been the healthy stock
To several fingers, to many more will be
Who reach to the sun.
No longer then bestride the threshold
But step in and stay
For good. We know the knife scars
Serrating down your back and front
Like the beak of the sword-fish,
And both your ears, notched
As a bondsman to this house,
Are all relics of your first comings.
Then step in, step in and stay
For her body is tired,
Tired, her milk going sour
Where many more mouths gladden the heart.

J. P. Clark

From *A Reed In the Tide* (London: Longman. 1965).
Copyright J. P. Clark. Reprinted with permission.

Abiku

Wanderer child. It is the same child who dies and returns again and again to plague the mother — Yoruba belief.

In vain your bangles cast
Charmed circles at my feet
I am Abiku, calling for the first
And the repeated time.

Must I weep for goats and cowries
For palm oil and sprinkled ash?
Yams do not sprout in amulets
To earth Abiku's limbs.

So when the snail is burnt in his shell,
Whet the heated fragment, brand me
Deeply on the breast—you must know him
When Abiku calls again.

I am the squirrel teeth, cracked
The riddle of the palm; remember
This, and dig me deeper still into
The god's swollen foot.

Once and the repeated time, ageless
Though I puke, and when you pour
Libations, each finger points me near
The way I came, where.

The ground is wet with mourning
White dew suckles flesh-birds
Evening befriends the spider, trapping
Flies in wine-froth;

Night, and Abiku sucks the oil
From lamps. Mothers! I'll be the
Suppliant snake coiled on the doorstep
Yours the killing cry.

> The ripe fruit was saddest;
> Where I crept, the warmth was cloying.
> In silence of webs, Abiku moan, shaping
> Mounds from the yolk.
>
> Wole Soyinka
>
> From *Idanre and Other Poems* (London: Methuen, 1967).
> Reprinted with permission.

In Soyinka's poem it is the Abiku child speaking, as is apparent from the lyrical and split-up form of children's language:

> In vain your bangles cast
> Charmed circles at my feet
> I am Abiku, calling for the first
> And the repeated time . . .

Whereas Clark's poem is a plea to Abiku for tenderness and sympathy toward the mother, Soyinka's is an assertion that the human spirit is indestructible. The functions of the language as well as the functional tenor of the writers as poets are evident in the language use. Hence Clark uses imperatives, pseudo-declaratives, declaratives, and semi-sentences:

> Do stay out . . .
> But step in and stay,
> We know the knife scars . . .
> Tired, her milk going sour . .

The many conjunctives, which are by no means loosely strung together, result in hypotactic structures. The elliptical sentences yield unusual structures characteristic of the language of poetry: p conj P.S. This initial positioning of the predicator foregrounds effectively the main idea of the poem, "coming and going."

Since Soyinka's poem is assertive, what we read are mainly declarative sentences with one interrogative:

I am Abiku...
Yams do not sprout in amulets...
I am the squirrel teeth...
Mothers! I'll be the
suppliant snake...

Instead of Clark's syllogism, there is much asyndeton. Apart from Soyinka's predilection for hypotactic structures, another socio-situational factor that accounts for his language is the influence of traditional incantatory poetry that revels in complex language, in elliptical and disjointed sentences. For example:

Night, and Abiku sucks the oil
From lamps...

The ellipted article before *Night* transforms it from a lexical item into a prominent symbol of fear, uncertainty, and death. Hence, structural ellipsis is a deliberate choice.

Words enter into a new collocational range because of the field and subject of discourse. Thus, *Abiku* collocates with *sacrifice* in Yoruba traditional belief, and all other words used within that religious register keep meaningful company with each other. In the first stanza of Soyinka's poem, *Abiku* reverberates in bangles and subsequently in *charmed circles*. What the poet does is a kind of magical play on words: the reification process from human Abiku to mere concrete but inanimate objects (bangles) and then to the pseudo-concrete (*circles*) is effectively employed in ridiculing the practice of using charmed bangles to compel Abiku to stay.

In the second stanza *goats, cowries, sprinkled ash,* and *amulets* are collocates of both *Abiku* and *bangles* since they are the sacrificial ingredients that go into the making of the bangles. Again, their company becomes meaningful only in the context of Soyinka's subject matter. Abiku's limbs are "earthed" like *yams* with *amulets* but *yams*, says the poet, "do not sprout in amulets." Soyinka's point is covertly made here that such charms do not sustain the life of mere yam tubers, let alone man or, worse still, an indestructible spirit like Abiku.

There is a central lexical thread that is skillfully interwoven by Soyinka to reflect the cyclic movement of Abiku, words like *bangles, circles,* and the *Earth. Earth,* in fact, is overloaded with meaning. In addition to its link with lexical items connoting round shape, it also collocates with *mound, yam,* and *sprout* — that is, the whole cyclic process of planting, which is a form of burying in the Earth and sprouting with new life. Because of this irony inherent in the concept of Abiku, a number of words in the poem are used with their full ironic import. *Whet,* for example, in addition to meaning "sharpen," is also a pun on *wet* since in this context sharpening tools with which to brand Abiku is like wetting or cooling them for a futile ritual. Similarly, "I'll be the *suppliant snake* . . . Yours the *killing cry"* is a deliberate choice that flouts the rules of selectional restriction and further highlights the irony in the poem: Abiku should be a *killing* rather than a *suppliant snake.* And the mother's cry, rather than being *suppliant,* is actually *killing* to Abiku since attempts made at placating it only result in its dying and coming back again to plague mother — an experience that is killing also to the mother.

The eighth stanza shows the same pattern:

. . . ripe fruit was saddest;
. . . warmth was cloying.

all pointing to Soyinka's economical use of words. By overloading the lines, he is able to say much within the short poem.

Part of the difficulty in tracing usual lexical collocates arises because the writer is grappling with the problem of expressing African ideas in a foreign language. "Abiku" the title is a transferred lexical item with no English equivalent. What Soyinka does is to explain the word extra-textually, while Clark integrates it into the opening lines.

Clark takes the more traditional view of Abiku, and he is therefore in sympathy with the mother. Words collocate in the context of these beliefs. Abiku is believed to dwell with *kindred spirits* in the other world on such omen-bearing trees as the *baobab. Owls* and *bats* link up with kindred spirits. Some lexical items keep meaningful company only in the context of Abiku's appalling state: "Knife scars" is an anaphoric reference to Abiku's ritual scars and also collocates with *notched, bondsman,* and *relics.*

Notching Abiku down the back with a knife binds the spirit. Different sets of collocates reflect Abiku's new world: *leaking . . . thatch, floods, brimmed banks, harmattan, bamboo walls, fresh fish,* and so on. Abiku keeps an ideational company with this set. They reflect changes in season from an extreme of floods to drought. These seasons come and go like Abiku. Since the paradox inherent in Abiku is part of a natural paradox even in this world, then Abiku should feel comfortable and "not bestride the threshold." Thus, the appeal to stay is made through reasoned argument. Clark's images are not just African but riverine and rural, reflecting Abiku's new home.

The function of the language in each poem affects the choice made by each poet. Hence Soyinka's images merge into each other, but Clark's ideas flow into each other. Clark's repeated use of a number of lexical items enables him to emphasize and persuade Abiku. His unique environment is reflected in the lexical choice too (for example, homely similes like "beak of a sword-fish").

For both poems, the most obvious socio-situational elements that distinguish them are the traditional figures of speech and images: "goats and cowries," "squirrel teeth," and "snail burnt in his shell." It is in these usages that each poem is unique and at the same time related. Both Soyinka and Clark have succeeded in communicating their ideas succinctly in spite of the fact that these ideas and experiences are written in a language foreign to them.

The foregoing analysis has revealed among other things that the poems differ in style. This makes a case against the view that content and style are inseparable. We have also tried to show that there is more to style; it goes even beyond the text, and the situational context comes into play as well as related texts.

BENDEL STATE UNIVERSITY, ABRAKA—NIGERIA

Note

1. The meaning here is related to the role being played by the language user in the language activity; the user's purposive role (field), medium relationship (mode), and addressee relationship (tenor).

Works Cited

Clark. J. P. *A Reed in the Tide.* London: Longman, 1965.
Enkvist, Nils Erij, John Spencer, and Michael Gregory. *Linguistics and Style.* London: Oxford University Press, 1964.
Gregory, M. "Aspects of Varieties Differentiation." *Journal of Linguistics* 3, (1967).
Halliday, M A K. "Language Structure and Language Function" In *New Horizons in Linguistics.* Ed. J. Lyons, Harmondsworth: Penguin, 1970.
Soyinka, W. *Idanre and Other Poems.* London: Methuen, 1967.
Young, P. The Language of West African Literature in English. In *The English Language in West Africa.* Ed. John Spencer, London: Longman, 1971.

DENSELY SPEAKING: TO DO OR NOT TO DO:
A COMPARATIVE STYLISTIC ANALYSIS OF SOYINKA'S AND CLARK'S POEMS

Mabel Osakwe

Density of speaking refers to the quality of texture of a text. It has to do with the cohesive devices used in the text which on interacting with the logical structure affects its realization as a text. When such devices are clustered, they are referred to as either 'tight' or 'dense' (c.f. Halliday and Hasan: 1976:296).

Poets in particular have a penchant for dense clusters of cohesive ties as an economical means of exploring the resources of their language. Density of speaking for poets varies from one level of simplicity through various gradations of simplicity and complexity to extreme obscurantism.

This paper presents a comparative stylistic analysis of the use of language by two Nigerian pioneer poets. Six texts (three by each poet) are brought under focus at four levels of analysis: intratextual, inter-textual, intra-authorial, and inter-authorial. These levels of analysis interact to produce a broad spectrum of stylistic analysis revealing the dynamic interaction between the logical structure and local texture as instances of the argument that:

(i) The choice to use or not to use densely clustered ties could be idiosyncratic arising from the author's talent, his : socializing agencies as well as manner and level of exposure to the L_2- idiolectal and Diatopic factors.

(ii) But some other contextual categories such as the subject matter, the addresser addressee relationship, point of view : and medium of addresser addressee relationship, point of view and medium of address (being aspects of 'Field' 'Tenor' and 'Mode' of Discourse or Diatypic Varieties, see Gregory 1967, Gregory and Carroll 1978, and Halliday 1978), contribute a large percentage to the choice of such usages.

(iii) Density of speaking is not synonymous with obscurantism, but the latter may be an instance of the former.

(iv) Obscurantism should be acceptable considered alongside (i) - (iii) above.

(v) Simplicity of language couched in dense clusters should be extolled for the same reasons.

The Nigerian civil war was one common experience which deeply pained these poets (either physically, emotionally or both) while it lasted and in its aftermath. Soyinka suffered detention, deprivations, and loss, while Clark smarted from the loss of his personal friends.

Clark mourned this sad event in his *Casualties*. In the poem 'Dirge' (see Clark 1970: 28) he chose to speak of it in very simple but dense style. In the seventeen-line verse paragraph the poet adopts the speaking voice of the self-comforting and the audience-comforting sage. The linguistic signals of this are observable first in the functional status of the sentences. Twelve out of the sixteen sentences are positive declaratives and axiomatic:

> Death is what you cannot undo.
> Tears do not water a land.
> Fear builds a place of ruin.

Two of the declaratives axioms are conveyed forcefully and indirectly in exclamatory and rhetorical questions:

> Show me a house where nobody has died
> Must the forest fall with it?

The other four sentences are emphatic imperatives which are admonitory:

O let us light the funeral pile
But let us not cut the clan!

Further structural ties which point away from addresser to the shared relationship with addressee (tenor) are seen in the choice of very simple structures, simple units that a mind in despair can absorb with ease. Thirteen out of the sixteen sentences belong to this simple and short type, ranging from the shortest (five-word) normal SPC structure, to the longest (nine-word) simple PSC inversion. The complex sentences are also short; two out of the three are even shorter than some of the simple ones and conform to the normal SPC structure, with simple 'yet' 'and' or relative clause subordination.

Apart from the lucidity engendered by the grammar of the poem, the simple lexis and collocations give additional density that help to convey meaning forcefully. There are hardly any syntactic ties between the lines. The poet depends a lot on lexical ties. The last word of a line is often reiterated anaphorically through its usual synonyms or near synonyms. For example the lexical item 'dies' which ends the first line of the poem is immediately reiterated in the initial word of the second line as 'Death' and as 'killed' on the third line. Similarly, 'Tree,' the final word of the fourth line, is picked up initially in line five as 'A tree' and in line six as 'forest.' And 'Desert,' the final lexeme of the seventh line, is stretched across the full length of the eighth line as it reverberates in its periphrastic reference, "A place of stones and bones."

In the succeeding five lines, 9–14, the most cohesive and powerful tie which integrates all the components of language is employed. The lines have an initial rhyme which repeats also the diphthong (/i ə/; a use of assonance which in addition to emphasizing the ideational link between tears and fears (their futile and limited outcomes) also reiterates phonologically the physiological ear /i ə/ which must listen now to these undisputable truths and these pleas that are being conveyed repeatedly in repetitive structures.

The ease with which the lexical resonances are traced stem from the fact that they conform to their usual collocational range. Other lexical chains that add to the density of the text are

"water" - "tears" - "fount from the heart"
"cut down" - "fall"
"build - "pile up" - "not cut down"
"light" - "faggot" - "charcoal"

Although the poet's usages are not entirely new, they are endowed with a special poise and novelty in their combination. This poise is further coloured by the rhetoric of the poet's L_1. The rhetoric is particularly noticeable at the conceptual level, signalled linguistically by the lexico-semantic choices and a few structural ones.

Out of one seed springs the tree (APS)
(A tree in a mad act is cut down) A (SAP)
Must the forest fall with it? P S P A

In those lines Clark explores the common pool of his two languages in the use of the word-order inversion which has regular colloquial usage in his L_1 and a more restricted poetic usage in the L_2.

A comparable level of simplicity of style is displayed in Soyinka's poem "Journey" (cf., Soyinka 1972:85). Soyinka in his preface to this anthology refers to the poems in this collection (except a few) as having a loom-shuttle unity and of the 'shuttle' he says that it is "a map of the course trodden by the mind . . . ." The shuttle symbol then is the context upon which "Journey" should also derive its meaning.

The overall design of the poem, both its layout and its lineation, is short and simple. It is a fourteen-line poem — a sonnet structured idiosyncratically into three discourse units or stanzas, seven + three + four lines each, to give it a Soyinkaesque touch. Although only three of the eight sentences constituting the text are simple, the poet uses simple coordinating and subordinating techniques to link the ideas:

I never feel I have arrived, though I come
To journey's end. I took the road
That loses crest to questions, yet . . .

The poem which speaks of man's sojourn on earth uses normal

lexical echoes of journey: 'road', 'my way', 'bear me down', 'home', 'welcome', and some lexical strings are repeated completely and serve as a cohesive tie among the three discourse units of the poem. For example,

> I passed them on my way

is repeated at the final line of the first and second stanzas while

> I never feel I have arrived

is carried forward from the first line of the septet to the same of the quatrian.

The unusual collocations are few and their meaning easy to tease out. They are the interweave of the positive and negative forces that propel the life force:

'Down the other homeward earth' means the grave; man's home at the end of life but which to the poet is viewed as a vault of creative mysteries like the vault of the shuttle as life's stitches are spurn by the movement between the lower thread of the shuttle and the upper thread. 'Love and welcome is considered a 'snare' as they might lure man to complacency.

The vicissitudes of life are conveyed in a down-to-earth manner:

> My flesh is nibbled clean, lost
> To fretful fish among rusted hulls - [Lines 5-6]
> ... I took the road
> That loses crest to question, ... [2-3]
> Usurpers hand my cup at every
> Feast.... [13-14]

The quoted lines convey his gradual weight loss and ego disintegration in gaol, the agony of a misjudgement of his positive traits, and the unlawful deprivation of his rights.

A major textual tie further employed by the poet is the use of the first person pronominal forms. There are nine usages of the subjective 'I,' four of the genitive 'my' and two of the objectives 'me' — twelve examples in a fourteen-line text, revealing a high density of linguistic markers of the speaker's personal involvement. The poet like Clark, actually adopts his own voice and echoes the speaking voice of Jesus Christ at the last supper by using his exact words 'my flesh', 'my cup.' These simple extra-textual allusions are so neatly integrated into the text that they yield meaning even without the biblical reference but become a more powerful, universal, and forceful means of reconciling feasting and suffering.

These two poems express the reaction of the poet to a traumatic experience. The poets opted for simplicity of style imbued with great potentials for expansiveness, each in his own way. Both poets are very much at home with their languages, which they explore. The analysis so far confirms the first and part of our third argument.

In "Abiku" (see Clark 1965: 5 and Soyinka 1967: 28-29) the same mythical subject attracts the attention of the poets. Abiku is the Yoruba wandering child who dies and returns repeatedly to plague the mother.

The first problem these bilingual writers had to resolve was that of the lexical item 'Abiku,' with no English equivalent. Whereas Soyinka explains the new items extra-textually, Clark integrates it into the opening lines—"coming and going...."

It would have been interesting to see them adopt the same viewpoint and by so doing open up another opportunity for the reader to observe more closely the idiolectal features of their style. But they adopt different viewpoints. Clark takes the more traditional view of Abiku, and he thus sympathizes with the mother:

> For her body is tired,
> Tired, her milk giving sour...

Soyinka's view is radical. He shows no sympathy to any of the parties, instead he asserts that the human spirit which Abiku represents is indestructible and it must of necessity come and go:

> In vain your bangles cast
> Charmed circles at my feet...
> Must I weep for goats and cowries...
> Yams do not sprout in amulets
> To earth Abiku's limbs.

In addition to tenor, then, the viewpoint also dictates the language function and consequently the style. The tenor and functional difference accounts for a significant difference in the two versions. For example, in their graphological lineation, Clark's is written in free-verse paragraphs and Soyinka's in eight quatrains. Clark's extended discourse reflects the adult speaking voice while its simple language shows that it is addressed to a child:

> Coming and going these several seasons
> Do stay out on the baobab tree . . .

In Soyinka's version we notice linguistic signals that it is the Abiku child speaking from the lyrical and split-up form of child language:

> I am Abiku, calling for the first
> And the repeated time . . .

An analysis elsewhere (Osakwe 1988) details these differences and also relates the texts as constituting related diatopic varieties of English by opening new collocational possibilities to reflect the traditional home (Soyinka's) and view (Clark's) of Abiku as well as the new home (Clark's, riverine Ijaw; English-speaking communities) and new view (Soyinka's + English speaking communities).

Both poems exhibit an easy complexity. The poets speak succinctly and meaningfully. Although Soyinka's is more obscure, Clark's idiosyncratic and contextual factors certainly come to play in the weighting of the complexity and simplicity as the case may be.

The styles of Abiku buttress the first three arguments. Soyinka's higher-level complexity and density is only partly idiolectal. The diatypic difference accounts for Soyinka's complexities. Behind the child language structure cited earlier is the poet's counter point of the indomitable spiritual force that needs to speak in more complex, more proverbial, and more incantatory language:

> . . . White den suckles flesh-birds
> Evening befriend the spider, trapping
> Flies in wine-froth

Soyinka overloads his lines and lexis with meaning:

> Whet the heated fragment, brand me
> Deeply on the breast—

In the single word 'whet' he phonologically evokes also its full ironic import in 'wet.' In the context of Abiku, sharpening tools ('whet') to brand Abiku is like wetting or cooling them for a futile ritual. The choice to speak in the manner he does here is the inevitable situation of the depth of mysticism needed to convey his new view point as he knits the ideas together to create an aesthetic unit.

Poetry for Soyinka is also mysticism, and the Yoruba pantheon is a major source for his literary activities. His creative muse Ogun engages his attention most of the time. In the longest poem of his first anthology (1967: 61-85), Soyinka celebrates the Ogun myth and the monumental hills of Idanre, relating them to existential problems of man on earth. The poem is often considered his grand example of obscurantism.

As we consider aspects of Soyinka's usages there, we shall also examine another instance of Clark's use of Yoruba myth in "The Imprisonment of Obatala" (Clark 1965: 6).

This is one of Clark's early poems. It is written in three sestet stanzas, each comprising an alternate rhyme quatrian and a couplet. His lexical choices are not as simple as we observed in the earlier cases considered. The complexity does not arise simply from the individual words (which pose no puzzle as seperate lexemes) but from the strange company they keep

> "lightning pit of alarms" "dart after"
> Him "daddy-long arms," "palace-sun"

and the extra-textual allusions: "Those stick insect figures!" "That mischievous stir" "Where ancestral eyes gleam."

Clark's subject matter has two referents: the first is the Obatala myth which claims that Obatala, the creation god of the Yoruba pantheon, having fallen victim to Esu mischief was sent to jail in error—an act which brought natural calamity to the earth. The other is the batik painting of the myth by Sussane Wenger. In describing the batik painting which constituted the major spectacle that inspired Clark's art, his visual sense is focused away from the mythical essence. Consequently the reference to the myth is exophoric at two levels and two removes from text. The use of exophoric reference has an inherent complexity of the cohesive tie being mediated extra-textually. This additional referent mediating between the initial referent and the present, adds yet another complexity to the text:

> These stick-insect figures! They rock the dance
> of snakes . . .

As a reference to the linear and jagged figures of Wenger's art, those lines hardly communicate the poet's meaning. The reader would need to see this painting which is a duplicate of the original art to enable him to reconcile it with the triplicate— Clark's art— and finally with the original—the Yoruba legend. It is only by so doing that '. . . Obatala' in its present form can communicate fully to the reader. Not even his extra-textual notes solve the problem.

While contemplating on the painting, the poet occasionally refers to the original as the duplicate setting, his riverine setting and even the parallel Pandora box myth intrude into the scene, resulting in obscurantism:

> And the mischievous stir, late sown or spilt
> On the way between homestead and esteem
> Well up in pots long stagnant on stilt
> Brims out to where ancestral eyes gleam

The use of complex and embedded structures contribute to the complexity of the text. The poem is made up of four complex sentences, each of the first two stanzas being a sentence and the final quatrain and couplet two separate sentences. Clark uses complex embedded structures. Below is an analysis of the shortest sentence

> (Sub)But(s) [the cry of a child at what is knows not]
> (P)Evokes trebly (A) there (C) the droop, (C) mud—
> crack and clot.

The subject of the sentence is a rankshifted group with interlocking embedding of prepositional and nominal groups and finally a rankshifted clause.

> (M) The (H) cry Q [(H) of (Cve) [(M) a (H) Child
> Q[(H) at
> (cve) [(Sub) what(s) it (P) knows not]

The use of asyndetic subordinators adds to the complexity:

> . . . they rock the dance
> of snakes, dart His daddy-long arms,
> Tangle their loping strides to mangrove stance

Even when there is simple subordination, grasp of the logical structure is made difficult by the unfamiliar exophoric reference.

> . . . ancestral eyes gleam
> Till angry waves dam the track
> *And* caterpillars riding break their back . . . . (italics mine)

On the whole the text neither has the simplicity of the 'Dirge' nor the complex ease of his 'Abiku.' Even his use of riverine images is stilted and questionable in this context. The style seems to suggest an attempt at imitating rigidly English poetic forms, which results in a less successful integration of his field and mode of discourse.

Most readers in a guess are likely to attribute this poem of Clark's to Wole Soyinka and that will puncture a strong argument on the idiosyncratic factor in style. But the analysis of 'Obatala' consolidates the second argument for contextual categories. The poet can also be viewed as an aspect of this context.

What the poem has in common with "Idanre" is the mythical subject matter and the obscure usages.

Wole Soyinka's usage deviates significantly from standard English. He does not fulfill expectations of usual graphology, syntax, and use of lexical collocations. There is also the influence of the rhetoric of his L_1.

The first noticeable deviation is the visual patterning of his verse. The stanzas do not reflect any form of grammatical coherence in their patterning. The seven sections of the poem also vary markedly in length, varying between the seven stanzas of the opening and shortest section to the forty stanzas of the fifth and longest section. No single pattern of lineation is maintained. Some of the lines are indented and others italicized. This apparently non-conformist pattern actually shows the poet integrating his oral tradition into his art. In its written form Yoruba oral poetry has an undefined verse line (see Olatunji 1970). He avails himself of this license to manipulate ideas with irregular lines and stanzas, a technique which also reflects the nature of the poet's vision at Idanre: so diversified and so nightmarish.

"Idanre" sentences are long and very complex. There is an average distribution of six clauses per sentence in "Idanre." Some of the sentences are ten lines. Apart from their length, the hypotactic and complex sentences add to the obscurantism. Let us examine just one:

(S) [(M) The (H) Sky (Q) [a slate (Q) [of scored lettering (Q) [of widening wounds (Q) [(P) eclipsed (A) in smoke,] (P) scabbed (A) From a pale cauterising hand (A) [to a jewelled (H) crucifix (Q) [(P) seared (A) in agonic purities]

There is multiple embedding and nesting of structures, which hinders comprehension. Soyinka describes the vision as it appears on his panoramic scenes, but without leaving obvious cohesive ties to enable the reader to perceive connecting threads.

Soyinka's use of collocation here is very unpredictable

Sunrise of his throat
Skeletons of speed

The connectiion between 'sunrise' and 'throat' is to be found in the poet's L_I where the pre-breakfast state of his body is referred to as the body's 'sunrise.' 'Skeletons' suggest scraps and wreckage. 'Speed' suggests 'development.' The collocation is therefore used to refer to and capture all that is negative and positive about modern technological development.

There are over fifty uncommon lexical items in the twenty-five-line poem and the readers may need good dictionaries of English as they encounter 'cavalcades,' 'pachyderms,' 'caryatid,' 'exorcism,' 'prestidigitator,' and related lexemes. But quite often the rhetoric of the traditional oríkì relieves the obscurantism and adds the extra local color that makes "Idanre" a truly African poem in English:

> My god Ogun, orphans shield, his home
> Is terraced hills self-surmounting to the skies
> Ogun path-maker, he who goes fore where no other gods
> Have turned. Shield of orphans, was your shield
> In-spiked that day on sheltering lives?

Soyinka's complexity provides a constraint on the language of this poem, partly by the vast subject matter and partly by the poet's assimilative talent. To what extent the style is idiosyncratic can not be fully explained here; all that could be said is that the poem's style is dense and obscure. The poem is best enjoyed as a complex linguistic puzzle-game.

These texts show that the poets choose to speak in obscure terms for related but different reasons. The entire analysis describes how poets of L_2 expression contribute to the growth of the English language. Soyinka's usages, their complexity notwithstanding, make a significant impact on the language, while Clark's 'Dirge' is an admirable linguistic spectacle.

BENDEL STATE UNIVERSITY, ABRAKA —NIGERIA

Works Cited

Banjo, A. "The Linguistic Factor in African Literature." A Keynote Address: Ibadan International Conference on African Literature, 1982.

Chinweizu, Jemine and Madubuike. *Towards the Decolonisation of African Literature.* Enugua: Fourth Dimension Publishers, 1980.

Clark, J.P. *A Reed in the Tide.*, London: Longman, 1965.

_____. *Casualties.* London: Longman, 1970.

Gregory, M. "Aspects of Varieties Differentiation" *Journal of Linguistics* 3 (1967).

Gregory, M. & S. Carroll *Language and Situation.* London: Routledge and Kegan Paul, 1978.

Halliday, M.A.K. *Language as Social Semiotics.* London: Edward Arnold, 1978.

Halliday M. A. K. and Hasan, Ruqaiya *Cohesion in English*. London: Longman, 1976.

Olatunji, O. *Characteristic Features of Yoruba Oral Poetry*. Ph.D. Thesis, University of Ibadan, 1970.

Osakwe, M. "The Styles of Abiku: Two Related Diatypes of English" *Language and Style* Vol. 21, No. 1 (1988).

Soyinka, W. *Idanre and Other Poems*. London: Eyre Methuen, 1967.

_____. *A Shuttle in the Crypt*. London: Rex Collings/Eyre Methuen, 1972.

THE SYNTAX AND SEMANTICS OF "IDANRE" NOUN PHRASES:
A LINGUISTIC SPECTACLE

Mabel Osakwe

The predictability of the linguistic items of a text to a greater or lesser extent constitutes its text-forming properties. Collocations are a type of such text forming devices involving predictable syntagmatic lexical relations. However, in Soyinka's poem "Idanre," collocations are highly unpredictable. This paper focuses on that premise in its analysis of the poet's noun-phrases.

The noun phrase is a convenient unit of analysis because of its syntactic and semantic spread within the collocational geography of the poem. Our aim therefore is to identify, describe, explain, and account for aspects of Soyinka's "Idanre" as well as assess the appropriateness of such bizarre usages in that poem.

The element of the sentence that functions typically as subject, object, and complement is the noun phrase (see Halliday 1961, Quirk et. al. 1972, Crystal 1980). It can be simply one word such as a pronoun or a noun. A noun-phrase can also take the form of so camplex a form as a sentential clause. This flexibility of form makes noun-phrases potentially indefinitely complex, Noun-phrases comprise a large segment of the grammar of the any language.

There are considerably more than seven hundred such phrases (noun phrases with a head and at least a modifier) in the 569- line poem. Each line on the average contains one or two noun phrases. Some lines exceed this number significantly, containing three or four:

   1.a. Red clay for his mould. In his hand the weapon
      (p. 71, line 4.)
     b. His sword an outer crescent of the sun
      (p. 75, line 1.)

This distribution is strikingly high, especially in a literary text that is otherwise sparing in its structure and lexis.

The stylistic deviations are more noticeable in phrase beyond the word level, but there are a few single word or compounds whose structural composition and usage constitute a linguistic spectacle as well. For example:

   2. a. whiteburns   (p. 61)   c. heartstone   (p. 70)
      b. Lungstream   (p. 71)   d. bird-pond   (p. 71)

By using the novel compound 'whiteburns' in 2a), the poet captures succinctly the dangers as well as the benefits inherent in the lightning as its white rays flash through the clouded horizon during a storm at Molete. 'Whiteburns' is therefore a new and more elastic variation of the hackneyed phrase the 'silver lining' of a cloud.

The phrase in 2b), 'lungstream,' is a variation of 'bloodstream'; the nodal item 'stream' collocates with 'blood.' 'Blood' in turn collocates with 'heart,' and 'heart' with 'lung' as organs of the human physiology. 'Lungstream' is used here as the respiratory mechanism of Ogun, located in the hills of Idanre and manifesting in the superhuman intensity of his breath in the erupting volcanic peaks. The poet in this new phrase verbalizes the union between man, nature, and the gods.

The contradictions in 2c), besides the echoing of 'hearthstone,' arise from the integration of near opposites into one lexical item: 'stone' is often contrasted with flesh, and 'heart' is often associated with flesh. But Soyinka's usage goes beyond a reiteration of 'heart' in physiological terms. A reference of the heart as the 'core' or 'center' of the body explains the phrase. Earth's 'heartstone' therefore, refers to the rock column of central significance in the Idanre hills. The new compound stretches its meaning beyond 'tombstone,' since it is not merely a monument of death but also of activity, creation, and destruction. Similarly, Soyinka in 2d), 'birdpond,' spans the apparent gulf between earth and sky. The novel noun phrase hyperbolically articulates the intensity of the 'deluge' as well as the supernatural forces responsible for the event. Beyond the word level there are series of fascinating structuring and usages of other noun phrases.

    3. a. Obsequious rites (p. 72)   b. Leprous sneer (p. 73)
        c. indifferent morsel (p. 76)   d. Omni-sentient
                                          cauldron (p. 81)

Structurally, 3a-d) display a surface adjectival style, but the deep structural style is adverbial, the focus being on the manner in which the thing is done. Other lexemes that are similarly structured are:

    4. a. white moments (p. 61)   b. Green deception (p. 64)
        c. gaunt corrosion (p. 65)   d. blind hunger   (p. 69)
        e. wet embrace   (p. 67)   f. agile wine   (p. 84)
        g. bronzed emergence (p. 82)
        h. parsimonious sifting (p. 84)

Each of the eight examples has an unusual adjectival modifier. Whereas such concrete modifiers are usually collocates of concrete nouns, here the modifiers are made to keep company with abstract nouns. Thus the colors 'white' and 'green' modify such non-visible nouns as 'moment' and 'deception'. After all, moments are built up by times (which can also be graduated) and by behaviors, events, and experiences, all of which are observable. Ogun's 'white moments,' then, are those pure and radiant moments when he manifests his creative energy.

    'Green deception' refers to the vegetation on Idanre hills which gives a deceptive impression of healthy growth but is actually a product of the fat manure from spilt human blood. This is one of Soyinka's ways of showing the inevitable link between life and death.

    In this context of death and decay 'gaunt corrosion' expresses the outcome of corrosive forces on the vegetation and consequently on man.

Human life and blood constitute Ogun's indiscriminate menu, being the only sacrifice that sates his appetite when he is blind with hunger. "Blind hunger," then, is a stastically deviant but apt phrase which expresses this strange craving of a god as manifested in road accidents and loss of lives. By transferring the epithet 'blind' to 'hunger' the poet also shifts the burden of man's destiny to the invisible gods.

'Wet embrace' seems to echo the familiar collocation 'warm embrace,' but it is actually its semantic counterfeit, as it is an embrace that "choked the world." The concretization of abstract nouns by the use of anomalous epithets, as in 'agile wind' and parsimonious sifting,' has the overall effect of establishing a link between the visible and invisible universe of the poem. Hence 'bronzed emergence' is the expectant outcome of the "ignited kilns." Here is a Soyinkaesque expression of the union between warring elements past and present civilization, as well as the fusion of the activity of the gods.

The poet also uses apparently deviant noun phrases to achieve ideational concord as well:

5. a. Cloud mirrors (p. 61) b. sun bubbles (p. 61)
   c. iron bellows (p. 67) d. Prestidigitator god
                                 (p. 74)

There are yet other instances of unequal yoking of lexemes within the noun phrase.

6. a. greying skull (p. 63)
   b. psalming feet (p. 63)
   c. dire reaped   (p. 84)

These usages are fascinating syntactic and semantic coinages. In 6a) and b), Soyinka has transferred the usual inflectional markings (of the verb class to the noun modifiers of the head. Consequently, the meanings of 'grey' and 'psalm' are extended beyond the static to a continuous process. Both 6a) and 6b) are instances of shift in word class by morphological processes.

However, in 6c), the poet shifts word class without the usual morphological procedures. The verb 'reaped' is the head of the noun phrase; Soyinka arrives at this shift not by the usual nominalisation process but by using a restrictive adjectval modifier, a practise which is reminiscent of Dylan Thomas' "he danced his did.'" 'Dire reaped,' therefore, echoes existing collocations such as 'dire need.' In its new environment it is imbued with the new meaning, 'terrible harvest.' Apart from effecting surprise, the new noun-phrase in the context of the collocational geography of the poem is endowed with an expansiveness that captures the nature of the metamorphosis taking place at Idanre, where men change to gods, and gods in turn change to men and other cosmic forces— a world where inanimates carry on lively activities, and the dead interact with the living.

Soyinka uses complex noun phrases which are modified by prepositional phrases. A wide range of prepositions are involved; for example:

7. a. priestess *at* fresh shrines (p. 66)
 b. Vines *on* nights's lam-post (p. 66)
 c. a time *beyond* memory of fallen leaves (p. 69)
 d. flames *in* fever fits (p. 70)
 e. the womb *of* energies (p. 71)
 f. parsimonious sifting *of* the sun (p. 84)

The usual dominance of prepositional phrases in the distribution pattern of noun phrase qualifiers is reflected in his usages. The *of*-phrase qualifier in turn significantly dominates the other prepositional phrase qualifiers. There are about a hundred and fifty such *of*-phrase qualifiers out of about two hundred prepositional phrases. Although it is also in keeping with the normal expectations of English usage to project *of*-phrases as the commonest type, the distribution here is overwhelmingly high. Apart from the significance of distribution, the rare collocability pattern of the phrases is also significant. Soyinka has exploited the advantage of the *of*-phrase for poetic effect. As a compress of the relative clause it is inherently an elliptical structure, dispossessed of major clause elements and therefore suited to a genre that strives after contracted forms of expression. Its lack of explicitness leads to ambiguities which also enriches the semantics of the poem.

Below is a sample of noun-phrase usages that display normal collocability:

8. a. warts of of electric coils (p. 64)
   b. terms of premium (p. 64)
   c. godfather of all souls (p. 65)
   d. a slate of scoured lettering (p. 66)
   e. shell of tortoise (p. 68)

In the above sample, the completive noun phrase (henceforth NP_2) of the prepositional phrase qualifier is a predictable companion of the antecedent noun phrase (NP_1). The NP_1 and NP_2 in each of the groups 7a through 7e are compatible and have regular commutation with - s genitive. Although other contextual features of the text make these normal usages unpredictable, they are still a reflection of the poet's surreal tendency of reconciling all features of life and living.

Some of the phrases have incompatible NP_1 and NP_2 but they are resonances of acceptable cliches of poetry:

9. a. wheels of death (p. 64)
   b. lip of sky (p. 62)
   c. archives of deities (p. 69)
   d. flakes of harvest rain (p. 65)

What is fascinating about these usages is their apparent acceptability, which underscores the fact that even obscure associations can achieve acceptability and appropriateness in language use.

One of the greatest linguistic feats performed by the poet emerges in the sample of a dozen anomalous bunches below.

10. a. lungstream of depleted pasture (p. 71)
    b. filigree of foliage veins (p. 73)
    c. winecup of my sheltering head (p. 79)
    d. blasphemy of my humanity (p. 79)
    e. breadth of indigo (p. 83)
    f. sunrise of his throat (p. 84)
    g. wrecks of last years super (p. 64)
    h. innocence of apocalyptic skies (p. 66)
    i. skeletons of speed (p. 65)
    j. surreal bowl of sounds (p. 68)
    k. one loop of time (p. 68)
    l. memory of fallen leaves (p. 69)

Each synaesthetic NP_2 is capable of further structural and ample semantic expansion. There are multi-level complexities arising from the incompatibility between NP_2 and its modifier (see b and c) as well as NP_1 and NP_2. Interpretational problems arise also from the resultant ambivalence of the NP swinging between regular commutation with -s genitive on the one hand, and the 'be' sentences on the other. The link between NP_1 and NP_2 in (f), for example, is mediated through the L_2 expression of the pre-breakfast state of the human body as the 'sunrise' of the body. Similarly, the syntagmatic link between 'wrecks' and 'super' is mediated through the translation of the sacrifice to the gods (including the sacrifice of human life) as 'super.' These usages enable the poet to reconcile apparent contradictions: the energetic influence of wine in man with solar energy and its influence on nature, and the indifference of the gods to man's plight about death (see g). The poet thus contrasts as well as reconciles divine pleasure with human sorrow.

Within the universe of the poem, absurdities and contradictions are suspended. The creation by the poet of a possibility for an acceptance of these linguistic anomalies as meaningful rests on his unequal yoking of the strings within its semiotics. Apparent human and divine states and events are contrasted and unified in expressions c, h, i and j. Life as lived in the poem becomes an unbroken string of the physical and spiritual essence (k and e). 'Indigo' is used to describe the life-protecting and life-sustaining force and its occasional polluting and suffocating tendency and aspect of the dual essence of the 'primal mechanic,' Ogun.

With samples 11a - d, we are faced with NPs that are structurally or lexically ambiguous:

11. a. sifting of the sun   (p. 84)
    b. blasting of the seed   (p. 64)
    c. heart of fire   (p. 76)
    d. Hands of camwood   (p. 83)

It is difficult to make a subjective-objective distinction in these phrases: a-c are cases of structural ambiguity, c and d of lexical ambiguity. Each phrase is at least double entendre; for example, the meaning of (a) includes inhibitions restricting full rays of the sun as well as the permeating sun rays serving as a searchlight.

In this poem the poet opens up new possibilities of collocability, as well as new structural complexity in noun-phrase forms. The most complex NP postmodification extends beyond two stanzas of ten lines (see Section 11: stanzas 22 and 23), and contains (among other qualifiers) two subordinate clauses and eleven post-modifying noun phrases, each of which is further post-modified by a prepositional phrase. 12a-12e provide samples of clausal NP qualifiers:

12 a. The dead whom fruit and oil await (p. 65)
   b. all souls who by road make the voyage home (p. 65)
   c. sacred leaf whose hollow gathers rains (p. 66)
   d. Light more than human frame can bear (p. 69)
   e. The vessel that was singly cast (p. 79)

These clausal qualifiers are mainly the relative-clause type, as in 12 a -12 c, or the reduced relative-clause type, as in 12d, whose structural complexity do not necessarily yield semantic complexity. In fact the structural and functional explicitness of the relative pronoun also yield explicit meaning. The interpretational problems that may arise with 12a and 12 b are resolved in the interplay between the poet's L_1 and L_2. The choice of the relative pronoun in 12a, for example, arises from a double constraint—the normal acceptability in English usage of that option in a context where the relative pronoun is not the subject of the relative clause, and the L1 interpretation of fruit and oil as sacrificial ingredients offered to the ancestors.

The foregoing analysis of noun-phrase usage in "Idanre" supports the earlier assumption that collocations are highly unpredictable. The spread and manner of usage of these noun phrases show how their indefinite complexity and potential flexibility has been exploited for poetic effect. Soyinka finds within this structure a means of reconciling the contradictions and absurdities of life. They accommodate his antithesis, his transferred epithets, and his use of oxymoron and synaesthetic phrases. All together, they constitute part of the sophisticated lexical device manufactured by this celebrated wordsmith to pull down the demarcating walls of life's experiences. These usages are aspects of what constitutes the 'arcane' poem "Idanre."

BENDEL STATE UNIVERSITY, ABRAKA—NIGERIA

Works Cited

Banjo, Ayo "On the stylistic study of Modern Nigerian Poetry." Seminar paper, Department of English, University of Ibadan, 1976

———. "The Linguistic Factor in African Literature." *Ibadan Journal of Humanities* 3 (1983).

Chinweizu, and Madubuike, *Towards the Decolonisation of African Literature*. Enugu: Fourth Dimension Publishers, 1980.

Crystal, David, and Derek Davy. *Investigating English Style*. London: Longman, 1969.

Crystal, David, *The First Dictionary of Linguistics and Phonetics*. London: Andre Deutsch Ltd., 1980.

Enkvist, Nils Erik, "On the Place of Style in Some Linguistic Theories." In Chatman, S. (ed.). *Literary Style: A Symposium*, 1971.

Halliday, M. A. K., "Categories of the Theory of 'Grammar.'" *Word*, 1. 17 No. 3 (1961).

———. *Explorations in the Functions of Language*. London: Edward Arnold, 1973.

Halliday, M.A.K. & Ruqaiya Hasan, *Cohesion in English*. London: Longman, 1976.

Jones, Eldred, *The Writing of Wole Soyinka*. London: Heinemann, 1973.

Moore G. *Wole Soyinka*. London: Evans, 1978.

Osakwe M. I., *The British Council Contemporary Issues in English Language and Literature*. Aberdeen Summer School Report, 1988

Quirk, Randolph, Sidney Greenbaum, Jan Svartvik & Geoffrey Leech. *A Grammar of Contemporary English*. London: Longman, 1972.

Soyinka, W. "Idanre" and Other Poems. London: Eyre Methuen, 1967.

Sinclair John, "Taking a Poem to Pieces." (Ed.) Roger Fowler, *Essays on Style and Language*. London: Routledge and Kegan Paul, 1966.

Udoeyop, No. *Three Nigerian Poets*. Ibadan: University Press, 1973.

Young, Pete, "The Language of West African Literature in English." *The English Language in W. Africa*. (Ed.) John Spencer. London: Longman, 1971.

THE DEPLOYMENT OF CODE IN SOYINKA'S *THE ROAD*:
A STYLISTIC ANALYSIS

Michael Cosser

Literary stylistics has been concerned largely with the analysis of monolingual works of literature. This study of Wole Soyinka's *The Road* will focus on a multilingual play that exploits a variety of language codes to dramatic effect.[1]

The emphasis on the stylistic analysis of monolingual literature is perhaps attributable to the development of stylistics within a Western literary tradition. Although the notion of code-switching is not foreign to that tradition, its application has been restricted to a conception of, for example, shifts between "standard and regional forms of English, between Welsh and English in parts of Wales, or between occupational and domestic varieties" (Crystal 1980:66). A more expansive perspective of code-switching is required in the study of what Gurr (1976:45) has called "Third-World drama" (the literature, essentially, of the underdeveloped nations of the world)[2]—a perspective that allows for a broader conception of code than that reflected by Crystal.

The notion of "Third-World drama" is, however, unfortunate, carrying with it the implication of an underdeveloped literature. From a linguistic perspective, Soyinka's work cannot be deemed "underdeveloped": the effectiveness of plays like *The Trials of Brother Jero* (1969) and *The Road* (1965) rests largely upon an adroit manipulation of language. As a drama critic for *The*

Observer once observed, "Wole Soyinka has done for our napping language what brigand dramatists from Ireland have done for centuries: looted it awake, rifled its pockets and scattered the loot into the middle of next week" (Gilliatt 1981:106). The linguistic achievement of *The Road* resides not merely in the deployment of language codes, but in the dramatic effectiveness of the interweaving of a variety of language strands into a coherent whole. This study will attempt to distinguish these strands, exemplify some of their characteristics, and establish the efficacy of the finished product.

The Deployment of Code

A Question of Terminology

The Road deploys as many language strands as it does characters (apart, that is, from the lay-abouts and the crowd): eight strands are discernible. A language strand may, depending on its realization, be a language, a dialect, a sociolect, or an idiolect. Crystal (1980) offers the following definitions of these terms: a language is a code unintelligible to all but its native speakers (110); a dialect is a "regionally or socially distinctive variety of a language" mutually intelligible with other varieties (110); a sociolect is a variety defined specifically on social (as opposed to regional) grounds (324); and an idiolect—a subdivision of a dialect—is the language of an individual speaker (179). The complexity of the interrelationship of these terms, it is claimed (110), is often disregarded: dialects, it can be argued, are occasionally mutually unintelligible (those of Chinese, for example: Mandarin, Cantonese, and Pekingese),[3] languages are occasionally mutually intelligible (Swedish, Norwegian, and Danish, for instance), and the distinction between dialect and sociolect is (since social class is often regionally determined) not always easy to draw.

Traditional notions of language, dialect, sociolect, and idiolect do appear difficult to uphold in the context of *The Road*—not for any nebulousness in the definitions themselves, but because of the mutual intelligibility, on a receptive level at least,[4] of all the codes deployed in the play, and the difficulty of defining the literary use of a code, unrepresentative as it may be of its spoken counterpart, according to extraliterary criteria. Language strands in *The Road* come closest to constituting idiolects, though this correspondence is complicated by the degree of code-switching that characterizes the language behavior of several of its characters. Code-switching, to complicate classification even further, may be monolingual (e.g., from formal English to colloquial English[5])—or bilingual (from English to Yoruba). Because of the terminological difficulty, therefore, the terms *code* and *strand* will be used to refer to the deployment of language strands in the play.

A Typology of Codes[6]

Codes 1 and 2: Standard English

Two varieties of standard English (SE) are manifested in *The Road*.[7] Professor uses both:

(1) There are dangers in the Quest I know, but the Word may be found companion not to life, but Death. (159)

(2) Do you think I spend every living moment looking for that? (188)

In (1), Professor uses a formal, slightly stilted variety of SE imbued with religious overtones—a variety which, because of its overt quality (the very esotericism of the language discloses its suitability for public oration) may be referred to as liturgical English (LE). (It might be argued that LE is distinct from SE in that, like the language of the King James Version of the Bible, it lacks vitality;[8] since Professor's speech lacks vitality only from a semantic perspective, however, we may classify LE as a species of the generic SE.) The majority of Professor's utterances are of the LE type.

A second SE language strand is evident in (2). Professor lapses into this equally formal nonliturgical speech style when annoyed (as here) or engaged in swift repartee (as with Salubi over the matter of forging a driver's license; 185). This style is characterized, like LE, by a lack of contraction (except for the occasional elision: "He'll" for He will; 180) and by a strict attention to syntactic regularity. Most of the SE conversation of

Samson, Salubi, Kotonu, and Chief-in-Town follows this rather stiff written-English pattern; vulgarity like Samson's "When you get on an endless stretch of road your buttocks open wide and you begin to fart on passengers in the first-class compartment" (156) is all the more striking for its accommodation within syntactic rigor. The notable absence in the play of the type of colloquial speech that characterizes a Joe Orton work, for example,[9] sets *The Road* and a second- language (L_2) English writer like Soyinka apart from their first-language (L_1) counterparts.

Code 3: American Colloquial English

A third strand woven into the linguistic tapestry of *The Road* is manifested in the following speech:

> A swell dame is gonna die on the road just so the next passenger kin smear her head in yam porrage? (172-73)

Say Tokyo Kid's stylized brand of American English—what Amankulor (54) calls "bastardized cow-boy language"—is characterized by lexical borrowings from American English ("swell" and "dame"), by elision ("gonna" for going to, where the *i* and *g* in *going* are elided in connected speech and the *to* reduced out of existence through the retrogressive assimilation of the *t* in *to* to the *n* in *going* to produce the gemination [Brown: 52] of *n*), and by reduction (the attempt to represent the weak form of the /œ/ in /kœn/ as i —"kin"—and generally to render this variety of English through an approximation to its phonological realization). Interestingly, by a process of what, to borrow the phonetic term, we might call discourse *assimilation*, Say Tokyo Kid's American colloquial English (ACE)[10] comes to exercise an influence over the speech of his interlocutors; Kotonu's "*Yeah, I suppose so*" (172; my italics) is the code-switching response to Say Tokyo Kid's timber speech (171-72).

Code 4: Simplified English

A fourth linguistic strand, exemplified by the speech of Samson and Salubi, is a simplified version of SE. Salubi's

> I take uniform impress all future employer. (152)

illustrates the type: determiners like articles (both definite and indefinite) are omitted ("take uniform," where the determiner might have been *a, the,* or a deictic like *this*), verbs are generally uninflected[11] ("take," an invariant simple present form, replaces the aorist took or the perfect *have taken*; the infinitive complementizer in *to impress* is omitted), and number agreement is dispensed with ("employer" for employers, the plural morpheme -*s* being omitted). Simplified English (SIME) typically exploits the redundancy of the language by discarding unnecessary information; since "all" already conveys plurality, the plural marker on "employer" is redundant and may be eliminated. Speech is therefore telescoped through the omission of grammatical words and a concomitant focus on lexis as a conveyor of essential meaning.

SIME has much in common with PE, and it is in practice difficult to distinguish the two in the speech of, for example, Samson and Salubi, both of whom switch from SE through SIME to pidgin English (PE). SIME appears to act, therefore, as a kind of catalytic medium between two codes. Since PE generally shows evidence of lexical borrowing from Yoruba (YOR) and differs from SE in that it is by and large unintelligible to code-bound SE speakers (PE is discussed further below), the two codes may for the present purposes be considered separate.

The following lines embody further characteristics of SIME:

> 3) I know I no get job, but I get uniform. (Salubi, 152)
> 4) Why you no mind your own business for heaven's sake! (Salubi, 153)
> 5) He get experience pass me? (Salubi, 154)
> 6) The man too clever. (Salubi, 154)
> 7) Which kind police? (Samson, 154)
> 8) It [your mouth] stinks so much that I will promote you Captain of my private bodyguard. (Samson, 156)

These examples indicate, respectively, positioning of the invariant negative particle "no" before the main verb "get" (3); a lack of *Do*-support in the formation of both negatives (3) and questions (4)—"Why you no mind" for *Why don't you mind?* (4); *Yes-No* and rhetorical question formation through intonation rather than through inversion—"He get experience" for *Does he [have] experience* (5); frequent omission of the copula—"The man too clever" for *The man is too clever* (6); frequent omission of the preposition *of* in *Wh*-question formation—"Which kind police?" for *Which kind of police?* (7); and omission of the preposition *to* obligatory before indirect objects after such verbs as *promote* ("I will promote you Captain" for *I will promote you to Captain*) (8). Other SIME features characterize PE also, and will be discussed below along with those features peculiar to PE.

Code 5: Yoruba

A fifth linguistic strand deployed in *The Road* constitutes both a dialect in the traditional sense and a fully autonomous language.[12] In his code-switching exchange with Say Tokyo Kid (170-71), Particulars Joe moves from the formulaic "Say Tokyo Kid!" and "No dirty timber" (170) to

> *Gbegi ma gbe'yawo!* (171)
> (Wedded, not to a wife but to timber!)

—a manifestation of the standard dialect of the Yoruba people.[13] The term *standard* requires qualification, however; standard YOR, a regional dialect, is not to be equated with SE, a nonregional dialect. YOR is, following Hill's classification (443), in conformity with the current view of dialect distribution a "dialect continuum"— a group of dialects, geographically contiguous and linguistically related, spoken, at the time of publication of *The Road* (1965), by some 12 million people in Western Nigeria, Lagos, Ilorin Province, and Dahomey. Since many of the approximately twenty YOR "dialects" (or more properly, perhaps, languages) are mutually unintelligible, it is claimed (Bamgbose 1966: 2), a *koine* based on the Òyó dialect is taken to be the standard—the YOR used in education, for writing, and as a contact language among persons speaking different dialects. For reasons of general intelligibility, standard YOR—the regional language that has become the lingua franca of the YOR-speaking realm[14] —is the variety Soyinka exploits in *The Road*.

Use of YOR is not extensive; Samson switches briefly from SIME to YOR (155, 225) or from SE to YOR (184, 197 [with Kotonu], 225), Particulars Joe and Say Tokyo Kid move from

ACE to conduct a five-line exchange in YOR (171), and the speech of Samson (whether SE, SIME, or PE)[15] is tinged with the occasional YOR word or expression (165, 185, 225). YOR is reserved chiefly for the songs of *The Road*, which constitute a sixth language strand.

Code 6: Yoruba Song

Apart from the poetic prose of Professor's LE, poetry is largely avoided in *The Road* in favor of what might in one sense be deemed a more accessible medium.[16] The blank verse of *A Dance of the Forests* (Soyinka 1963), for Moore (64) a language "rather loose" and "occasionally over-rich in its effects," gives way in *The Road* to a crisp, fast-moving prose. Poetry is retained, however, in the songs of the play, all of which exploit the standard YOR dialect.

A lay-about picks up a guitar, strums, and begins to sing:

Ona orun jin o eeeee
Ona orun jin dereba rora
E e dereba rora
E e dereba rora
Ona orun jin o eeeee
Eleda mi ma ma buru
Esin baba Bandele je l'odan
Won o gbefun o
Eleda mi ma ma buru
Esin baba Bandele je l'odan
Won o gbefun o. (165)
(It's a long long road to heaven
It's a long road to heaven, Driver
Go easy a-ah go easy driver
It's a long long road to heaven
My Creator, be not harsh on me
Bandele's horse galloped home a winner
But the race eluded him.) (230; Soyinka's translation)

The "Drivers' Dirge," as Soyinka calls it (230), exemplifies certain traits typical of Yoruba verse.[17] First, the length of line is based on balance of thought; the short, contrastive *"Won o gbefun o"* ("But the race eluded him"; my italics) is juxtaposed with the longer, assertive *"Esin baba Bandele je l'odan"* ("Bandele's horse galloped home a winner"). Second, repetition either of words (*"Ona orun jin"*), lines (*"E e dereba rora"*), or self-contained segments (*"Eleda mi ma ma buru/Esin baba Bandele je l'odan/Won o gbefun o"*) is apparently common in YOR songs. Third, there is a resemblance in some YOR poetry, and in this dirge in particular, to Western versification: the "Drivers' Dirge" resembles both the ballad in its narrative focus (see especially the continuation of the dirge, the "lewd verse"—166 and 166 s. d.) and repetition of epithets and phrases, and the elegy ("a poem of lament or of grave meditation"—Deutsch 1957: 46) in its thematic intent.[18] And though YOR is the medium of rendition, the song as genre constitutes an individual language strand of the play; like each of the other codes, the language of song—whether dirge, war-chant, or praise-song—is used as a stylistic device to achieve a particular dramatic effect.

Code 7: Silence

A seventh linguistic strand exploited by Soyinka is arguably the purest, certainly the most concise, "language"[19] of all; its use provides the perfect foil to the Professor's grandiloquence. Appropriately, the "language"of Professor's alter ego, Murano, is the language of silence, the language that shares none of the typological characteristics of SE[20] and yet which, as will be demonstrated below, speaks as loudly as any other in *The Road*.

Nigerian Pidgin English

The object of enquiry of the present section is threefold: identification of an eighth language strand as Nigerian pidgin English (NPE); analysis of the salient characteristics of this code; and, contingent upon these objectives, postulation of a specifically literary NPE distinct from extraliterary counterparts.

Toward a Definition of Pidgin

A brief consideration of the sphere of reference of the term *pidgin* will provide us with a framework for evaluating NPE and its realization in *The Road*. Several definitions of pidgin have been proposed:

1) a form of speech that usually has a *simplified* grammar and a *limited* often *mixed* vocabulary and is used principally for intergroup communication (*Webster's Third New International Dictionary* 1961:1712)[21]
2) a language which has arisen as the result of contact between peoples of different languages, usually formed from *mixing* of the languages (UNESCO 1963:46)
3) [a language] whose vocabulary is mainly provided by the language spoken by [the] upper stratum of a mixed society, adapted by the lower stratum to the grammar and morphology of their original language (Adler 1977:12)
4) a contact vernacular ... characterized by a *limited* vocabulary, an elimination of many grammatical devices such as number and gender, and a drastic reduction of redundant features (DeCamp 1971:15)
5) a marginal language which arises to fulfil certain *restricted* communication needs among people who have no common language (Todd 1974:1)

Though these definitions highlight the salient features of a pidgin— a *contact* language (2 and 4), *reduced* (4), more or less *restricted* in its reference (5)—a number of objections to the use of certain terms has been lodged. The first definition stresses the *simplified* grammatical structure of pidgins, giving rise (albeit inadvertently) to a confusion of *simplification* and *impoverishment* (as though the epithet *simplified*, connoting greater syntactic regularity, were transferred from *grammatical structure* to embrace the language itself) and confusion of *simplified* with *simplistic* (and, by analogy, *primitive*), to suggest a kind of referential poverty[22] (Mühlhäusler 1986: 4). Indeed, as DeCamp (15) points out, the reduced redundancy of pidgins may betoken complexity rather than simplicity. Similarly, the notion of a *limited* vocabulary (1 and 4) may connote the *limitations* of a pidgin as a language adequate to the linguistic needs of its speakers—may imply, that is, a language deficient in descriptive power.

A second objection concerns the notion of a pidgin as a mixed language. The lexicon of a pidgin, as (1) suggests, is the most mixed component of that language; the kind of mixing at a morpho-syntactic level implied by the inexplicitness of (2)— "mixing of the languages"—is rare in the initial stages of pidginization (Mühlhäusler 1986:5). Mixture suggests a lack of inner structure—an amorphous mélange of incongruous and possibly incompatible elements which, though characteristic of such pidgins as Fanagalo,[23] is not necessarily indicative of all pidgins. Allied to the objection surrounding the use of the term *mixed* is the problem of the degree of mixing. The assertion that the vocabulary of the pidgin is supplied chiefly by the socially dominant group (3: "upper stratum") is questionable. First, such an assertion downplays the mixed nature of the pidgin lexicon; and second, the implication that the lexicon rather than the morpho-syntactic framework is the base of the language is, arguably, unfounded (Dennis & Scott 1975:2; Mühlhäusler 1986:5).

A fourth problem is the extent to which a pidgin is restricted in its reference (5)—a question essentially of definition. If a pidgin is a "structurally reduced trade language" (Mühlhäusler 1986:3) native to none of its speakers, and a creole a pidgin that has become the L_1 of its speakers—a language no longer restricted to a specific purpose such as trade—the distinction between the two seems difficult to maintain. NPE, Mafeni claims (95), is a *lingua franca* for some and a mother tongue (hence, a creole) for others; either way it has transcended its original function as a trade language. If this claim is correct, however, *pidgin* is no longer an appropriate designation for the speech of those for whom the code has become a mothertongue: a creole is defined by its vitality.

Though the notion of a pidgin-creole continuum would seem to invalidate Todd's nice temporal distinction (Todd 1974: 5) between a "restricted" and an "extended" pidgin (the former *tending* to die out once the purpose for its origination— trade—has disappeared, the latter continuing to be used beyond its original limited function), the paradox is tenable: a pidgin may be simultaneously restricted in one of its varieties and extended in another. Fanagalo, for instance, may on a mine in the Orange Free State be extended, but in a domestic household in the Eastern Cape be restricted: the two varieties exist at different points along the pidgin-creole continuum. The reason for such a dualism is clear: if mother-tongue speakers vary, however little, in their control over their L_1, how much more will pidgin speakers vary in their control over an L_2? Pidginization is an ongoing process, and pidgins are therefore to be regarded "[as] examples of partially targeted or non-targeted second-language learning, developing from simpler to more complex systems as communicative requirements become more demanding" (Mülhäusler 1986:5).

In these terms a pidgin constitutes an interlanguage (IL), Selinker's term (1969) denoting an individual linguistic system (an idiolect) "based on the observable output which results from a learner's attempted production of a TL [target language][24] norm" (214). An IL, though separate in the sense that as a rule-governed system it is "distinct" (Nemser 1971:116) from both L_1 and L_2, shares characteristics of the codes between which it falls: the IL of any one learner exists at any one time along an "interlanguage continuum" (Ellis 1985: 54). NPE, then, constitutes an IL, an "approximative system" (Nemser 1971:116) between the speaker's L_1 (YOR, in *The Road*) and L_2 (SE, or Nigerian-educated English), showing in its lexicon some influence of Portuguese—from the days of trade with Portuguese sailors.

The notion of NPE as an IL is especially suggestive in the context of *The Road*. Though NPE is essentially a spoken medium, the fact that much Nigerian literature exploits NPE[25] signifies that a kind of petrification beyond Selinker's concept of fossilization[26] has taken place: though IL is inherently unstable, constituting an ongoing process (cf. Mühlhäusler's definition of a pidgin, above), a work of literature like *The Road*, by exploiting a medium like NPE, actually freezes that code for all time, enabling us to descry paradoxically for a brief moment and yet forever the internal consistency of a constantly changing medium. There is nothing in *The Road* to suggest, for example, that NPE is not the native language of Samson or of Salubi, so total is their command of the medium and so effortless the facility of their code-switching. Literature may creolize a pidgin merely through the petrification of a changing medium.

Nigerian Pidgin English in *The Road*

Though the petrification of an interlingual code within a literary work may imply a degree of internal consistency, that consistency has yet to be determined in relation to the changing medium that is the code's extraliterary counterpart. Soyinka himself may distinguish an individual NPE strand in The Road (230: "Glossary of *Pidgin* Words" [my italics]), but not every code that goes by the name of *pidgin* warrants the appellation. This section will attempt to ascertain the extent to which the NPE of the play manifests those characteristics indicative of true pidgins.

Any discussion of literary NPE must be premised upon the notion that NPE (as a contact language) exists primarily as a spoken medium, has been transmitted by oral tradition, and has no uniform orthography (Barbag-Stoll 1983: 51). This last factor greatly increases the difficulty involved in the analysis of literary NPE: since writers can hardly be expected to render pidgin elements in their works in phonetic transcription, and since neither the English nor any other orthographic system can represent faithfully the articulation of those elements, the pidgin analyst must resort at times to conjecture. For example, in *The Road* the name of Kotonu's and Samson's erstwhile passenger service is rendered by Soyinka as *"No Danger* No Delay" (148: my italics); phonologically Danger might be realized as [dendza]; however, the shift from the medial /eɪ/ of RP to /e/ and from the final /e/ of RP to a sound approximating /a/ features commonly in NPE as spoken by the Yoruba (Barbag-Stoll 1983: 69). While Soyinka has endeavored to represent NPE elements in the play through an approximation to their phonetic realization (depicted in a corresponding orthographic shift), no directions for pronunciation have been given the producer. Indeed, pronunciation difficulties aside, the "Glossary of Pidgin Words" included for the non-initiate's benefit at the end of the play (230) does little more than gloss fourteen pidgin words, aside from the translation of others in the text (cf., for example, Samson's speech on 225).[27]

A further difficulty involves the distinction between SIME and NPE and the identification of SIME as a separate language strand, as depicted above. The distinction might appear to be arbitrary, since NPE shares most if not all of the characteristics of SIME outlined earlier. Since the SIME code manifests a basic reductionism only, however, while reduction is only one of many distinguishing features of NPE, and since SIME appears to signify a transitional stage between SE and NPE, the distinction may be sustained. The line

> You dey like monkey wey stoway inside sailor suit
> (Samson, 152)

displays, besides the pronouns "*dey*" ("which, who") and "*wey*" ("which, who") peculiar to NPE, the omission of articles ("monkey" for *a monkey*; "sailor suit" for *a sailor suit*), lack of concord (the uninflected "stoway" for *stows away* [sic]), and general elimination of grammatical words characteristic of SIME. And Salubi's

> I no sabbe do am. You fit show me? (154)

displays, besides the "sabbe" ("know, understand"), "am" ("he, she, it"), and "fit" ("able to, can") characteristic of NPE, the type of negative formation (invariant positioning of "no" before the main verb, and lack of *Do*-support) and question formation (through intonation rather than through inversion) that characterize SIME. Similarly, Salubi's

> He get experience pass me? (154)

shares features of both SIME (question formation through intonation) and NPE ("pass," where apocope results in the loss of final alveolar *t* and, in this instance, gemination of *s*). The reduction in redundancy we have observed in SIME characterizes NPE also.

NPE is to be distinguished from SIME, moreover, partly in the constitution of its lexicon. While SIME is a variety of English, NPE is a new language, the product of contact between, in Ross's terminology (in Mafeni 1971: 97), a *base* language (English) and one or more *substrates* (chiefly YOR [especially in the Lagos area], but also Igbo [in Port Harcourt], other Nigerian languages like Hausa, and even European languages [Portuguese and French]). The sense in which English is the "base" language is significant: English has provided both the bulk of the NPE lexicon, chiefly through nonstandard varieties of English and only recently through SE (Mafeni 1971:

103; Barbag-Stoll 1983: 55)—thereby substantiating Adler's claim (12) insofar as it applies to English-based pidgins that the pidgin vocabulary "is mainly provided by the language spoken by [the] upper stratum [in the case of NPE, white settlers] of a mixed society"*and* the morpho-syntactic framework of NPE (giving substance to Hall's notion of a pidgin's constitution: in Mafeni 1971:103). While the lexicon may not constitute the base of a language, then (Dennis & Scott 1975: 2; in Mülhäusler 1986: 3), English remains the base language of NPE. Whatever the contribution of English to NPE, however—whether morpho-syntactic or lexical—NPE constitutes as an IL a distinctive code whose characteristics are demonstrably productive.

The NPE of *The Road* displays in its phonology, morphology, and semantics an internal consistency: with a few exceptions, each NPE feature Soyinka exploits is productive to the extent of ample exemplification in the text. The following analysis, based primarily on Barbag-Stoll's recent survey of NPE (Barbag-Stoll 1983: 51-100) and partially on Mafeni (1971), will consider those NPE features in the play corroborated by the NPE speech of YOR-speaking Nigerians over the past three decades (see Barbag-Stoll's sources: 121-28).

Nigerian Pidgin English: Phonology

The difficulties associated with a phonological analysis of NPE (the lack of a uniform orthography and the problem of phonetic representation) have been alluded to; despite these obstacles, certain phonological features of NPE can be described.

In *The Road* NPE is characterized, first, by reduction. Apocope (reduction, in this case of final syllable or consonant) is realized through a consonant cluster simplification involving the loss of final alveolars weakly realized in RP: Salubi's "I no fit count *pass* ten" and "He get experience *pass* me?" (154)[28] reveal not only the loss of final t but gemination (doubling of consonant *s*); Samson's "If you put pin for am 'e go *burs*'" (217) and "na you be de *las*'for enter" (225) similarly display loss of final *t*; and Salubi's "Which *kin*' bus for heaven?" (155) manifests the loss of final *d*. Sometimes such apocope is accompanied by the omission of the following preposition—"kin' bus" (155) for *kind of bus*. Another kind of reduction—aphesis—is evident in Salubi's "Why'e no kuku play the ting inself?" (162), where /h/ deletion is the concomitant to the elision of /h/ effected by the running together of *Why* and *he*. A clearer example of aphesis is contained in Samson's " *'e* done chop bribe in face dey shine like tomato" (225-26), where /h/ deletion is independent of other processes.

Besides reduction, the NPE of the play is characterized by insertion or intrusion. "Make you all *walka* this side" (Samson, 198) manifests the addition of a vowel at the end of a word to make an open syllable (YOR, like many African languages, favors the maintenance of open syllables), where the added vowel either copies or differs from the preceding root vowel ("walka" may be realized either as [waka] or as [wɔka]). A third kind of phonetic change evident in NPE is replacement, which may be analyzed in terms of paradigmatic and syntagmatic relations. Syntagmatically, RP /aʊ/ by a process of monophthongization is realized as /ɔ/: "*Siddon* here make we talk" (Samson, 165) reveals the running together of *sit* and *down* to produce, by a process of total regressive assimilation, "*Siddon*," and the accompanying vowel change to produce [sIdɔn]. Paradigmatically, final /e/ is replaced by /aʊ,/: [meʊte] becomes in Samson's speech—"I beg, if you see moto accident make you tell me" (218)—[meʊte,]. How productive this example of vowel replacement is remains uncertain, however, for there is only one such instance in the play.

More quantifiably productive is the evidence of what appears to constitute consonant replacement in the NPE of *The Road*, where NPE /d/ frequently subsumes /ð/. The process at work is not replacement, however, but conversion—a shift from the fricative /ð/ to the alveolar stop /d/. Consider these examples:

6) I no care whether the Governor and in aide-de-camp finish *de* same hymn since yesterday. (Samson, 217)
7) Abi when den born am *dem* tie steering wheel for in neck? (Salubi, 161).
8) Why you dey worry your head for *dat* kind person? (Salubi, 162)
9) Abi *dis* one craze. (1st Man, 174)

The italicized words above illustrate the shift: from /ð e/

to /de/ (6), /ðem/ to /dem/ (7), /ðæt/ to /dæt/ (8), and /ðIs/ to /dIs/ (9). This conversion process, characteristic of several varieties of English, is attested to by Labov (1978:77-78), who, in his study of black American English in New York City, records a shift from the "prestige form" /ð/, an interdental fricative, through /dð/, an affricative, to /d/, a lenis "dental" [sic] stop. The stop consonant is characterized by the absence of a "turbulent, fricative, or scraping sound" (78) in its articulation.

A similar conversion process is evident in the shift from RP /θ/ to NPE /t/, as examples 10 to 14 illustrate:

10) Abi you *tink* say Kotonu no sabbe de man dey craze. (Salubi, 162)
11) Why he dey come play dat *ting* every morning self? (Salubi, 162)
12) You no sabbe de ting wey man dey call class so shurrup your *mout*. (Samson, 162).
13) Bishop done *trow* bomb! (Samson, 163).
14) Another time the general send cablegram *wit'* in own hand. (Samson, 217).

Here /θIŋk/ is realized in (10) as [tIŋk], /θI/ as [tIŋ] (11), /mavθ/ as [mavt] (12), /θr/ as [tr] (13), and /wIθ/ as [wIt] (17). Related to the shift from /ð/ to /d/ and from /θ/ to /t/ is the conversion from RP /v/ to NPE /f/. Samson's speech exemplifies the change: "*Lef'* your load, I say *lef'* your dirty bundle" (198), where the /v/ ⟶ /f/ change is accompanied by a reduction of /i/ to /e/.

Finally, NPE in the play is characterized by the process of assimilation noted earlier: *sit down* becomes (sIdɔn) (165), and, by a similar process, *come out* becomes (kɔmɔt) ("Commot my friend," 165), gemination of *m* arising out of the progressive assimilation of the *m* in come to produce (kɔm) + (mɔt). Interestingly, assimilation appears to betoken a semantic shift also: "siddon" in the expression "Go siddon my friend" (Samson, 218) undergoes a semantic change from sit *down* to "take yourself away" (Soyinka 1965: 99), while "commot" too changes meaning—"Na so we dey sing am for army camp and if you no like am make you *commot* for church go talk Latin for Catholic church" (217) being rendered by Soyinka as "That is how we sang it in the army camp and if you don't like it *get out of here; go chant Latin in a Roman Catholic church*" (Soyinka 1965: 98; my italics).

Nigerian Pidgin English: Morphology

Some of the morphological processes at work in NPE we have considered under the umbrella of SIME. One of those is reduction of redundant features. Loss of the genitive 's morpheme is one such feature: since word order indicates which of the two nouns in a noun phrase is the head noun and which the modifier, a phrase like "millionaire face" ("To breathe into millionaire face"—Salubi, 156) cannot mean anything but *the face of [a] millionaire*. NPE, in the interests of economy, uses only the attributive construction, however. Similarly, retention of the *r* in the possessive pronoun *your* is considered redundant: "*You mout' stink like night-soil lorry*" (Samson, 184).

Whilst word formation in SE involves the use of "derivational suffixes" (Barbag-Stoll 1983: 75), NPE word formation apparently relies to a significant extent upon lexical tone, compounding, and reduplication. Lexical tone is a crucial differentiator of otherwise identical words; for example, the minimal pair *sísí* ("sister, girl, female") and *sísì* ("sixpence") illustrates, solely through the addition of tonal markers (´ for high, ` for low), a fundamental semantic distinction. Soyinka's NPE in *The Road* does not illustrate the distinction, and, were the context not of some assistance, Samson's "Sisi," repeated thrice in the course of his penultimate and longest speech (225-26), might be mistaken for "sixpence" did not Soyinka gloss the word for us (fn. on 225: "Sweetheart").

Lexical compounding, another word-formational process, is displayed in the NPE of the play in two examples already cited—"siddon" and "Commot" (165). Both are compounds of the *verb + preposition* type—"siddon" of *sit + down*, "Commot" of *come + out*. Some variation in orthography appears to be permissible: "*comot*" in the line "Call am make e comot onetime" (1st Man, 174) dispenses with the seemingly usual gemination, and carries a meaning identical to that of the SE *come out*.

The third word-formational process exploited in *The Road* is reduplication, the iteration of a word. Reduplication may be used for emphasis, repetition, and continuity of action, or the formation of new lexical items. In most full languages reduplication exists as an *alternative* to the use of, for example, intensifiers; in NPE it is frequently the *only* process at work, particularly in the formation of new lexical items. Examples 15 to 20 below illustrate the use of reduplication for emphasis, a process characteristic of several languages:

15) I mean no sah. *At all at all* sah. (Salubi, 156)
16) All the *fine-fine* girls just coming from offices, the young and tender faces fresh from school—give them lift to my house. (Samson, 156)
17) *Shoo shoo*, you no dey sleep for house? (Samson, 174)
18) I must get a license *now now*. (Salubi, 183)
19) I say *small small*—you tink say dis one na football game. (Samson, 203)
20) I say I do am *soft soft*. (Samson, 203)

Iteration here intensifies the meaning of the original word; thus "At all at all" (15) might be paraphrased as *By no means*, "fine fine" (16) as *"very pretty"* (Soyinka 1965: 97), "Shoo shoo" (17) as *Get out!*,[29] "now now" as *immediately*, "small small" (19) as *very little*, and "soft soft" (20) as *very gently*. Examples 21 and 22 illustrate the use of reduplication to indicate repetition and continuity of action:

21) *Moving moving* on greased wheels thank heavens. (Samson, 212)
22) I drive supply caravans, and I *turn-turn* this picken with one hand. (Samson, 216)

Iteration may also—one of its primary functions—create new lexical items. Mafeni (1971:104) records the following examples of reduplication as a method of word-derivation:

	ENGLISH ORIGIN	PIDGIN MEANING
ben-ben	bend	crooked, shady
katakata	scatter	confusion
waka-waka	walk	to wander about

While reduplication for emphasis or for continuity of action involves the iteration of adjectives ("fine-fine"), adverbs ("now now"), or verbs ("moving moving"), in the formation of lexical items reduplication of nouns also is utilized in NPE: reduplication of *san* ("sun"), for example, produces *sansan* ("sand"), the purpose of the iteration in this case to reduce the number of homophonous forms in the language (Todd 1974: 55).

Unfortunately *The Road* yields no such productive data, besides the use of *so-so*. Ordinarily "so-so" in NPE means "always" (Barbag-Stoll 1983: 79; Mafeni 1971: 104), though Soyinka glosses *so-so* in Samson's penultimate speech simply as "so":

Welcome o, how family sah, ah-ah, na you dey look so-so thin like sugar-cane so? (Samson, 225)

(Welcome sir, how is the family? Oh dear oh dear [reduplication for emphasis!], you look so thin, thin as a sugar-cane—Soyinka 1965: 99.)

While Soyinka's translation would suggest that reduplication here is purely for emphasis, either reading (*so* or *always*) is tenable in context.

Nigerian Pidgin English: Semantics

Moving beyond the morphological level, NPE makes use of circumlocution or periphrasis in fulfillment of the economy principle. Samson's

God I go *chop life* make I tell true (155)

exploits periphrasis in its use of "chop life" ("enjoy life"). In isolation *chop* denotes "eat," as Samson's earlier line—"You no chop this morning?" (155)—indicates; *chop* itself signifies a transfer, or semantic shift, from SE "chop" to NPE "eat." In combination with "life," *chop* assumes a new meaning: the circumlocution involves the notion of transfer from *eat life* to "enjoy life." By a similar extension of meaning, "cinema" in

Samson's "Na another man calamity you fit take look cinema" (198) comes to connote "entertainment," as Soyinka's translation indicates: "Another man's calamity fulfills your entertainment" (1965:98). Properly "cinema" is not an instance of circumlocution, however, but of metonymy (if "cinema" is merely associated with "entertainment") or of synecdoche (if the specificity of "cinema" is taken to represent the more generic "entertainment").

Nigerian Pidgin English: Lexicon

The lexicon of NPE comprises, besides a large proportion of English words and a quantity of YOR words, a few words of foreign origin. As Todd 1974 (15) observes, most pidgin Englishes possess a form of *saber* for "know" and *pequeno* for "little" or "offspring." In *The Road* Soyinka uses the Portuguese-derived "sabbe" and "picken" in the following ways:

23) I no *sabbe* do am. (Salubi, 154)
(I don't know how to do it.)
24) Na de kind ting person dey show small *picken*?
(Samson, 198)
(Is this the kind of thing to show small children?
—Soyinka 1965: 98)

NPE exploits, moreover, a form of the Portuguese *palavra* ("word, speech"), borrowed, together with *saber* and *pequeno*, into NPE in the fifteenth century when a Portuguese-based pidgin was spoken along the West Coast of Africa (Mafeni 1971 105). Samson's

No nonsense no palaver (225)
(No nonsense no trouble—Soyinka 1965: 99)

exemplifies the borrowing. Interestingly SE utilizes the same word: *palaver* was borrowed into English through Portuguese from the Late Latin *parabola* ("parable, speech") (*Webster's New Collegiate Dictionary* 1977:824), and is related in origin and meaning to such SE terms as *parley, parliament,* and *parlor*—all of which are derived from the Middle French *parler,* "to speak" (*Longman Dictionary of the English Language* 1984:1068). Soyinka's gloss of *palaver*—"trouble"—suggests a kind of extrapolation from the root meaning, "a talk, parley, conference, discussion: chiefly applied to conferences, with much talk, between African or other uncivilized natives, and traders or travellers" (*OED* 1933: 390), to "tedious or time-consuming business, especially when of a formal nature" (*Collins Concise Dictionary* 1982:813).

African loan-words in NPE, maintains Mafeni (105), account for some twelve percent of the lexicon. The NPE of *The Road* contains indeed but a small quantity of YOR words, substantiating Mafeni's contention. Terms for local objects, food, and religious artifacts tend to be borrowed from the dominant Nigerian language spoken in any given area; thus YOR terms like *"bolekaja"* (Salubi, 153), *"Ogiri"* ("Skunk"; Samson, 165), *"panla"* ("stockfish"; Salubi, 175), *"Oga"* ("Master"; Salubi, 184), *"omo agbepo"* ("son of the night scavenger"; Samson, 184), *"Ole ngboro"* ("Robber abroad"; Samson, 185), *"Iwin ogodo"* ("Imp of the swamp"; Samson, 185), *"agbada"* ("loose garment"—Bowen 1858; Particulars Joe, 210), *"Baba Agbero"* ("Master of Fornication"—Bowen, 1858; Salubi, 224), *"Ti o l'eru ese!"* ("Light travellers only: no burdens of sin!" Samson, 225), *"olopa"* (Samson, 225), *"onijibiti"* ("bloody crook"; Samson, 225), *"egungun"* (226: s.d.), and *"agemo"* ("a religious cult of flesh dissolution"—149; 226: s.d.) are interspersed chiefly amongst NPE but also amongst SE lines in the play.

The Case For Literary Nigerian Pidgin English

Soyinka's NPE in *The Road* exhibits a number of other features neither Barbag-Stoll (1983) nor Mafeni (1971), the two sources for this analysis, corroborates. In one sense it may be true to say that Soyinka's NPE is itself idiosyncratic enough to constitute an idiolect. Even in his use of SE Soyinka displays the occasional nonstandard quirk: mood-mixing, in conditional constructions, creeps into Samson's speech—"If I won something I *will* put it on a new lorry" (204; my italics)—and, unprecedentedly, into Professor's—"If you could see through that sealed church window you *will* see the lectern bearing the Word on bronze" (205; my italics).[30] NPE features like the use of "self" (161) and "kuku" (162) for emphasis, the use of *in* for *him* (for example, in reflexive pronoun constructions: "Why'e no kuku play the ting *inself*—Salubi, 162; my italics), and the use of numerous fillers (like the interjection "Haba!"—"Ha!" [161]—and the enigmatic "enh" [162]) might well be thought to characterize Soyinka's own brand of NPE. Moreover, since a work of literature is itself idiosyncratic in the sense that it is the personal creation of its author, the encapsulation of certain idiosyncratic features of a code within that work might be taken to signify a specifically literary exploitation of that code. That Soyinka's NPE is an idiolect, however, is tantamount to an affirmation of the play's idiosyncrasy. The use of Soyinkan NPE features, then, connotes not a divergence from 'standard' NPE (if indeed such a code exists), but an adaptation of a code according to the artistic needs of the author. The NPE of *The Road*, as this by no means exhaustive analysis has demonstrated, not only fulfills the requirements for a pidgin outlined earlier, but conforms in large measure to a variety of NPE in use in Nigeria. What Soyinka designates as NPE in the play, we must conclude, is pidgin indeed.

The Function of Code in *The Road*

The identification and description of linguistic strands in *The Road* has been achieved at the expense of a consideration of the significance of these strands, as though form and function were separable. A consideration of the uses to which the eight codes of the play are put has been postponed until now for two reasons: first, because of the multiplicity of linguistic media Soyinka exploits and the necessity of upholding what might appear to be tenuous distinctions among them and, second, because of a desire more clearly to illustrate the functional interrelatedness of the codes—the way they are woven into the fabric of the play. The object of this section is not a comprehensive discussion of the dramatic purpose of every speech that exemplifies a code, but a consideration of the kinds of purpose certain speeches representative of one or another code embody. In this sense the discussion offers a model according to which the use of code may be interpreted.

The deployment of eight separate codes within a single work might appear to be gratuitous, presupposing on the part of the reader or audience a receptive knowledge of every code.

Clark, himself a Nigerian writer, is disparaging of Soyinka's achievement, contending that in *The Road* "he [Soyinka] seems to have lost his way in the search for proper levels of speech for his odd collection of characters" (Clark 1970: 95-96). Unfortunate paronomasia aside (Soyinka's groping after "proper levels of speech" is likened to Professor's quest—"search"—for the Word, both of which are doomed to failure),[31] Clark's charge of inappropriateness is a contradiction in terms: if the characters of the play are odd, it is their language in part that makes them so, and Clark's prescriptivism—the notion of a "proper" language for each character—is misplaced. Moreover, as Probyn (36) in an illuminating article on *The Road* and Theatre of the Absurd observes, "a central feature of the play is the idea of delinquents treated as pillars of society, a technique of social satire and political alienation used when the artist feels most radically disaffiliated from society's norms." Oddity is a necessary evil in a world of inverted values where characters must find their own way amidst a plethora of misleading signs.

A useful starting point for a discussion of the function of the play's language, then, is to consider the deployment of idiolect as a vehicle of characterization. The precise matching of character and idiolect implied by Professor Higgins's "An Englishman's way of speaking absolutely classifies him" in "Why Can't the English?" (opening song of *My Fair Lady* [Lerner 1956]), is precluded in *The Road* by the degree of code-switching that marks the speech of several characters; it is possible, however, to match character and code in the speech of monolinguals like Kotonu and Chief-in-Town (who speak only non-liturgical SE), the Lay-abouts (who utilize YOR songs), and Murano (whose only language is silence). *Monolingual* is used in a restricted sense to designate one who has a productive knowledge of a code. (It is, perhaps, this distinction between productive and receptive code that has led critics like Clark to be skeptical about the linguistic achievement of the play.) Moreover, since code-switching in the play is not arbitrary—Samson, Salubi, and 1st, 2nd, and 3rd Man, for example, switch amongst SE, SIME, and NPE—a certain degree of character-code matching is possible even with respect to code-switchers.

Character-Code Identification

Kotonu and Chief-in-Town

Non-liturgical SE is the most widely exploited code in *The Road*, acting as medium for seven characters (nine if we consider the 1st, 2nd, and 3rd Man discretely) and sole medium for two. Kotonu and Chief-in-Town both utilize the code, and, because such monopoly is exceptional, Soyinka uses its deployment for their characterization. We might, for example, expect Kotonu—erstwhile driver of "'No Danger No Delay'", companion to Samson, and indolent lay-about amongst fellow lay-abouts (s.d. on 167: *"Kotonu slides back into his favourite position, lying by the wall of the store or sitting up against it . . . half-asleep, indifferent to what goes on around him"*)—to exploit the SIME, NPE, or ACE of his colleagues, yet his persistent use of SE distinguishes him from his fellows. The distinction is substantiated, moreover, in his apparent aloofness from Samson and his desire to escape the sordidness of the circumstances of his existence; Kotonu will not drive again, will not kill a dog on the road as a propiatory offering to Ogun (Samson, 165), and attempts constantly to distance himself from the contingencies of the road:

> A man gets tired of feeling too much (166)

is his excuse for giving up the road to take over Sergeant Burma's store, and his recognition that steeliness is the only answer to the harsh realities of the road underlies his comment on Sergeant Burma's seeming inhumanity in removing the tires from a lorry whose dead driver he recognized:

> A man must protect himself against the indifference of comrades who desert him. (167)

In these two examples, medium and message fuse to distinguish Kotonu's pragmatism from the idealism of Samson. Professor acknowledges Kotonu's superiority in his remark to Samson: "Your friend [Kotonu] appears, if I may say so, to have the edge on Burma" (200).

The short, clipped speech of Chief-in-Town, politician and organizer of thugs (168), likewise distinguishes him from the store's other frequenters; making only one brief appearance in the play (167-69), Chief-in-Town speaks with the voice of authority that bespeaks his hold over Say Tokyo Kid and his resolve in a world of vacuous irresolution:

> I need ten men. . . . How soon can you round them up? (168)

The use of SE as a monolingual code betokens a purposefulness that elevates Kotonu and Chief-in-Town, however amoral their perspectives, above the idle procrastinators of the play.

The Chorus

Though the structure of the play would suggest that the "gang" (166: s.d.) acts through song as a kind of Greek chorus commenting upon the action—dirge, war-chant, or praise-song, e.g., might appear to reinforce the action by unravelling the deeper significance behind Kotonu's refusal to kill a dog (165), Say Tokyo Kid's reverence for timber (172-73), Kokol'ori's fatal accident (190-91), or the succor Professor affords the group (219-20)—the resemblance is formal only. The gang sing and dance, but their songs fail to elucidate the meaning of the events they portray: the apt somberness of the "Driver's dirge" (165; 230) is offset by the levity of its lewd verse (166; 230-31), the esotericism of the "Thug's war-chant" (173; 231) is cryptic in its allusion (the significance of Oro and Esu remains a mystery to one not versed in the Yoruba pantheon), the sense in which Kokol'ori, Kotonu's father, was "A man among men" (231) appears merely to belittle the significance of his life ("Dirge for Kokol'ori"—191; 231), and the gratuitousness of "Professor's praise-song" (231)—"to restore [his] self-confidence" (220)—appears, in its assertion of Professor's demonic nature ("our being like demon"—231) and spiritual associations ("who holds discourse with spirits, who dines with the Ruler of Forests"—232), self-consciously to aggrandize the mythological significance of one already inflated beyond credibility. The songs serve, then, as foils to the action rather than commentaries upon it.

Murano

More illuminating than the songs is Murano's silence. Murano is the one person "in whom the Word reposes" (Professor, 186), and is therefore a fitting companion for Professor in his quest for the "elusive word" (Professor, 184). As the songs are to the action of *The Road*, the silence of Murano is to the verbosity of Professor: only silence can act as a foil to "the intolerable wrestle/With words and meanings" (Eliot 1944: 17) that characterizes Professor's relationship with the world. Ironically, Professor seeks meaning through language in a Word which resides in a mute; and while Professor's language merely obfuscates the reality that surrounds him, imprisoning him within a linguistic cage, Murano's silence is the fitting embodiment of the real object of Professor's quest—(to appropriate Eliot's words once more) "only a shell, a husk of meaning/From which the purpose breaks only when it is fulfilled/If at all" (36). The silence of Murano, empty as it is, is more meaningful than the vacuous verbiage of Professor, and is the more honest response in the face of the death and brokenness that accompanies any intercourse with the road.

Professor

Professor's relationship with the world is negotiated through two codes, LE and SE. The background to his exploitation of a liturgical code is located in his former involvement with the church and religious ritual, an association now abandoned: the Christian doctrine of the Incarnation—the Word made flesh—has been replaced by the Yoruba notion of flesh dissolution and the *agemo* through which it is realized. However, the substitution is not total: the Word, symbol of the Christian Incarnation, remains, albeit in another guise, the object of Professor's quest. In an ironic reversal, the Word becomes associated not with the Incarnation but with its antithesis, dissolution: Professor's

> There are dangers in the Quest I know, but the Word may
> be found companion not to life, but Death (159)

indicates not that the Word was made flesh, but, as Izevbaye (54) observes, that "all flesh becomes associated with the Word during the process of decomposition." Meaning is located not in life but in death—hence Professor's preoccupation through his quest for the Word with the dead and the dying (Murano is himself the embodiment, as it were, of one snatched from the jaws of death) and his reliance upon the road for its yield of human flesh.

Through his use of LE Professor cuts himself off from the world with which he must perforce engage, infusing everything with a spiritual significance and transforming the natural world into a supernatural stage. To Samson, perched (literally) above him, he says:

> Yes, you seem a knowing man, cutting yourself from common touch with earth. But this is a path away from true communion . . . the Word is not to be found in denial. (158)

The observation is misplaced: the irony is that Professor's language—LE—has cut *him* off from "common touch with earth," and that his quest for the Word entails the very isolation from "true communion" he advises against. Language, chief instrument of human communication, becomes the chief obstacle in the way of Professor's communion with the world. The spiritualization of as ordinary an event as the death of three persons in a motor accident—"all three of them crucified on rigid branches" (Professor, 159)—parodies, through the association of car accident and the crucifixion of Christ amid two thieves (Mark 15: 27), any notion of "true communion"[32] with the world.

Nonliturgical SE becomes Professor's medium of expression when he is annoyed, or when Soyinka exploits his obsession with metaphor to humorous effect. Professor's response to Samson's seemingly flippant suggestion that he (Professor) is preoccupied with finding the Word is the amazed

> Do you think I spend every living moment looking for that? What do you think I am—a madman? (188)

The questions are inadvertently rhetorical, the answer to both unequivocally in the affirmative. Soyinka uses SE also to ridicule Professor's confusion of levels of meaning. Consider the following exchanges:

> PROF: [*takes out his watch and looks at it.*]: Hm.
> SAMSON: Is it working now Professor?
> PROF.: No. But it still tells the time. (181)

SAMSON: I only said I kept my money there. [In a cigarette tin, in the churchyard.]
PROF.: So the dead are now your bank managers?
SAMSON: No sir, I . . .
PROF.: No harm in it, no harm in it. Do they give overdrafts though? (182)

And occasionally Professor's SE is the vehicle for the communication of a double-edged truth:
SAMSON: May I ask you something? A little personal?
PROF.: Why not? Even God submits himself to a weekly interrogation. (205)

Code-Switching

The Function of Yoruba

Professor's switching between LE and SE is on the whole unremarkable, and does not constitute a change of medium the switch from one language to another implies. Say Tokyo Kid's movement from ACE, his customary medium of expression, to YOR in conversation with Particulars Joe (170-71) is more noteworthy. Though Say Tokyo Kid's ACE merely distinguishes him as motor-park lay-about and conveyor of timber who has appropriated the American Southern drawl for self-aggrandizement—"I'm Say Tokyo Kid and I don't fear no son of man" (170)—his switch to YOR betrays a readiness to engage Particulars Joe in ritual insult. YOR becomes in his trance-like exchange with Particulars Joe—a "stick of weed" (170) has hastened the onset of the trance for the latter—a medium for formulaic showing another code would not allow. The code-switching is achieved effortlessly, from

PARTICULARS JOE: No dirty timber.
SAY T.: Thas me kid.

to

PARTICULARS JOE: *Egi dongboro lehin were!*
SAY T.: *Yio ba baba e.*
PARTICULARS JOE: *Gbegi ma gbe'yawo!*
SAY T.: *Yio ba 'ponri iya a'laiya e.*

PARTICULARS JOE: *Olomokuiya.*
[*Say Tokyo grins, both hands held in an insulting gesture.*]
(Nothing like a sound club on the back of a looney!
May it land on your father.
Wedded, not to a wife but to timber.
May it hit the fountainhead of your great grandmother.
Oh, what sufferings for such as give birth.) (171)

and immediately back again to the ACE of Say Tokyo Kid:

I mean, a man has gotta have his pride.... (171)

The Function of Nigerian Pidgin English

The code-switching of Samson and Salubi, and to a lesser extent of the 1st, 2nd, and 3rd Man, is not only the most productive but also the most interesting exemplification of medium exchange in the play. If it is deemed appropriate that a work of literature reflect in its use of language the linguistic environment that has led to its genesis, *The Road* succeeds in representing the multilingual nature of Nigerian society and the code-switching that must characterize the speech of many of its members. In this sense the switching amongst SE, SIME, and NPE of Samson and Salubi constitutes nothing more than part of Soyinka's attempt to represent the totality of Nigerian life through a linguistic window.

The deployment of NPE in a literary work may, as Obilade (1978:434) corroborates, signify such a representation only; Defoe's *The History and Remarkable Life of the Truly Honourable Colonel Jacque* (rpt. 1965) utilizes NPE (137), but not as a stylistic device. One object of this investigation into the use of NPE is to establish whether pidgin elements in *The Road* are to be regarded as foregrounded—elements that are stylistically productive. Clark (1970:95-96) has stated that Soyinka "in his use of pidgin English [in *The Road*] is aiming at special theatric effects, too esoteric for common understanding," a charge to which the adroit code-switching of Samson and Salubi, whose replacement of one medium with another might well appear arbitrary or gratuitous, is open. The establishment of the truth of this charge—difficult as it is in the absence of a first-hand knowledge of Nigerian society to determine the effect of such "esoteric" craftsmanship upon the average theatergoer, Nigerian or otherwise—constitutes a second object of enquiry.

NPE serves two important functions in *The Road*—facility of communication, and identification. Both Samson and Salubi resort to NPE as the medium through which they can best communicate forcefully: Samson's switch from the SE "May I ask you what you are?" (152) to the NPE "God almighty! You dey like monkey wey stoway inside sailor suit" (152) is matched by Salubi's shift from the SIME "A uniformed private driver—temporary unemploy" (152) to the NPE "Na common jealousy dey do you" (152), and Salubi's outburst—"Wes matter? Na me you take dream last night or na wetin" (153)—in response to Samson's advice about cleanliness (152) is uttered *"desperately"* (153: s.d.), and therefore in NPE.

Similarly, NPE is the medium through which Samson delivers the *coup de grace* to his tale about the bishop's outwitting of Professor (163-64); after relating the entire story of the "proper fight" (163) in SE—how the bishop, playing on Professor's penchant for bowing at every mention of "Jesus Christ," reduces Professor at last to one final bow—Samson declares:

> The bishop sermonized his head off, the church shook with reverberations from passionate grammar but na so Professor bend in head—'e no move one inch. *[Samson sits, shaking his head in admiration.]* (164)

The fluent transition from the SE of "the church shook with reverberations from passionate grammar" to the NPE of the following clause ("na so Professor bend in head—'e no move one inch") is masterful, the effect (matched by his final cessation of movement—*"Samson sits"*) incisive.

Again, NPE is the language in which Salubi seeks refuge when he finds himself the butt of Professor's virulence over the question of obtaining a driver's license. Never daring to lapse into NPE at any other time in addressing Professor, a desperate Salubi (*"prostrating flat on his belly"*—184: s.d.) breaks out inadvertently into the NPE

> Oga I beg you sir. I sorry too much (184)

and the plea to his companions,
> Tell Professor to take in curse commot for my head. (184)

The more embroiled a character becomes in a difficult situation and the tenser his position, the more natural his reversion to the comforting familiarity of NPE. Given this notion of familiarity, however, one cannot on the basis of fluency alone distinguish either NPE or SE as the mother-tongue of its speakers, however fluent the code-switching of Samson and Salubi.

If NPE is the more accessible medium in situations of emotional stress, it is the language of identification also—that code through which the drivers of the road, and their touts, identify with their passengers, their fellow Nigerians. NPE constitutes in this sense a unifying *lingua franca* that unites those speaking disparate languages—and more disparate than a lorry-load of languages traversing the pathways of a multilingual land one cannot get. In his recreation of the scene of an accident (198) Samson utilizes NPE, the language that has grown up amongst the people, to identify with the bemused witnesses of a gruesome spectacle, now to shepherd ("Make you all walka this side"), now to upbraid ("God punish you, you wretched woman, why you dey carry your picken look that kind thing?"), now to chide ("Commot my friend . . . a-ah, these people too foolish")—always to influence through the solicitude of a familiar medium.

For Samson, NPE in Part Two becomes chiefly the language of reminiscence, the medium through which he recalls for himself and for his audience such nostalgic events as his driving with Kotonu (202-03), Sergeant Burma's military exploits (216-18), and the superiority of his (Samson's) touting (225-26)—this last reminiscence delivered in a state of near inebriation. We are never quite sure, however, of the precise function of such reminiscing; Samson appears to use NPE both to recall the past and sardonically to parody it before our eyes. His

> Wetin? You tink say I get dat kind sentimentation? Me wey I done see dead body to tey I no fit chop meat unless den cook am to nonsense? (218)

> (What? You think I have time for sentimentality? I who have seen so many corpses that I cannot eat meat unless it is overdone?—Soyinka: 98-99)

suggests a cultivated stoicism akin to Kotonu's self-protection "against the indifference of comrades who desert" (167) we are not taken in by. Soyinka uses NPE in *The Road* for another purpose also—the expression of profound truths. Samson's "Haba! Justice no dey for white man world" (217) ("Ha! There is no justice in the white man's world"—Soyinka: 98) and "When person die, 'e done die and dat one done finish" (218) ("When a man dies, he's dead and that's the end of that"—Soyinka: 98) reflect perhaps Soyinka's perceptions about the colonial heritage of injustice post-independent Nigeria has merely embellished[33] and about the cessation of life upon death neither Professor's erstwhile Christianity nor his adopted Yoruba mythology can gainsay.

One final observation about the function of NPE in *The Road* concerns the influence NPE exerts upon the speech of various characters. No one speaks NPE to Professor, for example: besides Salubi's outburst over the question of obtaining a license (184), SE is the medium of expression among Professor, Samson, and Salubi (156-60). Samson and Salubi converse in NPE, but to his former driver, Kotonu, Samson speaks only SE: Kotonu is himself an exponent of SE only. This indicates that SE exerts a moderating influence over NPE speakers, actually determining the medium of conversation; syntagmatically, use of SE in addressing Professor is the natural concomitant to the decision to address him as "Professor" and as "sir" (for example, Samson, 179).

Conclusion

One approach to the variety of language codes in *The Road* is to consider the effect of such deployment in terms of a dialectical tension between confusion and harmony. The esotericism of Soyinka's use of NPE to which Clark (1970: 95-96) objects might be thought to embrace the other codes also, as though the final effect of a mixing of languages were the creation of a confusion Soyinka did not intend. According to this conception, the mere deployment of a multiplicity of codes recalls the tower of Babel (resembling theHebrew for "confusion"), the symbol of the confusion of languages effected by God's scattering of his people "upon the face of all the earth" (Genesis

11:9); *The Road*, by using disparate codes, reflects Nigeria's multilingual composition. Probyn's idea of character-code identification in the play reinforces this notion:

> In *The Road* individuals are individualists, fashioning their own language from a more or less rootless and anarchic social matrix built up painfully out of the deficient conventions of an inherited world. (37)

The sense of confusion engendered by a "rootless and anarchic social matrix" may, however, be intentional: if Probyn's analysis is accurate, the confusion is a product not of artistic failure but of a deliberate attempt to reflect the socio-political disorder of Nigerian society.[34] Soyinka's very characterization reflects a basic corruption of the time: Professor, "*proprietor etc. of the drivers' haven*" (Soyinka 1973: 148), is an overseer of lay-abouts, dabbler in road-death, and forger of drivers' licenses (188); Kotonu, "*a driver*" (148), is, in Samson's metaphor, a spider (169) lying in wait to claim the spare parts of the vehicles of victims of the road; Chief-in-Town, "*a politician*" (148), is an organizer of thugs and dealer in drugs (168-69), while Say Tokyo Kid is a "*captain of thugs*" (148); Particulars Joe, "*a policeman*" (148), is a sniffer of "weed" (170) whose approach to the law (209-15) constitutes a travesty of justice; and Samson and Salubi, like the thuggish lay-abouts, are unemployed "hangers-on" (Particulars Joe, 219) bound to the drivers' haven.

These characters are united not only through their connection with the drivers' haven, but through their common pursuit of meaning through language. Professor's quest for the Word epitomizes the (albeit more covert) search for meaning through speech evinced by all the characters besides Murano. Their journey along the road is as much spiritual as linguistic, each character's language marking his progress along a path toward death that Murano, the mute, has already travelled; and, appropriately, silence—symbol of one (Murano) who has glimpsed the secrets of the dead—embodies the emptiness of the search for meaning other wayfarers are yet to discover. The confusion suggested by the diversity of tongues and inversion of values is offset, then, by the harmonious juxtaposition of the languages of those engaged in a similar pursuit, the quest for meaning through language in a world that offers few signs and fewer rewards. Considered in this way, Soyinka's satirization, through language and characterization, of the Nigerian socio-political situation makes at once for linguistic confusion and dramatic harmony; the play is representative both linguistically and dramatically of the situation that led to its creation. Professor's assertion of unity—

> My task is to keep company with the fallen. . . . We must all stick together. Only the fallen have need of restitution. (220)

—is an ironic recognition of the need for unification of those fallen who were never mighty.

UNIVERSITY OF THE WITWATERSRAND—SOUTH AFRICA

Notes

I am indebted to Maurice Aldridge of the Department of Linguistics, University of the Witwatersrand, for his useful comments on early drafts of this paper.

1. *The Road* has been admired by a number of critics, but chiefly for its exploitation of the Yoruba mythology that underpins it. Studies by Larsen (1983: 64-76), Dingome (1980), Sekoni (1983), Gurr (1976), Mootry (1976), Katrak (1984: 71-90), and Edet (1984: 125-45) have contributed much to our understanding of Soyinka's use of the Yoruba pantheon, but make only cursory mention of its "literary distinction" (Yankowitz, 1966: 132). Three notable exceptions are: Probyn's "Waiting for the Word: Samuel Beckett and Wole Soyinka" (1981), valuable for its character-code identification; Barbag-Stoll's *Social and Linguistic History of Nigerian Pidgin English* (1983), the final chapter of which is devoted to a consideration of literary uses of pidgin English; and Obilade's "The Stylistic Function of Pidgin English in African Literature: Achebe and Soyinka" (1978), which provides a useful model, as far as it goes, for the stylistic analysis of multilingual works of literature.

2. One denotation of "Third World": see *Longman Dictionary of the English Language* (1984: 1562).

3. If mutually unintelligible, however, they are surely to be considered languages and not dialects.
4. Though the characters of the play do not evince a productive knowledge of all the codes deployed, they must, since no character's speech is challenged as code *per se* (Jakobson's conception of code as part of the speech act—1960: 353), be assumed to possess a receptive knowledge of every code.
5. Such a situation may constitute diglossic code-switching: see Bell (1976:133-35).
6. The following discussion of codes in the play is largely semantico-syntactic, given the difficulty surrounding the orthographic representation of phonological features and, in the case of Nigerian pidgin English (NPE), a lack of uniform orthography. Observations about phonology are, therefore, necessarily speculative.
7. All references to the play, unless otherwise stated, are to the 1973 edition—*Collected Plays* I.
8. Vitality, following Hymes's functional typology (in Bell 1976: 147-53), is a feature of SE: SE is the property of a mother-tongue community of users.
9. Orton's *Loot* (1976) abounds in the colloquial style.
10. ACE has been coined for the purposes of this study, and does not necessarily designate an actual variety of American English.
11. The influence of YOR is evident here: in YOR the verb is not conjugated—auxiliaries or contextual markers frequently determine verb tense (Ogunbowale 1970: 13).
12. See above.
13. The following discussion of YOR is tentative, relying, in the absence of firsthand knowledge, solely on the analyses of others.
14. A non-classical definition of *koine (Longman Dictionary of the English Language* 1984:814).
15. The relationship between PE and YOR will be examined later.
16. Poetic elements, in the form of riddles, songs, proverbs, and actual poetry, apparently characterize the everyday speech of the average Yoruban (Ogunbowale 1970:12); since poetry reputedly comes more naturally to the Yoruba than prose—the triple naming of infants seems to substantiate the claim (Beier 1970: 22)—it might be argued that poetry is the more

accessible medium. We are exposed in *A Dance of the Forests* to blank verse in *L2 English*, however, and inevitably YOR poesy is altered in the switch of codes.
17. For a discussion of the principles underlying Yoruba versification, see Ogunbowale (1970:173-80).
18. Despite the seeming lapse of tone introduced into the continuation of the "Drivers' dirge" through the switch from heaven to its carnal earthly equivalent, a brothel.
19. Silence is properly the absence of language; the use of inverted commas here and subsequently is intended to accommodate this notion.
20. Following Hymes's functional typology (Bell 1976:147-53).
21. In this and subsequent definitions, my italics.
22. Such a poverty is characteristic certainly of restricted pidgins—see Todd (1974: 5).
23. For a discussion of Fanagalo as a pidgin, see Heine (1973).
24. TL: L2.
25. See, for example, the novels of Achebe (1960, 1964, 1966) and other plays by Soyinka (1969). For further exemplification, see Barbag-Stoll (1983:101-18).
26. Because only an estimated five per cent of learners ever achieve native-speaker proficiency in the TL, most IL reflects "fossilized IL competences" (Selinker 1972:217).
27. The original edition (Soyinka 1975), though more helpful, is by no means exhaustive: terms like "E sa mi" (6), "den" (7, 14), "tief" (18), and "Commot" (18) are left unglossed, however easily their meanings may be gleaned from the context.
28. In this and subsequent quotations, italics unless otherwise stated are mine.
29. Some conjecture is involved in establishing the precise meaning of "Shoo," but the context seems to render "Get out!" plausible, Shoo acting as a kind of exclamation.
30. Quirks—unless *will* and *would* are not distinguished in YOR, in which case the use of *will* for *would* may be attributable to primitive-level translation (which, in the absence of evidence that these utterances are translations, seems unlikely). For a useful discussion of translation as a distinctive feature of African literature in English, see Adejare (1987:145-59).
31. See *The Road* (157), where Samson suggests that Professor has "missed [his] way" along what Professor deems "the true path

to the Word" (159).
32. Professor's use of "communion" is itself ironic: his association of "communion" and "Word" in the same sentence (158) recalls the commemoration of the death of Christ—the Word made flesh—in the rite of Holy Communion (cf. I Cor. 11:23-26).
33. A perception shared by at least two of his compatriots: Solarin (in Judd: 246), who remarked in 1963 that "one thing is clear in the minds of the young elements in our country: Nigeria is not being effectively governed.... Our government is a hydra-headed octopus that veers and backs, depending on the prevailing planets and political winds, and that oscillates and flounders and hopes, whatever happens, for the best. It is not purposive; it is not logical; it is not disciplined"; and Fagbure (in Davidson 1978:322), who simultaneously protested against "the appalling mismanagement of our public affairs, the lack of direction on the national level, the moral depravity of our society."
34. See Davidson (1978:323).

WORKS CITED

Achebe, Chinua. *No Longer at Ease.* London: Heinemann, 1960
___. *Arrow of God.* London: Heinemann, 1963.
___. *A Man of the People.* London: Heinemann, 1966.
Adejare, Oluwole "Translation: A Distinctive Feature of African Literature in English." *Language and Style* 20.2 (1987):145-59.
Adler, Max K. *Pidgins, Creoles and Lingua Francas.* Hamburg: H. Buske Verlag, 1977.
Aldridge, M.V. Unpublished recordings. Personal collection. Department of Linguistics, University of the Witwatersrand, Johannesburg (n.d.).
Amankulor, James Nduka "Dramatic Technique and Meaning in *The Road." Ba Shiru.* 7.1 (1976): 53-58.
Bamgbose, Ayo. *A Grammar of Yoruba.* London: Cambridge University Press, 1966.
Barbag-Stoll, Anna *Social and Linguistic History of Nigerian Pidgin English.* Tubingen: Stauffenberg Verlag, 1983.
Beckett, Samuel *Waiting for Godot.* London: Faber & Faber, 1965.
Beier, Ulli, ed. *Yoruba Poetry: An Anthology of Traditional Yoruba*

Poems. London: Cambridge University Press, 1970.
Bell, Roger T. *Sociolinguistics.* London: Batsford, 1976.
Bowen, T.J. "Grammar and Dictionary of the Yoruba Language." In *Smithsonian Contributions to Knowledge* (1858).
Brown, Gillian. *Listening to Spoken English.* Essex: Longman, 1977.
C. C. T. A. Symposium on Multilingualism. London: [n.p.], 1964.
Clark, J. P. *The Example of Shakespeare.* London: Longman, 1970.
The Collins Concise Dictionary London: Collins, 1982.
Crystal, David. *A First Dictionary of Linguistics and Phonetics.* London: Deutsch 1980.
Davidson, Basil *Africa in Modern History.* Harmondsworth: Penguin, 1978.
DeCamp, David "Introduction: The Study of Pidgin and Creole Languages." In Hymes (1971:13-39).
Defoe, Daniel *The History and Remarkable Life of the Truly Honourable Colonel Jacque.* [*1722]. London: Oxford University Press, 1965 [rpt.]
Dennis, Jamie & Jerrie Scott. "Creole Formation and Reorganization: Evidence for Diachronic Change in Synchronic Variation." Paper presented at the International Conference on Pidgins and Creoles, Honolulu, 1975.
Deutsch, Babette. *Poetry Handbook: A Dictionary of Terms.* London: Jonathan Cape, 1957.
Dingome, Jeanne. "Soyinka's *The Road* as Ritual Drama."*Kunapipi.* 2.1 (1980): 30-41.
Edet, R.N. *The Resilience of Religious Tradition in the Dramas of Wole Soyinka and James Ene Henshaw.* Ann Arbor, Michigan: University Microfilms International, 1984.
Eliot, T.S. *Four Quartets.* London: Faber & Faber, 1944.
Ellis, Rod. *Understanding Second Language Acquisition.* Oxford: Oxford University Press, 1985.
Fagbure, G. *Sunday Times.* 15 December, 1963. Lagos.
Fowler, Roger & Gunther Kress. "Critical Linguistics." In Fowler et al. (1979: 185-213).
Fowler, Roger, Bob Hodge, Gunther Kress, & Tony Trew *Language and Control.* London: Routledge & Kegan Paul, 1979.
Gibbs, James, ed. *Critical Perspectives on Wole Soyinka.* London: Heinemann Educational Books, 1981.
Gilliatt, Penelope "A Nigerian Original." In Gibbs (1981:106-07).
Gurr, Andrew "Third-World Drama: Soyinka and Tragedy." *Journal*

of Commonwealth Literature. 10.3 (1976): 45-52.
Hall, Robert A., Jr. "Pidgin Languages." *Scientific American.* 200.2 (1959).
Hancock, Ian F. *A List of Place Names in the Pacific North-West Derived from the Chinook Jargon with a Word-list of the Language.* Vancouver: Vancouver Public Library, 1972.
Heine, Bernd. *Pidgin-Sprachen im Bantu-Bereich.* Berlin: Dietrich Reimer Verlag, 1973.
Hill, Trevor "Institutional Linguistics." *Orbis.* 7.1-2 (1958): 441-455.
Hymes, Dell. "On Communicative Competence." In Pride & Holmes (1972: 269-93).
___. ed. *Pidginization and Creolization of Languages.* London: Cambridge University Press, 1971.
Izevbaye, D.S. "Language and Meaning in Soyinka's *The Road.*" Drama in Africa. 8 (1975): 52-65.
Jakobson, Roman "Linguistics and Poetics." In Sebeok (1960: 350-77).
Judd, P., ed. *African Independence.* New York: Dell, 1963.
Katrak, K.H. *The Tragic Drama of Wole Soyinka.* Ann Arbor, MI: University Microfilms International, 1984.
Kleinecke, David "An Etymology for 'Pidgin'." *International Journal of Applied Linguistics.* 25 (1959): 271-72.
Labov, William. *Sociolinguistic Patterns.* Oxford: Blackwell, 1978.
Larsen, Stephan. *A Writer and his Gods.* Stockholm: Minab/Gotab, 1983.
Lerner, A.J. *My Fair Lady.* London: CBS Masterworks, 1956.
Longman Dictionary of the English Language. Essex: Longman, 1984.
Mafeni, Bernard "Nigerian Pidgin." In Spencer (1971: 95-112).
Moore, Gerald *Wole Soyinka.* London: Evans Brothers, 1971.
Mootry, Maria K. "Soyinka and Yoruba Mythology." *Ba Shiru.* 7.1(1976): 23-32.
Mühlhäusler, Peter. *Pidgin and Creole Linguistics.* Oxford: Blackwell, 1986.
Nemser, W. "Approximative Systems of Foreign Language Learners." *International Review of Applied Linguistics* IX (1971): 115-23.
Obilade, Tony. "The Stylistic Function of Pidgin English in African Literature: Achebe and Soyinka." *Research in African Literatures.* 9.3 (1978): 433-44.
Ogunbowale, P.O. *The Essentials of the Yoruba Language.* London:

London University Press, 1970.
Oxford English Dictionary Oxford: Oxford University Press, 1933.
Penguin Plays: New English Dramatists [13] Middlesex: Penguin,(1968): 17-83.
Pride, J.B. & J. Holmes, eds. *Sociolinguistics: Selected Readings.* Harmondsworth: Penguin, 1972.
Probyn, Clive T. "Waiting for the Word: Samuel Beckett and Wole Soyinka." *Ariel* 12.3 (1981): 35-48.
Ross, A.S.C. "On the Historical Study of Pidgins." In C. C. T. A. (1964).
Sebeok, T., ed. *Style in Language.* Cambridge, MA: MIT Press, 1960.
Sekoni, 'Ropo. "Metaphor as Basis of Form in Soyinka's Drama." *Research in African Literatures.* 14.1 (1983): 45-57.
Selinker, L. "Language Transfer." *General Linguistics* 9(1969): 67-92.
___. "Interlanguage." *International Review of Applied Linguistics.* X (1972): 209-231.
Smithsonian Contributions to Knowledge. Vol. X, Article 4: 5-134. Washington: Smithsonian Institution, 1858.
Solarin, T. "A View of Nigerian Independence." In Judd (1963:246).
Soyinka, Wole. *A Dance of the Forests.* London: Oxford University Press, 1963.
___. *The Road.* London: Oxford Univ. Press, 1965.
___. *Three Short Plays.* London: Oxford Univ. Press, 1969.
___. *Collected Plays* I. Oxford: Oxford Univ. Press, 1973.
Spencer, John, ed. *The English Language in West Africa.* London: Longman, 1971.
Todd, Loreto. *Pidgins and Creoles.* London: Routledge & Kegan Paul, 1974.
Unesco. *The Use of Vernacular Languages in Education.* Monographs on Fundamental Education, 8. Paris: *Unesco,* 1963.
Webster's New Collegiate Dictionary, Springfield, MA.: Merriam, 1977.
Webster's Third New International Dictionary, Springfield, Massachusetts: Merriam, 1961.
Wilson, John. "The Relation of Master John Wilson of Wanstead in Essex, One of the Last Ten that Returned into England from Wiapoco in Guinea." *Purchas his Pilgrimes.* Book 4, ch. 14. (1625). Glasgow: James MacLehose & Sons, 1905-07 [rpt.]
Yankowitz, Susan. "The Plays of Wole Soyinka." *African Forum* I. 4(1966): 129-33.

RHETORICAL AND LINGUISTIC GAMES IN COMIC AESTHETICS

Taiwo Oloruntoba-Oju

By 'comic aesthetics' we mean that which excited amusement, culminating in laughter or similar expressions of comic feeling.

The stylistic appraisal of such comic material often falls back on certain descriptive 'tags' that are readily available in the traditional repertoire of Rhetorics. These include terms like 'pun,' 'paronomasia,' 'verbal humor,' and so on, and it is often convenient to slap them onto comic expressions.

This paper attempts to show that although the rhetorical game is relatively easy, it sometimes blurs stylistic enquiry into the precise nature of linguistic contribution to comic aesthetics. The rhetorical game should therefore be complementary to the linguistic game. As will be demonstrated, the latter involves checking for significant contribution to comic aesthetics at every level of linguistic analysis.

The Rhetorical Game

Linguistic structures and language-related situations are potentially comic and are generally amenable to comic exploitation. A wide range or rhetorical terms is available to describe the outcome of such exploitation: the following table indicates some potentially comic language-related situations and some rhetorical or 'more or less' rhetorical labels that correspond to the situations.

Dialectal Variation: 'norm' *vs* 'deviation' 'standard' *vs* 'variety,' colloquialism, slang, vernacular, Völapük, and so on.

Linguistic Affection: bombast, declamation, euphuism, grandiloquence, inflation, magniloquence, preciosity, sesquipedalianism, verbosity, overblown phrasing, and so on.

Linguistic Inadequacy: clanger, malapropism, misspelling, pidginisation, etc.(or deliberate subversion)

Word-Play/Stylistic Deviation: amphibology, anagram, badinage, banter, conundrum, drollery, epigram, enigma, equivocation, innuendo, jocosity, palindrome, paragram, parody, paronomasia, persiflage, pun, quibble, riposte, tergiversation, verbal humor, and so on.

The classification above is neither fixed nor exclusive. For instance, 'bombast' may in some cases reflect linguistic incompetence rather than linguistic affectation, while 'slang' may be a feature of affectation too. The classification is thus fluid and is meant to serve only as a rough guide. (See Cluett and Kampeas 1979 for explication on some of the more important labels.)

Although such labels are abundant, they are often inadequate as far as the proper stylistic investigation of comic aesthetics is concerned. To illustrate this inadequacy, we may consider the three examples below.

(1) Ask of me tomorrow and you will find me a grave man.
(Adapted from Shakespeare, *Romeo and Juliet.*)
Act 3, Scene 1, Line 91

(2) Hamlet: Whose grave is this, sirrah?
Gravedigger: Mine, Sir.
(Shakespeare, *Hamlet.* Act 5, Sc. 1, line 109f)

(3) Visiting relatives can be boring.
(Chomsky, *Syntactic Structures*)

Each of these examples can, *within the right context,* be described as a case of 'punning', 'word-play,' 'verbal humor,' and so on. Such description would however rob the stylistic enquirer of insights regarding the linguistic 'differentials' that constitute the precise contribution of linguistic elements in each case of 'pun.'

In (1), for instance, the pun is given by the ambiguity resulting (in semantic terms now) from the hyponymous character of the word 'grave.' In (2), however, the 'culprit' is not the word 'grave' as it might seem, and the pun is given, not by a semantic factor this time, but by a combination of semantic, syntactic and pragmatic factors.

Semantically, the possessive item 'mine' is characterized, again not by ambiguity as in (1), but by the vagueness of reference which casts doubt on the manner in which the 'grave' is 'possessed.' (See Kempson 1977:123-135 on differences between ambiguity and vagueness.) The doubt raised here is now cleared only by a recourse to pragmatic extrapolation and logical deconstruction (e.g., "since the man speaks and he is a gravedigger by profession he cannot mean that he is the dead man for whom the grave is being dug, except he is anticipating his demise and is performing this last duty on his own behalf for his personal benefit or satisfaction . . . or he would merely reside in the grave . . ." etc, etc). Such extensive pragmatic extrapolation is unnecessary in (1), for instance.[1]

Syntactic contribution to the comic in (2) comes mainly through the use of a structure that is capable of both subjective and objective referents, and is therefore capable of semantic and pragmatic manipulation. Apart from being an interrogative element, the item 'whose' in 'whose grave is this . . . .?' combines pronominal and genitive functions. This heightens the possibility of manipulation, since the referent of 'whose' is inexplicit. The syntactic nature of the contribution here is best appreciated when one compares the use of a pronominal/interrogative structure which, within this context, permits only an objective semantic referent in the response to the question, as in (4) or (5).

(4) *Who* are you digging this grave for?

(5) For *whom* is this grave being dug?

In (3), finally, the manipulation is entirely structural—'amphibological' in rhetorical terms. However, the manipulation in several other comic materials can be equally amphibological, such that the aspects of linguistic structure involved in such expressions can be elicited only through the linguistic game. Thus, in (3), it is a question of whether 'visiting' is a participial adjective functioning as pre-modifier to 'relatives' or it is a participial verb form functioning as a nominal head. The former can take a relativized form as its disambiguating paraphrase, while the latter takes a non-relativizable 'to-infinitive' form as its own paraphrase. Both alternatives are shown in (6) and (7) respectively.

(6) *Relatives who visit* can be boring
(or) *Relatives (who are) visiting* can be boring.

(7) *To visit relations* can be boring
(or) *Going to visit relations* can be boring.

It is evident from the brief sketch above that the rhetorical game must be supplemented by the linguistic game, for a meaningful stylistic analysis of comic expressions.

3.0 The Linguistic Game

A proper description in our context involves the naming of phonological, morphological, lexical, semantic, syntactic, and even graphological operations that seem contributive to the comic apprehension of a given comic expression. The sections below complement the brief sketch above by illustrating linguistic involvement in comic aesthetics at the various levels of analysis constituting the linguistic game.

3.1 Phonological

Here, we refer specifically to the marshalling of the sound properties of language, which are expressly amenable to comic manipulation.

Sometimes, such manipulation does not even require much exertion. For instance, the spontaneous realization of fun through the manipulation of phonological (and also morphological, etc) elements seems to be an aspect of the linguistic competence of the Yoruba in Nigeria. If an idea expressed by a speaker appears ridiculous or somewhat anomalous to the listener,[2] the latter spontaneously isolates the word expressing the idea. He alters the linguistic structure of this word such that, if the word is *Ax* originally it becomes *Ay* in the listener's response. *Ay* may be entirely meaningless. On the other hand it may express unrelated or inappropriate meaning—either way, it achieves the effect of ridiculing the idea and creating fun (or fury as the case may be). Suppose then that the words so involved are ló ('go'), *bíréékì* (brake), *ègbòn* ('jitters'), and so on, we would have such exchanges as the following:

(8) A: Mo n *lọ*. ('I am going.')
      Ax
    B: Ló ko *lò* ni. ('Not 'go' its ironed.')
      Ay ('not 'go' its 'ground.'[3])

(9) A: Waa te *bíréékì*. ('You'should step on the
                              brake 'pedal.')
      Ax
    B: Bíréékì ko, *bíríkì* ni. ('Not 'brake' 'brick'you mean.')
      Ay

(10) A: Mo da *ègbòn* bòó. ("I pour 'jitters'on him"
                        e.e. I rattled him'.)
      Ax
    B: Ègbòn ko, *ègbòngbòn* ni. ('Not jitters, its *ègbòngbon*').
      Ay

In (8) and (9) the tonal and segmental features respectively are altered. The words formulated in ridicule have 'meaning'but this is merely fortuitous. Such meaning is hardly ever contemplated by the utterer and it is discounted by the original speaker. In other words, the respondent 'B'in (8) does not intend that what he says should mean 'ironed'; neither does 'B'in (9) intend that what he says should mean 'brick' All they have done is alter the tonal and segmental features of the original words in order to ridicule them. It is only accidental that the words then have those meanings. It will be noticed for instance that these meanings are quite nonsensical within the context. The response in (10) is quintessential because *Ay*, which is reduplication of the morphological structure of the ridiculed item, is absolutely meaningless as an individual 'word.' Such examples then show just how easy it sometimes is to manipulate the sound properties of language in order to create fun. In artistic concerns, however, such manipulation requires careful, painstaking crafting, as in (11) and (12) among numerous other examples.

(11) You tief one kobo dem put you for pri*son*
You tief one million nat patrioti*sm*. (Wole Soyinka, 'Unlimited Liability'—a long-playing record)

(12) Fathers that *wear rags*
Do make their children *blind*
But fathers that *bear bags*
Shall see their children *kind*.
(Shakespeare, *King Lear*, Act 2, Sc 4, line 49f)

In (11), the difference in the amount of money involved in either case of theft is expected to be matched by a corresponding difference in the degree of *punishment to* be meted out to *both* culprits. This expectation is however violated. The 'bigger' thief who should have received bigger punishment is not even punished at all. Rather, he is rewarded, while the 'poor' thief is severely punished. This, in elementary terms, is 'funny.' The incongruity of this inherently warped sense of justice is reinforced and foregrounded by the rhythmical closeness of the juxtaposed items 'priso*n*'and 'patriotis*m*' In that fleeting musical medium through which the expression is rendered, this rhythmical closeness might even give the illusion of semantic closeness. The collapse of this illusion would then lead further to comic explosion.

The fun in (12) is equally accentuated by the manipulation of phonological elements. apart from the actual meaning of the statements made and their striking truthfulness (when considered either independently or against the background of Lear's discomfiture and the fact that the wise statements are uttered by Lear's 'fool'), the phonological manipulation referred to enhances the hearer's apprehension of the comic in the expression. Phonological similarity contrasts sharply, here again, with semantic disparity. It will be noticed for instance that b*ags*/ r*ags* and b*ear*/w*ear* are minimal pairs (diferring with regard to only one phoneme), while we have near minimal pairing in bl*ind*/k*ind*. The pragmatic import of the semantic differences between these elements, however, belies their structural closeness somewhat. It is yet another example of how the manipulation of phonological elements can contribute to comic aesthetics, and how stylistic analysis can elicit this contribution

3.2 Morphological

It will be recalled that a manipulation of morphological structures can provoke comic apprehension in some cases, as in the Yoruba examples for instance. Some other examples are noted below.

(13) Wed*lock* is pad*lock*
(John Gray, English Proverbs)

(14) You can get your original sin removed by John the Bo*po*dist....
Up Up my soul! This inaction is a*bom*i*na*ble.
Perhaps it is the result of disturbances a*bdom*in*able*
(Ogden Nash, "The New Decalogue")[4]

(15) *Teacher*: Use the word *indisposition* in a sentence
Learner: I am a goalkeeper and I like playing *in this position*.
("Mind your Language" London T.V. Series)

(16) *Officer*: I demand an immediate apology
Subordinate: I hereby tender my *un*conditional *un*mitigated, *un*warranted and *un*diluted apology.
Officer: Good.

(17) *Preacher*: And when Jesus saw the multitude

> *Interpreter:* Nigba ti Jesu si ri ti awon eniyan naa *tu*
> ("When Jesus saw that the people scattered")
> *Preacher:* He was surprised and *tan*talized
> *Interpreter:* Enu yaa, o si *ta* ko won.
> ("He was surprised and he opposed them")
> *Preacher:* And he shouted in a very loud voice
> *Interpreter:* O si kigbe ni ohun rara wipe
> ("And he shouted in a very loud voice")
> *Preacher:* Go away and *sin* no more
> *Interpreter:* E maa lo, ema se *sin* mi *mo*
> ("Go away, and worship me no more")
> (Anon.)

The juxtaposed items in (13) have similar morphological structures.

Wed + lock
pad + lock

This morphological likeness heightens the awareness of wedlock as some form of bondage: 'lock' in 'wedlock' and 'lock' in 'padlock' are also received as being of corresponding semantic quality. It will be noticed that the physical padlock whose image is mentally evoked is a direct icon of thraldom, and that the juxtaposition of the two morphological 'locks' evokes the same image for 'wedlock'.[5]

Examples (14) through (17) also manipulate morphological structures in ways that are quite obvious. (Notice that 'Bopodist' in (14) parodies 'Baptist', while '*un*warranted' in (16) does not accord semantically with other words in the series as it is disguised to appear. With (17) it is particularly interesting to note how the syllabic and morphological elements underlined in the English words suggest certain meanings to the barely literate interpreter. These meanings are borne in the interpreter's native tongue by words whose morphological structures happen to coincide with the syllabic morphological items isolated in the English words. The most interesting aspect of the manipulation here, it seems, is the way the wrong meanings generated by the isolated structures in one statement accord pragmatically with the wrong meanings generated by other structures isolated in the next statement, and so on. For instance, if the people 'scattered', Jesus might as well 'oppose' them.

3.3 Graphological

'Graphological' here refers to the entire writing system (including punctuation, etc) rather than to just orthography or the like (cf., Crystal and Davy, 1969).

Graphological units may also enhance the comic experience. Sometimes, there are phonological equivalents (though these may or may not produce similar effects). For instance, 'misspelling,' whose comic potential has been noted, may be expressed through both speech and writing, while another graphological element like the ellipsis mark may be equalized by a pause in speech. Also, in writing, the comic element is first visually apprehended before being decoded by the appropriate faculties. In some cases, however, the potentially comic graphological element (e.g., quaint or peculiar handwriting, incongruent capitalization, etc) is not realizable through other media.

Let us now assess the ellipsis mark in the following written discourse. The situation is that Samuel Sewall, Chief Justice of the colony in 17th-century America, made entries in his diary.[6] A widower in old age, he decides to marry again, and he makes a number of advances, mostly towards elderly widows. One Mrs. Denison is agreeable but she gives rather tall financial conditions, and Sewall writes: "My bowels yearn towards Mrs. Denison, but I think the Lord directs me in his providence to desist." There is another prospective bride, also a widow, and Sewall again records his encounter with her in his diary.

> (18) She was courteous to me but took occasion to speak pretty plainly about my keeping a coach. I said 'twould cost 100 pounds per annum, she said 'twould cost but 40 pounds ... Came away late.

This graphical representation of temporal passage is really striking. Into those three dots is packed all the haggling, the disagreement, the emotional torture, etc, about which we can only, but safely, speculate. Much comedy is equally packed into this graphological rendition. It is yet another example of how graphological elements can contribute to comic aesthetics.

3.4 Lexical and Semantic

Perhaps the vast majority of comic material can be apprehended mainly within lexical and semantic constructs, that is, in terms of the contribution made by the meaning of individual lexical items and by words in construction. It will be noticed for instance that even with those materials analyzed in terms of other linguistic levels above, reference is also made to their semantic content. We may consider other examples.

(18) A man, running in the street, trips and falls . . .
[People] laugh because he sits down
involuntarily . . .
[not] this abrupt change of posture but that
there is
something involuntary about the change.
(Bergson, 738)

(19) . . . twice abruptly, he measured his length on the ground.
(David Lodge, *Small World*, p. 241)

(20) How could one bear the thought of sleeping beside a wholly naked man?
(Molière, *Le Précieuses Ridicules*)

(21) *Lucio*: Why, how now Claudio? Whence cometh this restraint?
Claudio: From too much liberty, my Lucio
(Shakespeare, *Measure For Measure*)

(22) The woman in the black dress, or should I say half out of it?
(David Lodge, *Small World*, p. 9)

(23) As Tom and his wife were discussing one day
Of their several faults in a bantering way.

Said she: "Though my wit you disparage,
I am sure, my dear husband, our friends will attest
This much at least—that my judgement is best."
Quoth Tom: "So they said at our marriage."
(John Saxe)[7]

(24) *Teacher:* What do you call a pig after it has been killed?
Foreign Learner: Dead pig
("Mind Your Language")

(25) (In this example the interlocutors are a boy and a girl, the former [fairly local] seeing the latter [who is fairly exposed] off at the rail station.)

Girl (as the train moves, waving): So long.

Boy (embarrassed, angry, glancing round and down, shouting after her): So deep and so wide.

The item 'sit' in (18) is semantically anomalous in relation to the actual state of affairs (i.e., falling down). The contradiction it entails invests the circumstance with the force of ridicule, leading to laughter. It is the same for 'measured his length' in (19).

Also, 'change of posture' in (18) can be viewed in a number of ways. Rhetorics would call it euphemism, or tergiversation, while in pragmatics it would be regarded as a violation of two of Grice's maxims: a reduction on the necessary amount of information (Quantity) and corresponding lack of clarity in expression (Manner) (cf., Grice 1975). The linguistic mechanism is nonetheless semantic, that is, the vagueness of the phrase is deliberately crafted to achieve a non-commital but suggestive stance. Ridicule is implied and laughter enhanced. Again, each of 'this abrupt change of posture,' (18) and 'twice measured his length' (19), is ambiguous between voluntary and forced motion. This also heightens the sense of ridicule and the fun. It will be noticed that a structural (syntactic) mechanism also comes into play. For instance, passivisation would disambiguate the units and at least remove the question on agenture, whether this is voluntary or not, as in

His posture was abruptly changed
His length was abruptly measured on the ground.

In (20), the idea expressed is intuitively comic and there seems to be no specially marked linguistic imput. However, 'wholly,' in (20) is semantically 'superfluous' or redundant, and perhaps this heightens the incongruity and ridicule inherent in the query. Also, the preposition, 'beside', is locative, and the coy evasiveness it suggests is striking. It is the alternative preposition, 'with', that really implicates coition (the coyly evaded activity), and a non-cooperative interlocutor may respond: "What is wrong with sleeping *beside* a naked man when no one has asked you to sleep *with* him?" Though seemingly innocuous, these items and such a construction could indeed be deeply marked.

In (21) 'liberty' and 'restraint' are direct antonyms, and one does not normally or logically flow from or generate the other (i.e., 'restraint' leading to 'liberty' or vice-versa) except in a pragmatic sort of way. A sudden realization of this pragmatic implication may then further intensify comic feeling. The mechanism here therefore is the juxtaposition of antonymous elements where one would expect semantic or logical correspondence (e.g., expecting the punishment [restraint] to result from 'too much whoring', from 'recklessness', and so on).

It is a similar mechanism in (22). For instance, 'in' is the opposite of 'out of' but both are 'the same thing' here, in a pragmatic way.

Tom's response in (23) is the comic motivator. Short, but full of pith, it is an innuendo, enigmatic and epigrammatic, an instant riposte contrasting sharply with, and nullifying the wife's rambling argument. So much for rhetorical frenzy. In semantic terms, 'so they said' has the structure of affirmation whereas it is actually employed to negate. Simply then, we have external, pragmatic negation clashing with internal (grammatical) affirmation, leading to comic explosion within the context. Also, "Quoth he" consists of an archaic lexical item and archaic syntactic structure both of which seem to contribute to comic feeling in a way. For instance, it gives that air of an ancient pronouncement which, not unexpectedly (at least in retrospect), turns out to be quite devastating.

For its part, (23) seems quite self-explanatory.

"So long" in (24) is a fixed, formulaic expression whose pragmatic referent the 'Boy' is unaware of. He fails to make the required transfer of meaning (from the spatial to the temporal concept of length and from semantic fact to pragmatic implication), thus making the wrong inference, with 'disastrous' though comic consequences.

3.5. Syntactic

Some examples of this mechanism in comic expression have been used above, in (3), (4), (17), (18), (12), and their elucidation. A few more examples are presented below.

(26) I will not tell anyone that we spent the weekend together . . . because we did not.
(27) *A*: Abe Lincoln did not die in vain.
   B: No. he died in Washington.
(28) I never touch alcohol at all . . . except it's chilled.

Examples (25) and (27) fall within the semantic construct described as the 'denial use of negation', where a presupposition properly contracted in the first part of a sentence is negated in the second. It will be noticed, however, that this is possible only because of the syntactic arrangements in each of the expressions. The virtually unrestricted mobility of the adverbial clause is exploited to good effect here. For instance, if the negating adjuncts are moved to sentence-initial positions, this might prove negative as far as the comic is concerned.

In (26), structurally similar units (i.e., the prepositional phrases) are juxtaposed to give the illusion of semantic similarity within the context. The difference of these structures below the surface is representable thus:

in vain =P.P. —) P. + Adj.
in Washington=P.P. —) P. + N

What is further exploited is the unlimited paratactic potential of the preposition (i.e., its ability to combine with words belonging to different word classes) as well as its functional volatility (i.e., its ability to perform different functions). This twin potential is exhibited below.

	Word-Class Combination	Function
in vain	P + Adj	Manner Adjunct
In Washington	P + N.	Place Adjunct
in a moment	P + Det. + N	Time Adjunct
wife-in-waiting	N + P + Ving.	Nominal

Such variability, and the consequent combination in (26) go into the creation of an illusion, the collapse of which causes comic explosion.

4. Conclusion

The point may be reiterated here that it is not only interesting but also very useful to analyze comic expressions in terms of core linguistic operations exhibited by the expressions. The foregoing demonstrates that such analysis benefits the stylistic enterprise more than a mere bandying of generalized rhetorical labels. Rhetorical labels would of course serve to complement linguistic analysis, as also demonstrated above.

Two already implied caveats must however be explicity stated here. The first is the inter-dependence of linguistic and contextual elements in comic aesthetics. Such phrases as 'potentially-comic', 'within the appropriate context', and so on., have been used advisedly in several instances in our analyzes. The effectiveness of one linguistic machination or another depends a lot on their being recognized by an interlocutor and their making an appeal to this interlocutor's comic imagination. Several contextual factors are implicated here and the stylistic investigator must take note of them. His analysis would simulate or assume an ideal speaker/hearer situation, and the appropriate pragmatic extensions.

The second caveat is that the empirical fact of linguistic *presences* in a given comic expression may not always be a guarantee that these linguistic elements have contributed in such-and-such degrees to comic effect. It seems that the elicitation of certain linguistic structures in a comic expression only makes a *prima facie* case. Such structures must then be submitted to further tests by the stylistic investigator, before he can credibly assert that comic effect in a certain comic expression is indeed due to, or is enhanced by, certain linguistic operations. In short, with comic aesthetics, the analyst's task is not ended with describing the structures of a comic expression. He has to test the relevance of these structures. (See Oloruntoba-Oju (forthcoming): 'Testing Linguistic Imput to Comic Aesthetics').

UNIVERSITY OF ILORIN—NIGERIA

Notes

1. The word 'grave' in (1) is two-ways ambiguous—a straightforward kind of opposition. The speaker who is a natural, well-known gester utters the entire statement after receiving a wound that turns out to be fatal. The statement could mean that he would by tomorrow become a serious person or he would become a dead man. It turns out to be the latter. It must be noted of course that the comic value of the statement diminishes in view of the grave danger attending the situation: the statement is at the same time a disheartening prognosis and an uncomfortable joke. The humor is wry, the comedy 'dark' in the manner of Styan (1968).
2. As noted elsewhere (Oloruntoba-Oju 1968), comic theorists ascribe comic feeling to a perception of a certain incongruity or anomaly in the comic situation.
3. Ground: past tense of grind. The point of course is that these items are nonsensical.
4. In Bishop (1974: 287).
5. According to C.S. Peirce, the icon is the most direct means of representing an image. (cf., Silverman 1983: 32).
6. In Wright (1974: 23-25).
7. In Bishop (1974: 281).

Works Cited

Bergson, H. "Laughter," in Dukore, B.F. (ed.)*Dramatic Theory and Criticism: From Greeks to Grotowski* New York: Holt, Rinehart and Winston, Inc. 1974.

Bishop, M. "Light Verse in America," in Robin, 1974.

Cluett, R. & Kampeas, R. *Grossly Speaking*. Toronto: Discourse

Associates, 1979.
Crystal & Davy. *Investigating English Style.* Bloomington, Indiana: Indiana University Press, 1969.
Grice, H.P. "Logic and Conversation," in Cole, P. and J. Morgan. (eds.), *Syntax and Semantics 3: Speech Acts.* New York: Academic Press, 1975.
Kempson, R. *Semantic Theory.* London: Cambridge University Press, 1977.
Lodge, D. *Small World.* New York: Macmillan, 1984.
Oloruntoba-Oju, T. "Comic Theory and Stylistic Enquiry." Manuscript, 1986.
Oluruntoba-Oju, T. "Testing Linguistic Input to Comic Aesthetics." Manuscript, 1988.
Robin, L.D. Jnr. (ed.): *The Comic Imagination in American Literature.* V.O.A. Forum Series, 1974.
Silverman, K. *The Subject of Semiotics.* New York/Oxford: Oxford University Press, 1983.
Styan, J.L. *The Dark Comedy.* London: Cambridge University Press, 1968.
Wright, L.B. "Human Comedy in Early America," in Robin, 1974.

INDIRECTNESS IN DISCOURSE:
A STUDY IN PARADOXICAL COMMUNICATION AMONG THE IGBOS

Bertram A. Okolo

Oral communication is fundamental to our lives. Without speech we remain in near seclusion, unable to communicate our feelings, thoughts, wishes, or needs. Our gift of speech does not benefit us unless we have the ability to speak with reasonable effectiveness. Communication—when defined as the process of sending and receiving messages—implies that there will be a response to a message. Thus, communication is a two-way process. Successful transmission of ideas depends on mutual understanding between the communicator and the communicatee.

We recognize that language serves a variety of purposes. Hence what a linguistic expression means may not be the same meaning the speaker intends to convey. This is what Givon (1979:xiii) probably has in mind when he states:

> most interesting questions about the grammar of human language, namely, why it is the way it is; how it got to be that way; what function it serves; and how it relates to the use of human language as an instrument of information processing, storage, retrieval, and, above all, communication.

In other words, the inadequacies of autonomous syntax and semantics have necessitated the shift to the study of language in conversational settings. The study of language in social context has given rise to the consideration of the communicative intent in conversational interactions.

Theoretical Background

Grice (1975) states that certain inferences we make from utterances arise from our expectations concerning everyday conversational behavior. Participants in a conversation are expected to conform to certain conversational maxims, which, according to Grice, hold universally. One such maxim is that of cooperation: "make your conversational contribution such as is required, at the stage at which it occurs, by the accepted purpose or direction of the talk exchange in which you are engaged" (45). Cooperation, in this sense, may be taken to mean a principle by which both participants agree to a definition of the relationship they are involved in, and to its limits. This agreement may not be overtly discussed but may be the result of one or both participants not challenging the relationship-defining maneuvers of the other. Thus, cooperation in speech becomes nonchallenging conversational behavior.

Gordon and Lakoff (1975), in extending the ideas of Grice, establish some *reasonableness conditions* in conversational management. Among others, they state that "a request is reasonable only if the speaker has a reason for wanting it done" (90). This can be extended to statements as well: a statement is reasonable only if the speaker has a reason for wanting it said or made. Therefore, any statement made by a conversational partner is relevant (whether or not it is to the hearer) as long as the speaker has an intention or reason in making the statement.

Searle (1969) described the two parts of the speech act as the proposition and the illocutionary force. The proposition consists of the predicate and the argument, while the illocutionary force consists of the speaker's intent. Dore (1975, 1979), Stampe (1975), and others elaborate on the view that the illocutionary force is the speaker's intention. Dore (1979) explains that the speaker's intention produces effects on the hearer by the hearer recognizing the status of the utterance and also recognizing what the speaker intends for the hearer to do.

Two important observations could be made from these works. In the first place, it is often difficult to determine the intention or reason of a speaker in any conversational maneuver, and yet this is crucial if the hearer must cooperate. Take, for example, a simple case where a friend of yours is ridiculing or saying something dishonorable about you in the presence of people. You don't like what he is saying, and you ask him why he is saying those things. He replies:

1. "I'm kidding" or "I'm just playing." There are two options you could take: accept the statement of his intentions or assume he is lying about his real intentions, and that he is, in fact, not playing. In either case, it is difficult for the hearer to prove what the speaker's intentions are in uttering X, for intentionality lies within the speaker's mind.

Second, since the hearer may not know the intentions of a speaker in making an utterance, the hearer cannot prove the relevance or irrelevance of an utterance since the ability to do so depends on the hearer being able to determine the intentions of the speaker. If, therefore, the speaker's intentions are not accessible to the hearer, communication will break down.

In this study, I shall concern myself with such conversational utterances where the intentions of the speaker are, to a reasonable degree, accessible to the hearer, and as a result, the hearer responds appropriately. I am primarily concerned with conversational exchanges (which I am referring to as *paradoxical*) in which speakers manipulate the principles of cooperation and reasonableness conditions to their own advantage as a discourse strategy. In effect, I shall look at the situations that favor the use of such communicative strategy, the functional uses, and its implications in a theory of natural language.

Indirectness in Igbo Discourse

Participants in a conversation often control each other's behavior by the indirectness of their utterances without appearing to do so. The content of the message in an utterance is not always to be taken literally, but may require a higher level processing effort for a proper interpretation. This higher level may be referred to as meta-communicative level: a level that must be present for us to derive the intended content of an utterance by a speaker. For example, I shall assume that it is this meta-communicative level that induces us to interpret an utterance as, say, satirical, ironical, or sarcastic. If this is so, it follows that language encodes many levels of messages in contextualizing an utterance. A message that is not expressly verbalized then becomes a message that may be congruent or incongruent with the content message.

One of the strategies frequently employed by interactants in Igbo discourses is the use of indirectness. (Here, I am using indirect strategy to refer to a communicative behavior that uses incongruency to deny one or more meanings generated within a particular utterance.) In this use, a speaker makes an assertion, but most of the time the intended meaning of the speaker is incongruent with what has been expressly asserted. As Searle (1975) states,

> in indirect speech acts, the speaker communicates to the hearer more than he actually says by way of relying on this mutually shared background information, both linguistic and non-linguistic, together with the general powers of rationality and inference on the part of the hearer. (60-61)

Three main types of indirectness in Igbo discourse can be identified. In the first type, the indirectness (which is commonly referred to as reported speech) is just an alternative version of the direct speech. For example, if a speaker says

2. *Agaghi m abia nzuko ahu.* (I will not attend the meeting.)

this statement could be reported by the hearer thus:

3. *O si na ya agaghi abia nzuko ahu.* (He said that he would not attend the meeting.)

A feature of this type is that the initial statement of the speaker has the same message content as the version reported by the hearer; and as a result, the speaker's statement is congruent with the message content of the reported version.

In the second type of indirectness, the content of the message of the utterance is interpreted as the exact opposite of what appears on the surface. In other words, the intended message of the speaker runs counter to what has been overtly expressed. Take, for example, a situation where a mother tells her daughter:

4. *Kuwasia afere ahu ma i na-asa ha.* (Break those plates while washing them.)

Naturally, this will not be interpreted literally to mean that the mother actually wants those plates broken, but that the hearer should take care in washing them. The speaker believes the hearer has the ability to understand the intended meaning and to respond accordingly. If, however, the hearer fails to perceive the intended meaning of the speaker, and actually breaks the plates, then there is a communication breakdown because the hearer has not cooperated. Therefore, for such communication to be sustained, there must be, in the Gricean sense, cooperation and mutual understanding.

The third type of indirectness, which is the main focus of this study, is the one that often leads to a paradox. Take a situation where a wife went to the market but failed to come back in time to prepare supper. The following dialogue takes place:

Husband: *I lotakazi osiso.* (You came back so early.)
Wife: *Biko gbaghara m. O teela mu akaalotagori, ma ahughi m moto maka strike ndi taxi.*
(Please, forgive me. I should have been home long ago but I didn't get a vehicle because of the taxi drivers' strike.)
Husband: *Anaghi m ata gi uta. M chere ma obuzikwa ahia ka i gara.*
(I am not blaming you. I was wondering whether it was not the market you went to.)

The first utterance of the husband criticizes by implication. The wife recognizes the implied criticism and addresses her response to the criticism. The husband, in his last utterance, then denies having intended the level of interpretation perceived by the wife. This example is paradoxical from the wife's perspective because the husband seems to be saying one thing at one level while denying what he said covertly at another level—an instance of systematic disjunction between levels of message.

That this is a paradox rather than a contradiction is evident in the fact that the husband has not negated what he said, but rather is denying an implication of what he said. This strategy is possible because the husband is in a position to imply a criticism and then deny having intended the criticism since his intentions are not directly accessible to the wife. Paradox therefore occurs, for the husband invokes two communicative levels: he denies implying x on the basis of not having asserted x.

Paradoxical Communication as a Discourse Strategy

Paradoxical communication abounds in Igbo discourse. However, it is not a communicative strategy that one employs exclusively and in all conversational or verbal behavioral relationship situations. Bearing in mind that all conversational interactions are guided by the existing relationship between the interactants, this relationship is usually defined in one way or another before conversations can take place. In other words, the territorial parameters of the partners are established even before communication starts, and each partner knows where he/she stands in relation to the parameter before the conversation. Heringer (1972) and Lakoff (1977) refer to these parameters as politeness phenomena.

Among the Igbos this relationship manifests itself in several spheres (e. g., husband/wife; parent/child; elder/younger; teacher/student; employer/employee; boss/worker; peer/peer, and so on.), but in each case the position of a conversational partner in a particular relationship sphere will influence verbal behavior. Such behavioral relationships are evident, for example, in greeting ceremonies:

Student: Good morning, Sir.
Teacher: Good morning. How're you?
Student: I'm fine, Sir.
Teacher: What can I do for you?
Student: Please, Sir, could you lend me a book on Phonology?

From this common example, it could be seen that phatic communion functions primarily to define a relationship rather than message content. The use of Sir by the student is not only regarded as a mark of respect in the community but also as a recognition of the status of the person being addressed relative to that of the speaker. Once this recognition is established, communication is then directed toward and controlled by the established relationship.

Three types of verbal behavioral relationships among the Igbos can be distinguished. In the first type, one conversational partner usually dominates the other (e. g., in teacher/student or boss/worker relationships), say, by acquiring a particular status. In this type (which I shall refer to as *dominance relationship*), the dominating partner not only bosses the other all the time, but is free to use language in a way that leaves no one in doubt as to his or her position in the relationship. There is no competition as to who is the boss. Paradoxical communication as a discourse strategy is common in this type of relationship. An example is the following segment between a boss and one of the duty clerks at a local government secretariat:

Boss: *Gini ka i na-eme na machine?*
(What are you doing on the machine?)
Clerk: *M na a-type circular a i dobere na table.*
(I am typing this circular you left on the table.)
Boss: *A ma m na i na-ataipukari Felix.*
(I know you type better than Felix)
Clerk: *Oga, a na m ataipukwanu ofuma. M mesia, m gosi gi ka i kwere ihe m na-agwa gi.*
(Sir, I really type very well. When I finish, I show you so that you believe what I am telling you.)
Boss: *Asighi m na i naghi a-type fuma. Onweghikwa ego anyi nwere iji go machine.*
(I didn't say you don't type very well. We don't have any money to buy a machine.)

In this example, paradoxical communication is possible because of the status relationship. Here, such a communicative strategy is usually unidirectional: employed by the dominating partner on the dominated; it could, however, be bidirectional if there were another level of relationship existing between them. For example, a worker who is friendly with the boss can use this speech style in communicating with the boss without disrupting the relationship. The worker's use of paradoxical communication is simply an attempt to direct without challenging the structure of the relationship in which their interaction takes place. However, in a purely ideal situation, it would be considered disrespectful and rude should the dominated use it in addressing the dominating partner.

The situation is different in the second type, which I shall call *competitive relationship*. In this type, there is always a struggle between partners for dominance; if one partner does something, the other tries to do it as well. Conversations of this type are replete with moves and counter-moves, challenges and replies, all aimed at asserting dominance or superiority. An example is this dialogue that took place between friends, all businessmen. One of them had earlier boasted that he was going to buy a videotape recorder no matter the cost. On his return, the other friend took him up on the issue:

Speaker 1: *I gotaziri video obu?*
(Did you still buy the video?)

Speaker 2: *I na-ekwu na mu enwezughi ego video? Nna, oburu mkpari, achoghi, m ya. I choo ego, m nye gi.*
(Are you saying I don't have enough money for the video? If it is an insult, I don't want it. If you want money, I give you.)

Speaker 1: *Asighi m na i nweghi ego video. O-kwa ajuju ka m juru gi? I chokwaa ego ya, ka m nye gi.*
(I didn't say you don't have money for the video. Was it not a question that I asked? If you even want the money for the video, I will give you.)

In this example, though Speaker 1's utterance sounds like a mere question on the surface, Speaker 2 captured the implication of the question and directs his defense at that. Considering Speaker 1's utterance as an insult, he boasts that he could even give him the money he set aside for the video if he so desired. Speaker 1 consequently denies implying Speaker 2's interpretation contending that he merely asked a question, and equally volunteered to lend him money. Thus, we find in the dialogue a struggle between the partners for dominance. Within this type of relationship, cooperation in the sense of non-challenging is usually regarded as a defeat to which either will not yield very easily.

The third type of relationship that affects verbal behavior and within which paradoxical communication can occur, is what I have called *reciprocal relationship*. In this type, although the relationship-defining parameters exist, verbal behavioral relationships are not strictly adhered to in relation to the established parameters. Conversational interactions are managed in such a way as to accommodate all the partners. This is the type of relationship that exists between family members where, though there exists a dominating partner, this dominance is not strictly observed all the time. In other words, dominance and competitive relationships can possibly merge. That this is sometimes the case is seen in the fact that a wife can challenge the husband on some issues, just as children can challenge their parents and get away with it. Full cooperation is, therefore, not always enjoyed by the dominating partner. Consider this dialogue between husband and wife. The wife left a pot of soup cooking in the fire and went to give the baby a bath. As she came out from the bathroom she smelt burning, and this communication took place:

Wife: *Ofe m siiri n'oku agbaa oku.*
(The soup I left in the fire is burning.)
Husband: *Ewoo! Uche m adighi n'ebe ahu ncha ncha. M na-ege ihe ha na-agu na News.*
(Oh! My mind wasn't there at all. I was listening to the news.)
Wife: *Anaghi m ata gi uta. O-o akpomuche m.*
(I am not blaming you. It is my forgetfulness.)

Here, the wife's initial utterance appears on the surface as a mere exclamation, but it indirectly criticizes the husband's inability to watch over the pot of soup. The husband directs his response at defending this 'inability' by providing a reason for his distraction, which makes us believe that the wife's statement criticizes by implication. However, the wife denies the implied criticism and shifts the blame on herself. Here, we could see that the use of paradoxical speech style could be bidirectional (assuming the husband still remains the dominating partner) without causing any damage to the relationship.

Another example of this bidirectionality can be seen in the following conversation between mother and daughter. The daughter had just finished dressing and the mother was waiting in the car, ready to drop her off at school:

Mother: *Akwa akwukwo gi a na-egbukeri ka isi anyanwu.*
(Your school uniform shines
[dazzles the eyes] like the sun.)

Daughter: *O-kwa m suru ya na Friday.*
(But I washed it on Friday.)

Mother: *Ekwughi m na i sughi ya. Ihe soro gi yiri.*
Nke ahu agbasaghi m.
(I didn't say you didn't wash it. Wear whatever you like.
That does not concern me.)

Daughter: *Mama, i gotasialu m akwa m ga-eji na-agbanwe ya i kwere m na nkwa.*
(Mama, you have really bought me the spare clothes you promised me.)

Mother: *O-o igota nke ohuru bu idebe nke i nwere ocha?*
(Is buying a new one keeping the one you have neat?)

Daughter: *Asighi m na o bu, kama i debere nkwa i kwere.*
(I didn't say it is, but you kept your promise.)

In this example, the mother, as the dominating partner makes a statement directed at the condition of the daughter's clothes. The daughter understands the implication of the statement and responds accordingly and goes on to challenge the mother for the non-fulfillment of her promise to buy her new clothes, a type of verbal behavior that would be unexpected in a truly dominance relationship. Thus, we see that in a reciprocal relationship, the relationship-defining parameters recede in importance while content is given more prominence. This is why a violation of relationship-defining behavior could be tolerated without the relationship being jeopardized. It is a feature of this type of relationship that any partner in the conversation can employ the strategic use of indirectness irrespective of his/her stand in relation to the parameters defining the relationship. However, this bidirectionality should not be taken to mean that the position of the dominating partner is completely eroded or neutralized, for, depending on the type of communication and the situation, the principle of non-challenging behavior can still be fully invoked by the dominating partner.

One factor that is crucial in generating paradoxical communication is the hearer's ability to perceive the implied criticism and to respond cooperatively. Even in situations controlled by the relationship-defining parameters exemplified above, paradoxical communication will not be achieved if the speaker fails in getting the hearer to recognize that he/she is being criticized. Failure to perceive the criticism, therefore, paralyzes the strategy. For example, let us assume that our earlier example of the dialogue between a husband and a wife, after the wife returned late from the market, was this:

Husband: You came back so early.
Wife: Well, thanks.

Here, the wife responds to the husband's statement on the literal content level only, thereby giving the husband negative feedback. This response is counter to the husband's intentions, and consequently frustrates his desire to communicate by implication. Paradox will not be achieved because the wife has not cooperated within the framework of indirect communication. That this is true is seen in the fact that even if the husband wants to repair this, say, by adding:

Husband: You really did!

paradox will still not result. Thus, it becomes clear that in all paradoxical communication (whatever the relationship-defining parameters are), the hearer must cooperate by perceiving the intention of the speaker to communicate by implication and respond accordingly for paradox to be sustained.

Functional Uses of Paradoxical Communication

One of the primary uses of paradoxical speech style is to criticize. Usually this criticism is indirect or else paradox will not obtain. If, for example, a conversational partner decides to criticize the other directly in the course of a conversation, there will be no implication attached to the statement of criticism. As a result, the literal content of the message will be congruent with what has been expressed, and paradox will not result. Paradoxical communication arises because the strategy is aimed at criticizing indirectly without challenging the existing parameters of the relationship in which the interaction takes place. For example, when a husband criticizes the wife indirectly, it is mainly to respect the structure of the existing relationship between them. Therefore, indirectness is used when a speaker finds it difficult to be more direct without disturbing the existing relationship.

On the other hand, where a conversational partner is at the lower end of a relationship, paradoxical communication can be used without appearing uncooperative in the framework of the speech situation. When it is used in a dominance relationship by the dominating partner, the strategy sort of softens the dominance, thus creating a more conducive and friendly atmosphere for a more harmonious relationship. For example, it is likely that a boss who criticizes by implication would be more preferred to one who asserts his dominance by criticizing directly, even when he has the authority to do so.

Another use of paradoxical speech style might be to ridicule the other conversational partner. This use is common in competitive relationship where partners are almost always engaged in a struggle for dominance. It will be more appropriate in this type of relationship to make a direct criticism rather than an indirect one since the partners' moves and counter-moves are directed toward subduing the other in quest of dominance. Therefore, when an unexpected form (i. e., indirectness) is employed, it is more likely to be as a ridicule rather than criticism.

Interactants equally use paradoxical communication with

the intention of directing the addressee to change his or her behavior. For example, criticizing an aspect of one's behavior might induce the addressee to straighten up. On the other hand, paradoxical speech style might signal the speaker's inability to force the addressee to change behavior. Take, for example, a situation where the speaker may have made repeated attempts to induce a partner to change a habit. Since direct appeal has yielded no results, the speaker opts for an indirect strategy to imply that in spite of repeated attempts, the annoying behavior still lingers. In this case, paradoxical speech style communicates a frustration of the speaker's attempt at effecting changes in behavior through direct appeals.

From all these it becomes clear that paradoxical speech style is a discourse strategy employed in situations which are in one way or another determined by the relationship-defining parameters existing within a particular conversational framework.

Implications of Paradoxical Communication in a Theory of Natural Languages

Until recently, studies of natural language samples have concentrated on the analysis of the information content of a message, thereby ignoring the part played by pragmatics in the understanding and interpretation of natural language utterances. If we relied only on the literal interpretation of the message content in our analysis of paradoxical utterances, we would be unable to capture the implications intended by the speaker. This study, therefore, clearly demonstrates that understanding the way speakers manipulate language in conversational interaction will help in the proper analysis and interpretation of natural language utterances in their social context. Analysis of message content and speech usage should be given equal consideration in any theory of natural language.

Studies on direct and indirect speech acts abound in the literature (cf., Gordon & Lakoff, 1975; Davidson 1973, 1975; Sadock, 1970; Searle 1969, 1975; Dore & McDermott, 1982; and so on.). Most of these works looked at indirect speech acts from the point of view of the illocutionary act as suggested by the surface form, or on the actual illocutionary force of the speech act. However, this fails to note or predict the semantic differences between indirect speech acts and direct ones. Indirect speech forms, even when they have the same sentence meaning as the direct ones, have in addition speaker meaning attached to them. On the other hand, relying on the actual illocutionary force of an utterance fails to note the relationship between the surface form and the conditions necessary for performing the act conveyed, and treats the surface form as a case of idiomatic substitution. In other words, direct and indirect speech forms are regarded as mere alternative forms having the same content. Levinson (1983) even admits that the illocutionary force approach will run into problems in accounting for indirect speech acts. In discussing the notions of 'Thesis' and 'Antithesis,' he states that these can only make sense if we subscribe to the view that illocutionary force is built into the sentence form, and since what people do with sentences are quite unrestricted by the surface form, there has to be a way of deriving, say, a request force from sentence forms that are prototypically assertions and questions rather than requests.

This study clearly reveals that indirect speech acts are, in fact, not always alternative forms of the direct ones. It follows that any explanation of indirect speech forms must also explain why a more indirect form may be used rather than merely mapping a surface form to an implied form. Therefore, indirect speech forms are not usually substitutable for direct ones since different relationship-defining parameters are involved in each usage.

Conclusion

In this limited study, an attempt has been made to describe paradoxical speech style as it occurs among the Igbos. In spite of its shortcomings, this study highlights many things that are often ignored or taken for granted in the study of natural language utterances.

Communication presupposes the cooperation of the partners engaged in the conversational exchange. This cooperation, among other things, implies that the hearer should, to a reasonable degree, be able to ascertain the intentions of the speaker in making the utterance, and to respond appropriately (although the hearer may not always be able to prove the relevance or irrelevance of an utterance since this is tied to the speaker's intention, which is not directly accessible). In other words, cooperation is a positive feedback to a particular communicative strategy within a behavioral system. Lack of cooperation or negative feedback paralyzes paradoxical communication.

Conversations are not to be judged solely on the basis of their message content, but on the relationship-defining parameters that define the limits or range of a particular verbal behavior, and make conversational strategies possible within a particular behavioral system. It is really the relationship-defining parameters that explain why a particular discourse strategy is possible in one situation and not in another. Thus, the content of a message and the relationship surrounding an utterance are inseparable, and should be given equal treatment in any analysis of natural language discourse.

Finally, indirect speech styles are not always mere substitutes for direct ones. Indirect speech may feed paradoxical communication, and when this happens, there is no longer any straightforward mapping to the surface form. Furthermore, in most situations, indirect speech forms function differently from direct ones, thereby showing that both are not in all cases substitutable.

UNIVERSITY OF BENIN—NIGERIA

Works Cited

Cole, P. and J. Morgan, eds., *Syntax and Semantics, Vol. 3:Speech Acts.* New York: Academic Press, 1975.

Davidson, Alice, "Performatives, Felicity Conditions and Adverbs." Ph.D. Dissertation, University of Chicago, 1973.

——— "Indirect Speech Acts and What to Do with Them." In Cole and Morgan (eds.), 1975:143-85.

Dore, J., "Holophrases, Speech Acts and Language Universals." *Journal of Child Language,* 2, 1975:21-40.

———. "Conversational Acts and the Acquisition of Language." In E. Ochs and B. Schiefflin (eds.), *Developmental Pragmatics.* New York: Academic Press, 1979:239-362.

Dore, J. and R.P. McDermott, "Linguistic Indeterminacy and Social Context in Utterance Interpretation." *Language,* 1982:374-98.

Givón, T., *On Understanding Grammar.* New York: Academic Press,

1979.

Gordon, D. and G. Lakoff, "Conversational Postulates." In Cole and Morgan (eds.), 1975:83-106.

Grice, H. P. "Logic and Conversation." In Cole and Morgan (eds.), 1975:41-58.

Heringer, J., "Some Grammatical Correlates of Felicity Conditions and Presuppositions." *Working Papers in Linguistics*, No. 11. Columbus: Ohio State University, Department of Linguistics, 1972:1-110.

Lakoff, R., "Language and Society." In R. Wardhaugh and H. D. Brown (eds.), *A Survey of Applied Linguistics*. Ann Arbor: University of Michigan Press, 1977:207-28.

Levinson, S. C., *Pragmatics*. New York: Columbia University Press, 1983.

Sadock, J. M., "Whimperatives." In J. Sadock and A. Vanel (eds.), *Studies Presented to Robert B. Lees*. Edmonton, Alberta and Champaign, Illinois: Linguistic Research, 1970:223-38.

Searle, J. R., Speech Acts. New York: Columbia University Press, 1969.

——— "Indirect Speech Acts." In Cole and Morgan (eds.), 1975:59-82.

Stampe, D. T., "Meaning and Truth in the Theory of Speech Acts." In Cole and Morgan (eds.), 1975:1-39.

D. O. FAGUNWA'S NARRATIVES:
A RHETORICAL ANALYSIS

※

Gabriel A. Ajadi

African writers' local medium of verbal expression facilitates their articulation of the specifically African ethos. In addition, it actually makes possible a compelling portrayal of its aesthetics. As Abiola Irele rightly observes, "Traditional African literature is something which exists in our indigenous languages and which is related to our traditional societies and cultures"(9).

This observation is basically accurate when one contemplates D.O. Fagunwa's way with words in the expression of his creative imagination: the general African cosmology as well as the Yoruba particular cosmography and cosmogony are presented in his novels with seasoned narrative pattern enhanced by his rhetorical prowess. It is thus a useful exercise to subject the narratives to a rhetorical analysis, using his first two novels (for they typically exemplify his rhetorical power) as the basis for such analysis. For this reason, Fagunwa's first novel, *Ogboju Ode Ninu Igbo Irunmale* (1939), which Wole Soyinka translates as *The Forest of A Thousand Daemons: A Hunter's Saga*, and Fagunwa's *Igbo Olodumare*, a title which in a previous work I translate as *The Forest of God*, form the basis of the analysis in this paper.

A purely rhetorical analysis of an African literary work of art is relatively new within the arena of African literary scholarship; perhaps it is necessary to define rhetoric briefly.

There are several definitions of the art of rhetoric, but the classical definition by Aristotle combined with that of George

Campbell will suit the purpose here. Aristotle defines rhetoric as "The faculty of discovering all the available means of persuasion;" (in Corbett:3-14) while Campbell defines rhetoric in his assertion that "all the ends of speaking are reducible to four; every speech intended to enlighten the understanding, to please the imagination, to move the passion or to influence the will." (14) Both aspects of rhetoric are relevant in analyzing Fagunwa's works, and they are also in consonance with his intention for his art—he seeks to instruct. Didacticism is not accidental in his works—it is intentional. However, as he instructs, he instructs persuasively, and through the medium of his language he pleases the imagination.

What the present rhetorical analysis entails is the examination of the way Fagunwa uses rhetorical means to achieve his objectives. This procedure is pertinent to what Pratt thinks a rhetorical analyst does:

> Whenever we try to grasp not only the substance of what we read, but its effective relation to the structure and the style, we are making a rhetorical analysis. . . (375)

Fagunwa's means by which he projects the Yoruba world-view in particular and the African ethos in general is neatly woven into the total fabric of his creative imagination. Fagunwa's art "moves," in Irele's words "towards the definition, in and through literature, of an imaginative apprehensions and embodiment of an African spirit." (1975:75) Fagunwa, therefore, uses his natural rhetorical skill to communicate this African spirit effectively through his specific Yoruba cosmography, mythology, and that ethnic group's collective apprehension of the universe (Ajadi:xv). Thus, his works "explore the supernatural and the abnormal with gripping suspense," as Conklin writes (vi).

Obviously, Fagunwa's aesthetic vision, artistic prowess, vividness of imagination, and all his literary excellence are manifested in his powerful and compelling use of language. His Yoruba is impeccable; he is a master of his mother tongue. It is almost impossible to read through his works without catching many glimpses of his dazzling and delightful use of language as he employs a full range of rhetorical means, such as metaphors, symbols, proverbs, epigrams, parallelism, and so on.

Most of his critics cannot but notice his way with words. Beier thus observes that

> Fagunwa is fond of rhetoric. He likes words. He likes to pile them up, say the same thing over and over again in infinite variation.He is a master of rhetoric, who can mke repetitions and variations swing in a mountainous rhythm, like Yoruba drumming. (53).

At the outset of his first novel, *Ogboju*, he employs both metaphor and proverb in a single breath, to capture the attention of his reader. He addresses his readers, his audience, as friends. This is a typical device of a skillful Yoruba story-teller:

> *Enyin ore mi, bi owe bi owe ni a lu*
> *ilu agidigbo, ologbon ni i joo*
> *omoran ni si mo. Itan ti ngo so yi*
> *ilu agidigbo ni; emi ni eniti yio lu*
> *ilu na, enyin si ni ologbon ti yio*
> *jo, enyin ni omoran ti yio mo o pelu. (Ogboju Ode*, p. 1).

> My friends all, like a sonorous proverb
> do we drum the agidigbo; it is the wise
> who dance to it, and the learned who
> understand its language. The word which
> follows is a veritable agidigbo; it is I
> who will drum it, and you the wise who
> will interpret it. (Trans. Soyinka)

This address to the audience is an effective means by which to kindle the interest of his readers. Fagunwa invites his audience to go with him on his imaginative journey. Plainly, he is stating that the story is an allegory, a device from medieval and Renaissance style which began to fall out of fashion in the seventeenth century. The metaphorical thought now follows: Fagunwa, as the story-teller, is the drummer, and his story becomes the agidigbo. In the two elements of metaphor—the tenor and the vehicle—Fagunwa's mind here is the tenor, while *agidigbo* is the vehicle. The sound of his voice, his words, is the drum; the speaker becomes the drummer. The reader is thus the dancer who dances to the tune of the drum. The drum can only be danced to by a wise dancer who is also learned enough to be able to decipher the tenor, the meaning, of that drum. This, I believe, is an economical way of saying that "my story is both parabolic and allegorical; it is supposed to mean something other than the surface would indicate." In this way, Fagunwa arrests the interest of his readers. This uses the rhetorical device that Aristotle describes as the basic introduction to a discourse—the exordium—a crucial part of a discourse of any kind. It is important to put the audience or the readers in a "receptive frame of mind," as Corbett asserts in his analysis of the speech in the *Iliad* in which Odysseus tries to persuade Achilles to fight once more for the Greeks (26).

Through the same rhetorical device, Fagunwa also advises his audience that he is about to impart something of value through the medium of his literary art. Fagunwa does not seem to subscribe to the idea of "art for art's sake"; he believes that art is a didactic medium, as Beier rightly observes:

> Fagunwa's moralizing is often too deliberate and it would be difficultfor the adult reader to take if I was not done with such charm. No event takes place, no situation is described from which we are not supposed to learn something. A nauseating idea. Yet who could object to being "improved" in such a charming manner . . . ? (53)

In the first few lines quoted from *Ogboju*, we can hear Fagunwa's soft voice as he whispers his intention through the rhetorical medium: "Come with me as I journey to the *Forest* of the universe; reason with me, as I penetrate into the abyss of the human soul." The audience or the readers are lured into the realm of the unseen world—a mythical world—through the rhetorical devices of metaphor, proverb, and epigram. In an earlier essay, I asserted that

> didacticism is not accidental nor a residue of his naivete in his works, but an accomplishment of a purpose. His basic purpose is to teach—to teach delightfully through the verbal gymnastics and a dazzling rhetoric—as vehicle which conveys the reader so smoothly, that he forgets the pain of the bumpy roads of "sermons" and proverbs that are intended to teach morals. Thus, in spite of the modern reader's resentment, he is lured to read along by Fagunwa's rhetorical prowess. (230, 382n.)

It is not amiss, then, to suggest that the meaning of Fagunwa's message is borne by the grandeur of his language—the language which is ornamented by rhetorical aptness. An example of Fagunwa's deliberate intention to teach, albeit pleasingly, is pronounced in the following passage—a passage in which Fagunwa demonstrates "verbal gymnastics":

> ... *bi o ti wa ni aiye nigbana a ma te oro yi mo wa leti nigbakugba pe, 'Okunrin ti o ji ni kutukutu ojo aiye re ti o gbe oran obinrin le ibi pataki okan aiya re ko ni di pataki lailai; Obinrin ti o ji ni kutukutu ti o gbe oran okunrin le ibi pataki okan aiya re ko ni di pataki lailai; okunrin ti o to akoko ati ni obinrin ti o gbe oran obinrin re ti o ni le ibi pataki okan aiya re yio di pataki lailai; obinrin ti o to akoko ati ni oko ti o gbe oran oko re ti o ni le ibi pataki okan aiya re yio di pataki lailai; okunrin alabosi ti o fe alabosi obinrin ti o gbe oran alabosi na le ibi pataki okan aiya re ko ni di pataki lailai; obinrin alabosi ti o fe alabosi okunrin ti o gbe oran alabosi na le ibi pataki okan aiya re ko ni di pataki lailai; okunrin pataki ti o fe alabosi obinrin ti ko gbe oran alabosi na le ibi pataki okan aiya re yio di pataki lailai; obinrin pataki ti o fe alabosi okunrin ti ko gbe oran alabosi na le ibi pataki okan aiya re yio di pataki lailai; enikeni pataki ti o gbe oran elomiran le ibi pataki okan aiya re yio di pataki lailai.* (*Igbo*, pp. 6-10)

. . . When he was alive, he used to impress this on our minds very often that

1. A man who wakes up early in the morning
     of his life,
   And gives an important place in his heart
     to a woman's matter
   Will not become important forever.
2. A woman who wakes up early in the morning
     of her life,
   And gives an important place in her heart
     to a man's matter
   Will not become important forever.
3. A man who is mature enough to get married
   And gives an important place in his heart
     to his woman's matter
   Will become important forever.
4. A woman who is mature enough to get married
   And gives an important place in her heart
     to her husband's matter
   Will become important forever.
5. A deceitful man who marries a deceitful woman
   And gives an important place in his heart to
     deceit
   Will never become important forever.
6. A deceitful woman who marries a deceitful man
   And gives an important place in her heart to
     deceit
   Will not become important forever.
7. An important woman who marries a deceitful man
   And does not give an important place in her
     heart to the deceitful one
   Will become important forever.
8. Whoever is important and gives an important
     place in his heart to others who are important
   Will become important forever.

The above passage exemplifies Fagunwa's epigrammatic use of language. He is fond of this kind of structure. He believes in exploiting Yoruba language; thus, he employs all of the parameters of its beauty here: the sound effect of the language is fully utilized. Note the words *kutukutu, pataki, lailai* in lines 3-9; the repetition of these words creates a sort of rhythm that is akin to Yoruba rhythmical drumming.

*'Okunrin ti o ji ni **kutukutu** ojo*
aiye re ti o gbe oran obinrin le
*ibi **pataki** okan aiya re ko ni di*
***pataki** **lailai**; Obinrin ti o ji ni*
***kutukutu** ti o gbe oran okunrin le*
*ibi **pataki** okan aiya re ko ni di*
pataki** **lailai (ll. 3-9)

Kutukutu ("early") is ideophonic, and contains a reduplication of Yoruba low tone, followed by *pataki* ("important") another low tone which does not contain reduplication These are followed by another ideophone *lailai* ("forever"), which contains a reduplication of high tone. The first word *kutukutu* appears in the line 3, and the second word *pataki* in line 5, while *pataki* and *lailai* ("forever") co-occur in line 6, with *lailai* in the final position. The pattern is repeated in lines 7-9. This pattern of repetition creates the rhythm, and also the near tongue-twisting form which I have called verbal gymnastics.

Thus, through the sound of the language, Fagunwa catches the attention of his readers and boldly prints the socio-ethical philosophy of the Yoruba people on the tablet of their hearts. He does not merely express what he feels alone, he wants to influence the attitude of the readers, persuade them, and ultimately change them. In this way, he projects the collective Yoruba sensibility, and serves as the conscience of the society as well. Thus he harmonizes ethics and aesthetics in an artistic–hence a delightful–way: his readers' minds are instructed, and their imaginations pleased.

Fagunwa also exploits other rhetorical devices through which he engages in that mode of rhetoric which the classical rhetoricians labeled *deliberative oratory*. "Aristotle pointed out," as Corbett reminds us,

> . . . that deliberative oratory is concerned with future time; that the means used in this kind of oratory are exhortation and dissuasion; and that the special topics that figure prominently in this kind of discourse are the

expedient and *in-expedient* or the advantageous and the injurious. (26)

Thus the speech or the passage displays the ingredients of deliberative oratory. In the first place, there is a note of dissuasion: both young man and young woman are urged not to place a premium on frivolous immoral activities and premature marital thoughts that could be injurious to their personhood, and, ultimately, impede their growth; hence their achievement of an authentic selfhood in life. In other words, there is an element of cause and effect in the passage: if a young man who is not old enough to begin to think about the opposite sex engages his time in doing that, thereby filling his thoughts with the filth of 'fornication,' that young man will not become important forever. Properly set in a rhetorical perspective, one can catch the message or the implication of the passage.

The implication is that if a male youth puts another female youth into a family way, while both of them should be in school studying and preparing for their adulthood, they would find themselves in all kinds of troubles that will impede their progress in life.

This idea is in consonance with Fagunwa's cultural background: most Africans, especially the Yoruba people, believe that a young man must wait until he is able to support a family, morally, emotionally, psychologically, and economically, before he thinks about getting married, or dating for that matter. Besides Fagunwa's cultural background that propels such an exhortation, there is his Judeo-Christian Puritan-like morality that impels him to sound such note of warning in the ears of the young reader.

The pronouncement against the youth, male or female, that goes against such mores is very emphatic: that youth will not become important forever! What every youth desires is to be somebody, to be famous and important in the society. Thus, by showing this in terms of cause and effect—the effect of playing with immoral activities or taking marital matters frivolously, which no one desires—Fagunwa is able to convince his young reader that the choice of waiting to get matured before such activities is the most noble choice, for he says:

> A man who is matured enough to get married
> And gives an important place in his heart
>   to his woman's matter,
> Will become important forever.
>
> A woman who is matured enough to get married
> And gives an important place in her heart to
>   her husband's matter
> Will become important forever.

Knowing this, therefore, it is then expedient for a youth to wait and get ready physically, emotionally, even spiritually, and economically before he gets into family matters in life.

In the second place, there is the promise of "abundant life," if a youth obeys this injunction; the abundant life will come in terms of being or becoming important forever. Here, again, Corbett's analysis of Homer's passage in which the envoys plead with Achilles to return to the battle is helpful:

> Whenever we try to persuade someone to do something, we try to show him the benefits that will result from his action. Some of the goods that most men agree upon as contributing to happiness are such external goods as a respected family, loyal friends, wealth, fame, honor, and such personal excellences as health, beauty, strength. (27)

This constitutes a sort of reward that is always promised in deliberative oratory. The action that is sought for in the passage, however, is both for the present and the future, for we know that deliberative oratory is concerned with the future. The future in this passage impinges upon the present as far as the action that is encouraged is concerned. The youth should start thinking from the present moment in order to reap the reward of such right thinking and right action in the future.

However, it is important to still discuss some other rhetorical devices in this passage, such as balancing and parallelism. For example, the first stanza talks about a woman; thus it balances the second that talks about a man, hence effecting a structural balancing between man and woman. This structural balancing is seen throughout the eight stanzas of the epigram. Also, closely related to this idea of structural balancing is the balancing of ideas, thus allowing the form to inform the content. This balancing occurs between being matured (ready) enough to get married and not being matured or ready to get married. For a man to achieve an authentic selfhood in life, he has to do the right thing at the right time, and the same thing goes for a woman. Such an important social activity must be approached with maturity and soundness of mind on the part of a woman and a man.

We also have another rhetorical device in the passage—parallelism. Fagunwa achieves parallelism by the use of antonyms:' man,' for example, parallels 'woman.' By the use of negations, "will not become important" parallels "will become important forever," as found in stanzas three and four. Fagunwa returns to parallelism achieved by opposites in stanzas five and six. The seventh stanza parallels the sixth, for both stand as a pair of opposites: the sixth stanza, for example, reads:

> A deceitful woman who marries a
> deceitful man
> And gives an important place in her heart
> to the deceitful one
> *Will not become* important forever

and the seventh stanza stands out as the opposite of the sixth, reading:

> An important man who marries a deceitful woman
> And does not give an important place in his
> heart to the deceitful one
> *Will become* important forever.

Though the intention here is clearly didactic, even tiresome, in Beier's opinion, yet I cannot find fault here with the author, for the lesson is presented in such a "charming manner."

Parallelism, of course, is preponderant in Fagunwa's narrative style. Consider this passage from *Ogboju*::

> Mo ni iyawo nko ka apa re, mo nse bi
> oko lasan. Ohun ti emi iba se nko se,
> ona ti emi iba gba nko gba. (*Ogboju*, p. 4)
> I have a wife, whom I cannot control,
> I am behaving like a mere (uneffective)
> husband. What *I should have done I did
> not do; the path that I could have
> I did not take.*

I have disussed the kind of parallelism that he achieves by negation; this makes him sound basically poetic, hence aesthetically compelling.

His expression of simple ideas is done in such a way that it will give a ring of oratory and uniqueness to it. Talking about his competence as a hunter, before the death of his father, his hero hunter says:

> *Mi o to ku pelu, mo ti npa erin,*
> *owo mi si ti nba efon; sasa eranko*
> *ni ibon mi ko tile ti ipa. (Ogboju,* p. 6)

> Before he (his father) died also, *I had*
> *been killing elephant; my hand had been*
> *clenching buffalo,* the kinds of animals
> that my gun had not killed were few.

Note the italicized sentences that are strung together for poetic effect. The description of the ordinary act of shooting is done with onomatopoeia. Akara-Ogun, in relating his father's shooting of the deer, says:

> *Nigbati agbonrin kan jade lati inu*
> *okiti ogan na ti o bo si inu oko ti*
> *on ka ila je, ni baba mi ba da oju*
> *ibon koo o wo ina moo lori . . . (Ogboju,* pp. 4-5)

> When a deer emerged from the mound of
> the ant hill, and darted into the farm,
> and started plucking *okro* to eat, my
> father turned the face of the gun towards
> him, and *crushed* fire on his head.

At times Fagunwa will describe the same thing in various ways. For example, when Akara-Ogun's father encounters a gnome, who becomes disgruntled because of the odor of tobacco that the father is smoking. When the father is challenged by the gnome, he responds: ". . . *ngo da ina mo o lori.*" " I will kindle fire on your head." (Ogboju, p. 9)

Fagunwa also uses proverbs effectively:

> *opelope ejika ti ko je ki ewu o bo*
> *(Ogboju,* p. 29)

Thanks be to the shoulders that prevent the garment from
falling off.
Okere gun ori iroko oju ode da . . .
(Ogboju, p. 88)
Squirrel climbs *iroko* tree; the hunter's eyes
become vacant.

*Mo titori egan mo legberin ore, bi irinwo ba nbu mi, irinwo a si
ma yin mi. (Ogboju,* p. 36)
I, because of reproach had eight hndred friends; if four
hundred are abusing one, four hundred will be
praising one.

Fagunwa also employs epigrams:
*Bi arugbo ba ni ki on ka ohun ti oju ohun ri ki o to gbo sinu
aiye, awon omode miran iba ma gbadura ki won ku lewe*
(p. 5)
If an old man says he will recount all that his eyes had seen
before he became old in the world, some children will be praying to die young.

When Akara-Ogun scolds the gnome (dwarf) who disturbs him when he is looking for game in the forest, the gnome's response is an epigram:

*Oa yi ni eyin omo araiye ma nse, eyin
aforesunise, awa a ma wo yin, oju yin
ko gbe ibikan, enba hilahilo kiri.*

*. . . gege bi iwa eda yin pelu, okan
yin ki ibale; eniti inu re ba dun
loni, awon eniyan re ko ni simi lola;
oni iku, ola arun, oni ija, ola
airoju, oni ekun, ola obanuje ni omo
araiye ma nba kiri . . . (Ogboju,* p. 9)

This is the way you children of the world behave, you who cause one to be weary of well-doing. We always observe you: your eyes never rest in one place; you go about restlessly . . . in consonance with your nature, your minds never rest. If one is happy today, his people

will not rest tomorrow: death today, disease tomorrow,
fight today, pressure tomorrow, weeping today, sorrow
tomorrow (these) are the menace of the children of the
world.

Here Fagunwa tries to deal with the natural existential experience of man: his frivolity, his search for security, and the corresponding frailty and existential instability. He also uses hyperbole in describing the gnome that his hero Akara-Ogun encounters during his first expedition—his journey to Igbo Irunmale:

> ... mo ngburo bo niwaju mi bi enipe enia
> mefa mbo; ase ewele oloju merindinlogun
> ni ... o de fila irin o wo ewu oje o si
> `wo sokoto penpe kan bayi ti a fi awo se ...
> lati idodo re de ekiti idi, kiki onde ni ...
> aye ejo mbe ninu won, won a ma yo ahon re
> bere bi agbako banlo (Ogboju, p. 12)

> I was hearing his movement in front of me as if six persons were coming; O! it was a monster with sixteen eyes
> .... he wore a cap of iron; he put on a garment of lead, and he wore a short pant made of leather... from his belly button to his waist, he wore girdles ... live snakes were there, and they were sticking out their tongues when *agbako* was going.

The purpose of this vivid hyperbolic description is to achieve rhetorical effect. These and many other rhetorical devices he employs in order to communicate and portray the world-view and the myth of his people—in a mythopoetic language.

A rhetorical analysis of Fagunwa's narrative could not ignore his basic symbols which are in all of his works—the *forest* and the *hunter*. The basic setting for all of Fagunwa's works—the Forest—is a metaphorical, archetypal, and symbolic element of his works. The forest represents the existential experience of all peoples in the world, for in his imaginative journey into the forest, he is able to explore the psycho-philosophical dimension of human experience and as such, through the myth and ethos of Yoruba cosmography, he is able to probe to the depths of the human psyche. He is able to fathom the abysses of the human soul.

Thus the symbolic element of the Forest is articulated in a clear deliberative oratory in the epilogue to his *Igbo Olodumare* (*The Forest of God*), as he warns his reader:

*E mase gbagbe pe bi aiye ti dun to
bena ni isoro inu re po to, igbati
enia ba ri isoro kan soso nigba miran
a dabi enipe ki oluware ku lekan . . .
Mo fe ki gbogbo enia fisi okan pe ko*

*si eniti ko ni Igbo Olodumare tire lati
lo ninu aiye, Igbo Olodumare ti enikan
yato si ti enikeji; ki Olodumare jeki
olukuluku ti Igbo Olodumare tire de
laini ipalara.* (*Igbo*, p. 163)

> Do not forget that the sweeter the world is, the more its difficulties. When one experiences difficulty one time, it often seems as if one should die immediately: I want all the people to know that thereis no one who does not have his own Forest of God to go in the world. One's Forest of God is different from the other's; may God grant that every-one would come back from his own Forest of God without being wounded.

The Forest of God, in this sense, becomes the symbol of the ups and downs or the phantasmagoria of the existential experience of man. This is the universal import of Fagunwa's aesthetics.

By the same token, the image of a hunter which pervades his works symbolizes the adventurous spirit of man that is not daunted by the awe of the unknown—the basic characteristic of a typical Yoruba hunter. The fact that his hero-hunters always conquer in the end after a selfless search for the key that unlocks the gate of peace and ease of the community, helps his reader to conceptualize and consequently internalize the fact that it is the one whose spirit grows not weary in the face of trials and tribulations that man inevitably encounters in an archetypal journal into the wilderness of the universe, that will survive in the end. The hunter imagery, therefore, symbolizes the unconquerable spirit of man. Through this symbolism, Fagunwa transcends his culture; he thus universalizes his aesthetics.

A rhetorical analysis of Fagunwa's narrative should not neglect his demonstration of the vividness of imagination, especially in his account of the tension between the inhabitants of the divided universe of his creative imagination. When in *Igbo Olodumare (The Forest of God)* Olowo-aiye wants to enter the Forest of God, Esukekere-Ode tries to stop him. Esukekere-Ode, armed by diabolic power and bravery, asks some soul-searching questions as he confronts Olowo-aiye, in a language that is charged, not only with rhetorical aptness, but psychic energy as well. Esukekere-Ode asks:

> *Tani o? Ki lo jamo?*
> *Kilo jasi? Ki lo nwa? Kilo nfe?*
> *Kilo nri? Ki lo nro? Kini se o?*
> *Nibo l'o mbo? Nibo lo nre?*
> *Nibo l'ongbe? Nibo lo nrin?*
> *Da mi lohun! Omo enia da mi lohun*
> *ni gbolohun kan. (Igbo,* p. 14)

> Who are you? What are you?
> What do you amount to?
> What have you become?
> What are you up to?
> What do you want? What are you looking at?
> What are you seeing?
> What are you thinking?
> What's the matter with you?
> From where are you coming?
> Where are you walking? Answer me!
> The son of man, answer me in a sentence.

In what is nothing less than verbal gymnastics and a virtuoso display of wit and rhetorical skill, Olowo-aiye gives a stern rejoinder, in which he makes it clear to the gnome that man is the head of all the created beings in the world. Thus the rejoinder echoes the story of creation in the Bible:

> ... *Ebora ti o ba fi oju di mi yio ma*
> *ti orun de orun ni, emi okunrin ni mo*
> *wi be; oni ni ngo so fun enyin ebora*
> *Igbo Olodumare pe, nigbati Eleda da*
> *ohun gbogbo ti mbe ninu aiye tan, o fi*

> *enia se olori gbogbo won. Mo fe ki
> iwo mo loni pe, igberaga ni ibere
> iparun, on ni ibere isubu o lodi si
> ofin enia, o si yato si ilana Olorun Oba.*
> *(Igbo,* p. 6)

> ... the troll that underrates me would
> fall headlong from one heaven to the
> other. I, the very man (of all men),
> had thus spoken; today I am going to tell
> you trolls of Igbo Olodumare, that when
> the Creator created everything, in the
> universe, he made Man the head of them
> all; I want you to know today, that pride
> is the beginning of (Man's) fall; it is
> against the law of Man, and it is different
> from the plan of God, the (Heavenly) King.

As I maintained in an earlier work, this passage exemplifies Fagunwa's dichotomized Universe—the unseen world and the world we can see. The seen world is the world in which we move and exist. The unseen universe is inhabited by the gnome, the troll, and various kinds of spirits, including the spirits of the departed. Because of the theocentric and anthropocentric nature of Fagunwa's narratives, he proves that Man who inhabits the seen world is superior to the inhabitants of the unseen world. He thus never allows Man to be relegated to the background. In order to prove his point, Fagunwa allows poetic justice to take its course: Olowo-aiye overcomes the troll—a victory for Man, and a vindication of God's plan, an affirmation of the superiority of Man over the inhabitants of the unseen world. This is basically a theistic consciousness that is woven into the total fabric of his art.

Another area in which Fagunwa shows his rhetorical skill is in the area of description. His vivid description of events and landscapes is powerful and compelling. Several passages in his novels can be cited to support this point, but a magnificent pictorial description of natural imagery in his Ogboju will be sufficient here:

Ni owuro ojo dara dara kan bayi ni:
oju ojo mo kedere; ikuku lo si ile re;
awon eranko igbe si sunlo; awon
eranko ile nje amuwa Olorun, awon eiye
si nyin Eleda won; ategun alafia nfe
lu awon eweko igbe; gbogbo won dudu
mirinmirin; orun yo ni ila orun ninu
ola ti Olorun fi fun u; o tan imole
sinu aiye awon omo enia si bere si
irinkerindo won . . . (Ogboju, pp. 1-2).

It was in the morning of one beautiful day, such it was: the face of the daywas bright; the cloud had gone to its abode; the animals of the bush were asleep; the domestic animals were eating that which God had provided (for them); the birds were praising their Creator (in songs); the peaceful breeze was blowing on the plant of the bush; all of them were very green indeed. The sun emerged from the east in its God-given honour; it illuminated the earth, and the children of men resumed their up-and-down movements . . .

It is obvious here that when Fagunwa describes anything, you more than see it, you feel it too—to use Samuel Johnson's terms. This kind of craftsmanship is noted by most of the critics who have dealt with Fagunwa's works. This is because of ". . . his use of language," for "Fagunwa shows an incredible feeling for words and their effects," as Bamgbose aptly remarks (130). Olabimitan also believes that

[b]y his use of beautiful expressions and his vivid descriptions of events and places, by his ability to blend romance with realism nicely, and by his use of both traditional materials. . . he towers about (sic) all creative writers in Yoruba before him, and wins for himself an eminent position among all Yoruba writers. (14)

A critic of Fagunwa's works can conclude by saying that Fagunwa, through a compelling creative power, vividness of imagination, rhetorical prowess—manifested in his use of proverbs, metaphor, epigram, symbols, and parallelism—is able to articulate through his mother-tongue the mythology and ethos of his Yoruba ethnic group and its collective, apprehension of reality. Samuel Johnson writes that "the end of writing is to instruct; the end of poetry is to instruct by pleasing" (137). I believe that Fagunwa, in his writing, demonstrates this dictum to be true by his rhetorical prowess and, more so, through his mytho-poetic expression.

UNIVERSITY OF ILORIN—NIGERIA

Works Cited

Ajadi, Gabriel A. "A Critical Introduction for and An Annotated Translation of D. O. Fagunwa's *Igbo Olodumare (The Forest of God)*." Diss. Ball State University, Muncie, Indiana, 1984.
Bamgbose, Ayo. *The Novels of D. O. Fagunwa*. Benin City: Ethiope Publishing Corporation, 1974.
Beier, Ulli. "Fagunwa:A Yoruba Novelist." *Black Orpheus* (1965):53.
Black, Edwin. *Rhetorical Criticism:A Study in Method*. Madison: Univ. of Wisconsin Press, 1978.
Campbell, George. *The Philosophy of Rhetoric*. Oxford: 1838. In Black 1978.
Conklin, Groff. "Introduction" to Edgar Allan Poe's *Ten Great Mysteries* (New York: Scholastic Book Services, 1960).
Corbett, Edward P. J. *Classical Rhetoric for Modern Students*. 2nd ed., New York : Oxford University Press, 1971.
Fagunwa, D.O. *The Forest of A Thousand Daemons:A Hunter's Saga*. Trans.Wole Soyinka, London:Nelson, 1958.
Irele, Abiola. "Tradition and the Yoruba Writer: D.O. Fagunwa, Amos Tutuola and Wole Soyinka. *ODU:Journal of West Afrixcan Studies*. 11 (January 1975):75.
———. "Criticism of Modern African Literature." In *Perspectives on African Literature*, ed. Christopher Heywood. London:Heinemann Educational Books Ltd., 1977.
Johnson, Samuel. "Preface to Shakespeare." In *English Critical Texts: 16th Century to 20th Century*, ed. D. J. Enright and Ernst De Chickera. London: Oxford Univ. Press, 1962.
Olabimitan, Afolabi. "Daniel Fagunwa." In *Perspectives on Nigerian Literature 1700 to the Present*, Vol. 2, ed. by Yemi Ogunbiyi. Lagos:Guardian Books Nigeria Limited, 1988.
Pratt, William. *The College Writer:Essays for Composition*. New York: Charles Scribner's Sons, 1969.

EAST AFRICAN LITERATURE

✱

LEXICAL COHESION IN OKOT P'BITEK'S *SONG OF PRISONER*

Ogo A. Ofuani

Despite numerous studies by critics and literary scholars, the effectiveness and aesthetic use of language in Okot p'Bitek's *Song of Prisoner* (1971) have remained largely unexplored. Scholars have made contributions to our understanding of p'Bitek's themes, images, historical and biographical background, and traditional poetic devices, but have devoted little time to linguistic/stylistic analyzes of his language (see Ofuani 1985). The issue that tends to dominate all others has been the controversial one of the number of prisoners contained in this Song (see Ogunyemi 1982 : Wanambisi 1984). The linguistic clues that should resolve this issue are often neglected, and critical analyzes have suffered from a deplorable vagueness and lack of depth (Ofuani 1988).

By looking at the lexical cohesive properties of a specific text, instead of all of p'Bitek's *Songs*, this essay will help establish some of the special properties of *Song of Prisoner*.[1] It ought to be possible to state some of the grounds upon which readers or critics of a literary work base their estimation of the work's stylistically significant features. On a more general level, this essay hopes to supplement the larger corpus of literary critical analyzes in which linguistic explanations of literary impressions, intuitions, and judgments about this text are either completely absent or glossed over in generalizations.[2]

I

The concept of *cohesion* is semantic: "it refers to relations of meaning that exist within the text, and that define it as a text" (Halliday and Hasan: 4). Cohesion occurs where the interpretation of one element in the discourse is dependent on that of another. The one presupposes the other in the sense that it cannot be effectively decoded except by recourse to it. When this happens, a relation of cohesion is set up, and the two elements—the presupposing and the presupposed—are thereby at least potentially integrated into a text. In another related definition, cohesion is seen as

> the relations obtaining among the sentences and clauses of a text. These relations, which occur on the grammatic stratum, are signalled by certain grammatical and lexical features reflecting discourse structure on a higher semiologic stratum. These features, such as anaphora, subordination and coordination . . . account for what may be referred to as the textual connectivity of sentences and clauses. (Gutwinski: 26)

Cohesion is part of the system of a language. The potential for it lies in the systematic resources of reference, ellipsis, and so on that are built into the language itself. In any given instance, however, cohesion depends not merely on the selection of some option from these resources, but also on the presence of some other element that resolves the presuppositions set up.

Like other semantic relations, cohesion is expressed through the strata organization of language. Language can be explained as multiple coding systems, or strata: the semantic (meanings), the lexicogrammatical (forms), and the phonological and orthographic (expressions) (Leech 1969:37). Meanings are realized (coded) as forms, and forms are in turn realized (recoded) as expressions. There is no hard-and-fast division between vocabulary and grammar; the guiding principle is that more general meanings are expressed through the grammar and more specific meanings through the vocabulary. Cohesive relations fit into the same overall pattern. Cohesion is expressed partly through the grammar and partly through the vocabulary.

We can refer, therefore, to *grammatical cohesion* and *lexical cohesion*. The distinction is really one of degree, and we need not make much of it here. There is no sharp line between grammar and vocabulary: the vocabulary, or lexis, is simply the open-ended and most delicate aspect of the grammar of a language.

Lexical cohesion is the cohesive effect achieved by the selection of vocabulary. It is not a single homolithic entity or phenomenon but involves a complex of interrelationships in the choice and use of words within a text, the cohesive effect of this choice and use deriving from the various semantic effects they yield (Halliday and Hasan 1976:74).

Lexical cohesion could be achieved through *reiteration, lexical relations,* and *collocation*. Reiteration involves the repetition of a lexical item, at one end of the scale; the use of a general word to refer back to a lexical item, at the other end of the scale; and a number of things in between: the use of synonym, near-synonym, a superordinate, or a general word; and in most cases it is accompanied by a reference item, typically *the.* This kind of reiteration involves reasonable reference to the same referent. But a lexical item may cohere with a preceding occurrence of the same item whether or not the two have the same referent, or indeed whether or not there is any referential relationship between them. The possibilities may be, as far as reference is concerned, identical, inclusive, exclusive, or simply unrelated. At another level, there is always the possibility of cohesion between any pair of lexical items that are in some ways associated with each other in the language. The cohesive effect of such pairs depends not so much on any systematic relationship as on their tendency to share the same lexical environment, to occur in collocation with one another. In general, any two lexical items having similar patterns of collocation—that is, tending to appear in similar context—will generate a cohesive force if they occur in adjacent sentences. However, it should be borne in mind that collocation is simply a cover term for the cohesion that results from the co-occurrence of lexical items that are in some way or other associated with one another, because they tend to occur in similar environments: the specific kinds of co-occurrence relations are variable and complex, and would have to be interpreted in the light of a general semantic description of the English language (see the essays by Halliday and Sinclair in Bazell 1966).

II

Song of Prisoner is a poem about African society after Independence (lo Liyong 1971:59-61). It explores further the theme of post- colonial disenchantment raised in the earlier *Song of Lawino* (1966) and *Song of Ocol* (1970). The prisoner's anger is the anger of the class of East Africans he represents: the poor who contributed immensely to the Independence efforts but are now relegated to pre-Independence subjugation and humiliation. They have lost their pride and dignity through the wiles and violence of the new black African masters.

It is "a generalized satire" (Roscoe 1977:54), almost allegorical: Prisoner has no name, the politician he murdered is unnamed too. Prisoner has no identity; he is one of a type. This makes him pathetic and symbolic. He is married with children and comes from a minority tribe. He has played an unspecified role in the Independence struggle. Now, he is a spokesman for the disillusioned majority: the rural poor, neglected minority groups, the unemployed, the underdogs. He is arrested and imprisoned for that and now talks to us from his cell (which he describes as "hell"). He does not expect to be and is not fairly treated by the judge and his jailers, whom he addresses as "Brothers." At times he talks like a man from "the wrong clan," a man outside the system he criticizes, but at others he talks like a man who once belonged. He accuses and condemns the politicians and their thugs, the prison guards, and his own weaknesses.

But his motives are suspect. He has plenty of reasons to be bitter: he has fought for "Uhuru," and those now in power have betrayed what he fought for. He is still poor, his children are still sick, hungry, and uneducated; his matrimonial bed is desecrated by the "Big Chief" (44); and he sees nothing but violence, corruption, and tribalism. His anger seems justified. But he is also motivated by hatred and despair, and we do not find it easy to separate his personal motives from his social vision. His description of the man he killed (66-74) lacks social significance; we do not immediately see whether he killed him to avenge his own disappointment. His descriptive tone turns into a sadistic venture: as if he killed for killing's sake.

There is a general tone of complaint in the poem as Prisoner catalogs, in each section, the ways he and his class have been maltreated.[3] In the enraged state of mind in which he finds himself after being beaten and tortured, he digresses now and again and repeats what he has said before in his effort to elaborate, substantiate, and prove his allegations or justify his actions. He looks for analogies to his physical situation. In spite of his digressions and repetitions, and in spite of the length of this monologue, the poem is a coherent unit. Cohesion, particularly lexical cohesion, helps to make the poem what it is.

III

Song of Prisoner, in the tradition of p'Bitek's other poems, is in fifteen movements or sections.[4] Consequently, an analysis of the type intended here would be cumbersome if all its movements were subjected to analysis. The first (under the subtitle "dung of chicken") is representative enough of the other movements and so provides the corpus for the present analysis. Where necessary, incursions will be made into other movements to depict the relationship between all of them. This restriction of data is, however, not a defect if a detailed microstylistic analysis is to be achieved.

The title of the poem contributes significantly to its general cohesive pattern. *Song of Prisoner* is a nominal phrase of the Head ("song") and Qualifier ("of prisoner") type,[5] in which the article, whether definite or indefinite, has been deliberately omitted. The Head and the Qualifier are both capable of taking the article, the addition of which should have changed the form and, therefore, the significance of the title. The omission is paradigmatic. There are four possibilities: "the song of a prisoner," "the song of the prisoner," "a song of a prisoner," and "a song of the prisoner." If the qualifying element of the title is crucial, then two possibilities are likely: "song of a prisoner" and "song of the prisoner." If the meanings of these two latter versions are considered, the omission of the article will be seen to be stylistically significant.

If the indefinite article *a* is taken as given, the prisoner will have an almost allegorical quality, referring to *any* one prisoner who finds himself immersed in the kinds of experiences narrated in the poem. Phonological cohesion can also help here to suggest only *one* prisoner known to the poem ("Song of a Prisoner").[6] The choice of the definite article *the*, on the other hand, suggests a *specific* prisoner. *The* will make the title lose its allegorical tone by exophorically referring to a prisoner already known to the poet but not known or assumed not to have been known to the reader.

Okot p'Bitek's deliberate omission of the article is a grammatically cohesive device that operates at two levels: the level of exophora, where it is assumed the reader has foreknowledge of *which* prisoner, and at the level of ellipsis, involving the omission of the deictic element of the noun phrase. It is also lexical because it involves the omission of a lexical item of the closed set whose absence consequently ambiguates the meaning of the title. This omission could, therefore, have been partly responsible for the different interpretations given to the persona(e) in this poem. Some critics believe there is only one prisoner who on some occasions involves himself in the confusion and self-deception that create the impression that there are two prisoners (especially in the seventh movement, "voice of a dove," which seems out of tune with the others). Other critics feel there are two prisoners (a poor one whose voice re-echoes throughout the poem, the misused political assassin and hero of Uhuru who is angry and pleads to all kinds of repression, the defenseless and badly beaten prisoner of all the movements, except the seventh; and the rich, satisfied, unperturbed prisoner of the seventh, whose detention is only momentary). (See Gathungu 1973; Heron 1976; Marshment 1972; Ofuani 1985; and Ojuka 1973.) Edward Blishen (1971: 6-35) even suggests that there are three voices and personalities, though he fails to establish the existence of three separate masks. It is worth mentioning here that in *Two Songs*, p'Bitek reveals a significant consistency in the non-use of the article in headings. In *Song of Prisoner* the word "Prisoner," as used, makes concrete reference, and the feeling of cohesion is achieved through the play with the semantic features of nouns. "Prisoner" is a common noun but the omission of the article and its capitalization give it the status of a proper noun, make it a name, thus giving it specificity, and identity. Prisoner is now a person, not a class. The same goes for the persona in *Song of Malaya*.

The kind of cohesive pattern traced in the poem's title is also present in the subtitle of the first movement: "dung of chicken." It is a noun phrase, made up of a Head ("dung") and Qualifier ("of chicken"). The interpretive significance is that, as a heading, it carries the main statement about the state-of-affairs described in the section: corruption, brutality, mercilessness, and violence. All these associations are signalled by the connotations of foulness, fetid odor, putrefaction, repulsion and so on that "dung of chicken" brings to the reader's mind. We are, therefore, psychologically prepared for the brutality the prisoner says he is subjected to.

The first movement has, for convenience, been divided into eighteen stanzas determined by the poet's use of the conventional breaks between strand so on.hes of verse. This movement starts with a description of the prisoner's discomfort:

> 1) The stone floor
> Lifts her powerful arms
> In cold embrace
> To welcome me
> As I sit on her navel. (11)

The discomfort described here is conveyed in the rest of the movement through a combination of the various facets of lexical cohesion. There is, for instance, a concentration of phrases with different kinds of collocation: words with negative meanings whose effects contrast and tend to negate other positive ones with which they co-occur ("cold embrace . . . welcome"); personifications involving suggestions of animacy for inanimate objects ("stone . . . lifts . . . powerful arms"; "stone floor . . . her navel"), and so on. The stone floor's "cold embrace" is negative and immediately contrasts with "welcome me" (positive). The "cold embrace," if explained as a sexual image, has all the connotations of detached and unresponsive relations and so negates the effect of warmth suggested by "welcome." Human associations are significantly used to describe the effect of the bare floor ("her navel") on the prisoner's bare body. The several attributes in 1), whether anatomical or merely attributive, are unnaturally ascribed to the different portions of the prisoner's cell, giving them volition, a degree of deliberateness, a sense of purpose that is almost human in their effects on the prisoner. It is as if Prisoner believes the cell has acquired the physical features of the human beings whose invention it is. Most of the images are erotic and female, suggesting the extra softness and tenderness expected of a woman that starkly contrast with the hardness and coldness of the cell.

Other human associations given to inanimate objects include their ability to exhibit emotions. For instance, in the third stanza the prisoner describes "the brow/Of the weeping stone floor" (12). The wetness (and cold comfort) of the stone floor that increases the prisoner's discomfort is likened to a human face and given the capability to express human emotions (to weep). Most of these metaphors arise from a deviation in lexical collocation at the syntagmatic level, and the negative interpretations we give to their associations derive from this deviational pattern. For example, stone walls have no arms they can lift, irrespective of the effect of these arms, whether they are "cold" or really intending to "welcome" the prisoner, or to increase his discomfort. "Arms" should collocate with "man." This kind of deviant collocation heightens, in its absurdity and unexpectedness, the unnatural and unjust atmosphere of the prisoner's situation. The inappropriate collocations bolster this distortion of the natural order of pity and mercy. In addition, cohesion is aided through the provision of one consistent imagery. There is a progression in noun reference from inanimate to animate; from animacy to personification; and from human to proper.

The sense of discomfort aroused by the contrasts created by the collocational patterning of the personifications and metaphors is also carried by the similes. In the ninth stanza, the prisoner describes the profuse bleeding of his nose as follows:

2) My nose
Is a broken dam
Youthful blood leaps
Like a cheetah
After a duiker . . . (14)

Passage 2) is significant at several interrelated linguistic levels. First, is the prisoner's use of the equative copula verb *be* (line 2) such that we have the structure x = y, "My nose" (x) "is" (=) "a broken dam" (y). But x is not exactly y. "My nose" would normally make us expect a trickle since nostrils are small; but "a broken dam" carries the suggestion of a deluge. So there is exaggeration (hyperbole) in the discrepancy between "nose" and "dam" (especially as the declarative nature of lines 1 and 2 makes them look like a statement of fact). The prisoner also exaggerates in the simile following "broken dam" ("Youthful blood leaps/Like a cheetah"). "Blood," because of its liquid nature, does not "leap" but Prisoner states so as if it were true. "Leaps" and "cheetah" seem to form a lexical set, stressing intense agility. The cheetah is known for its speed and lethal accuracy in tracking down its prey. Its agility ties with "youthful" and "leaps." These associations are blood-curdling when used to describe the flow of the prisoner's blood. For his situation, the comparison is apt, more so as it describes one aspect of the outward manifestation (the result) of the cruelty and manhandling he has gone through.

A similar simile is in the tenth stanza:

3) Brother
How could I
So poor
Cold
Limping
Hungry like an empty tomb . . .
Inspire you
To such heights
Of brutality? (15)

Line 6 above is significant. The attributive/stative adjective "hungry" is animate, and if used for a "tomb" suggests personification as the question that arises is "Could the tomb be hungry?" But in the context of Prisoner's starvation, the comparison describes the insatiability of graves (their unending reception of the dead), likened to his hunger. "Tomb," therefore, ties anaphorically with the description of his imminent death through loss of blood in 2).

Lexical cohesion is also achieved by a concentration of

items whose semantic description involves the contrast between want and avoidance (approach-avoidance), as evidenced in the following pairs:

>   cold embrace-welcome (11)
>   colorless-rainbow (12)

Several such pairs occur in other sections. The significance of the first pair is explained here. The approach-avoidance syndrome can be related to the sexual images explained above (in relation to passage 1), and describe the kind of situation where the erotic man-woman effect that pervades the movement is equivalent to the effect of the cold on the prisoner. His initial acceptance by the stone wall ("embrace," "welcome," "kisses") contrasts with the numbness and pain the wall offers him after the seduction ("shoots freezing bullets/Through my bones").

The real effect of the contrast is that there is a significant play on words. Irony is expected here because the stone wall as an inanimate object has no volition and is incapable of initiating the kind of actions ascribed to it. The ironic intention is to show the similarity between Prisoner's suffering (coming directly from the cold wall and floor) and that meted out to him by his torturers (the guards). The referent involved (the stone wall) is static, fixed, and passive.7 Its effects on the prisoner can therefore be blamed on the jailers. But the "rejection," symbolic of the rejection and lack of protection from those who paid him to assassinate others and who have not kept him out of jail, makes him rigid with anger, his throat burns, his heart gets riddled "with the arrows/Of despair"; he is "drowning/In the deep lake of hatred." Bruised and bleeding, he marvels at the extent of the jailers' brutality against a poor defenseless man in spite of his services to Uhuru:

>   4) A young tree
>   Burnt out
>   By the fierce wild fire
>   Of Uhuru. (15)

His despair is heightened by the concatenation of words that have associations of lifelessness: *stone, cold, whitewashed, shoots, freezing*, and so on. *Shoots* in the third stanza, for instance, refers forward through cataphora to elements of pain and destruction in the fourth: *fiery hailstones, punching holes*, and so on., all of which reveal harshness and brutality.

Cohesion is achieved also in the first movement with words suggesting motionlessness, and there is progression in their occurrence from the first stanza: *sit* (1), *rests* (2), *dizzy* (6), *bed* (12), *sleep* (13) and *asleep* (17). These words arouse in our imagination the difference between pain and death. The contrast is sharper because psychological torture is increased by a combination of physical pain, the glare of the harsh lights in the prison cell, the restricted movement ("tie my hands/And feet/With this rope"), and the numerous images through which the prisoner describes their effect (*bullets, hailstones, white, hot, melting, drowning, break, killed, cracked, broken, fire, slap, ram, red-whirlwind, venom, mamba*). Sleep is impossible, but that image (sleep) and then death keep coming to Prisoner's tortured mind, as if death should logically follow sleep in this situation. Hence the sequence of "my father/Is asleep" (penultimate stanza) and "my father's/Grave" (last stanza). In his present state, he is a contrast to his father, who is in a kind of restful sleep in his grave,

5) Unseeing
Unhearing
Undreaming. (17)

There is a cohesive effect in the repetitive pattern of the lines in 5), in which the senses of sight, hearing, and cognition (perception) are concentrated. The cohesion is syntactical (morphological) and also lexical. There is a kind of Cummingsian touch in the role of morphology here, in the derivation of stative nouns through a combination of the use of the negative prefix *un-* and the gerunding suffix *-ing*. The *un-* prefix is reversitive, implying that the states of *seeing, hearing,* and *dreaming* have been reversed. These *-ing* forms are stative nouns rather than progressive verbs suggesting ongoing processes. There is a degree of permanence in the new states created with the aid of the prefix, thus giving the prisoner's lament a tone of finality, futility, and irredeemable sorrow. His father's states contrast with his own.

Most significant of the words in 5) is *undreaming* which, in this context, has several possible meanings. Literally, it means his father is "not dreaming" (he is not conscious, completely dead, unfeeling). At another figurative level, it means his father no longer has delusions—he now knows more about reality, hence his detached objectivity, unlike the prisoner who still has delusions about release, rewards, Uhuru and its promises, revenge, and so on. At a third level, the *un-* prefix could be interpreted to mean that in his new state of detachment achieved at death, his father is now "changing his old dreams, re-living his past," taking stock and seeing his past from a new perspective (perhaps the proper one!). He has achieved a moment of proper focus that is not and cannot anymore be distorted by pain, or the senses.

The last stanza is a single sentence that begins with a line of command:

6) Listen to the footsteps
Of the wizard
Dancing on my father's
Grave. (15)

The verb "listen" draws attention to the wizard's desecration of the prisoner's father's grave, overturning those sacred things he holds dear. This verb has no immediate subject and so applies to both the singular and plural *you* (the tormentors as well as the reader). The prisoner is, in prison, more perceptive than his tormentors to imaginatively "hear" the desecration of his father's grave. His views are no longer distorted by dreams of Uhuru that have been "burnt out." He no longer has illusions. If the analogy is drawn between the "unseeing," "unhearing," "undreaming" state of his dead father and his own apparent "life-in-death" state of pain and torture, he may be implying some kind of cathartic effect of the pain for himself, responsible for his sensitive nature. He has experienced a purgation of his earlier trust for his "brothers" in the fight for Uhuru, for whom he no longer has any regard. This could explain the sarcasm with which he attacks their misdeeds, in his own admission of being guilty of the murder of the politician but confessing to other "crimes," such as impotence within the new order, deafness, blindness, fear, joblessness, landlessness, sickness, orphandom, and hatred for those who exploit the poor—the deprivations caused by the new African post-Uhuru leaders. The last stanza ends on a note of pessimism struck by the grammatical form of the verb that, at the paradigmatic level, is a lexical item. Whatever the meaning read into the end of this movement, it tallies with the note of negativisim with which it started. The first movement as a whole sets the general tone for the other movements, which are composed along the same lines, cataloging the ills the prisoner laments about. Lexical cohesion is not internal to this movement but is tied with the other movements. Most of the patterns discussed in the first recur in the others.

IV

Examining a text, especially one as long and intense as *Song of Prisoner*, can often reveal sources of cohesion we might not otherwise notice and can help us discover recurrent themes and images. In any discourse, lexical choice is intimately associated with— and partly limited by— choice of subject matter. Lexical choices that result most directly from choice of subject matter are likely to be the least striking stylistically. This means that the choices, to the extent that they are likely in the context (i. e., if they are normally associated with the subject matter), are not foregrounded, not attention-drawing, and therefore not as stylistically significant as the foregrounded elements.

Song of Prisoner illustrates some of the usual kinds of lexical foregrounding. A number of words, word-groups, and even clauses stand out by virtue of their rarity or their novelty in the context in which they are used. These elements are often striking because of the associations they carry. In the first movement, the following occurrences are some of the most striking:

> i) "freezing bullets" (12). The bullets here are not real bullets but bullets of cold; cold ("freezing") contrasts with bullets, which are usually propelled by the heat of gunpowder combustion; here bullets refer to the piercing effect of the cold on the prisoner's bare body.

> ii) "fiery hailstones" (12). Hailstones are drops of iced rain; they should be cold but the ones dropping from the

roof of the prisoner's cell are unusual—they are "fiery," not in their coldness but in their glare and persistence (they refer to the harsh electric light on the roof). Hailstones can never be fiery, hence their unusual collocation. The continuous drop of these masses of iced rain can literally cause discomfort and pain.

iii) "colorless rainbow" (12). Another unusual collocation that is reminiscent of Chomsky's (1965) "colorless green ideas," describes the blood-spattered walls of his prison cell. Could it be a reference to the monochrome effect of his blood on the walls and floor?

The sense of ii) and iii) could be seen if placed in the full context of the utterance in which Prisoner exhibits his usual predilection for exaggerations:

7) That giant firefly
On the high ceiling
Rains *fiery hailstones*
Into my closed eyes
Punching holes
Through the thatch,
There is a *colorless rainbow*
On the bleak white walls . . .
And on the brow
Of the weeping stone floor . . . (12)

A poet's use of deviant expression and unusual collocations is usually called "poetic license." As Geoffrey Leech explains (1969: 37), in the phrase "poetic license" we concede the poet's right to ignore rules and conventions generally observed by users of the language. But in the grammar of a language, there are usually constraints imposed on the use of words in certain environments. Such "selectional restrictions" govern the selection of lexical items for insertion into underlying structures (Chomsky 1965). The three examples above are instances of apparently meaningless collocations involving contradictions because they say something is both x and not-x at the same time (Traugott & Pratt 1980:206). In iii), for instance, the contradiction lies in the fact that *rainbow* is colorful but is here being claimed to be colorless.

Examples iv) and xi) below are in a different class as metaphorical forms, with their areas of semantic transference divergent. Metaphors may be anomalous but they do not fail to communicate-they are to some extent "meaningful." When our knowledge of language and the world will not let us take a meaning literally, we do not give up, but rather "make sense" of the anomalies by allowing certain features to override others in particular contexts. These examples further illustrate Prisoner's hyperbolic disposition; their contexts are provided to make their senses clearer:

iv) I am drowning/In the *deep lake/Of hatred*... (13)
v) My heart is riddled/With the *arrows/Of despair*... (13)
vi) I am engulfed/By a red *whirlwind/Of pains*... (17)
vii) Do you see/The *beads of blood/*On my legs and feet? (14)
viii) Look at *the laughing wound/*In my head... (14)
ix) The dark *silence/Urinates fire/*Into my wounds... (16)
x) My *brain is melting*... (13)

All the examples can be given different explanations, and have been italicized to show the areas of transference. Texts iv) to vi) are concretive metaphors that attribute physical existence to abstractions. The abstract "hatred," "despair," and "pains" that describe sensory perceptions or feelings are equated to the physical forms "lake," "arrows," and "whirlwind," respectively. The semantic transference lies in their equations (lake = hatred; arrows = despair; whirlwind = pains). Example vii) involves the equation of two physical entities that are in different states ("beads," solid; "blood," liquid). Beads are ornamental but these are not jewelry, only the clotted blood on his lips. The brutality he received is nauseating, yet he describes it with an ironic matter-of-fact tone that makes the result more telling (as if he says, "see how they decorate me with my blood").

The situation in viii) is equally serious. His "wounds" are made to "laugh." Maybe in personifying his "wounds," he really wants them to laugh at human callousness. He sees a parallel between the shape of a laughing mouth and the depth of his wound. Text ix) is deviant at two levels. The abstract "silence" is ascribed an animate characteristic to "urinate," an impossibility made more tenuous by the nature of the product of this excremental process: "fire." The verb "urinates" collocates with and predicts/anticipates water. "Fire" is therefore aberrant here, even if the silence literally can urinate. It is difficult to perceive the grounds of Prisoner's usage here.

Lastly, text x) adds a climactic note to Prisoner's frustration: his physical "brain" is said to thaw, to melt, to become liquid (like ice). The reduction he describes refers to the unbearable pain, mental torture, and pressure he is subjected to, particularly when later he screams, "I am/Mad,/Can't you see?" (24). The ground for his complaint is not farfand so on.hed.

These unusual forms also occur in the second movement, whose preoccupation is with hunger and its effects: "infant pregnancies" (in reference to the prisoner's children's malnutrition and kwashiorkor—22); "their stomachs/Drum sleep off" (reference to the disturbing effect of hunger and starvation—23); "javelins/Inside my stomach" (descriptive of the burning effects of hunger in his stomach—23).

One cannot fail to notice the use of shock words, especially the references to sexual organs, physiological processes, and excrement. This kind of "obscene" language is not a mere attempt at reproducing street language; it serves a fundamental use in the expression of anger and hate. It is often directed toward some person or thing the narrator loathes (see Luce 1977; Collins 1979). Examples abound in the first movement: *penis, breasts, bosom, belly-button, buttocks* (12); *stark naked, in bed with your wife, raping your mother* (15). These words and expressions are used in the questions asked by the prisoner in which he suggests (rather naively?) that only such sexual misdeeds should occasion the kind of punishment meted to him. He uses them to advance his argument about his innocence and not because he intended to be vulgar and obscene. His only "outrageous" crime, he suggests, is his loyalty to the Party and commitment to Uhuru.

There are also other references to physiological processes: *urinates* (16), *pangs/Of childbirth* (17). These sexual images progress from a mere anatomical description of the effect of the cold on his body couched in the images of sexual foreplay, to those of intercourse (whether cooperatively accepted by the jailer's wife or forcibly imposed on his mother) and then on the finality of childbirth: *embrace: kisses: naked: bed: raping: sleep: urinates: childbirth.* These words form a lexical set whose meanings are interrelated. In this context, *urinates* could be a euphemism for the more offensive *ejaculation*. "Childbirth" in the sixteenth stanza is immediately followed by "my children" in the penultimate stanza, as if the mere mention of "pangs of childbirth" reminds him of the prolonged suffering of his wife and children (who form the subject of the second movement). After the pains of childbirth should come the joys of motherhood but this natural order is perverted as the "lullaby is stuck/In their mother's throat" (17), and he remembers the death of his own father. His children, like himself, will soon be orphans at his own death. This refers forward to the helplessness of his wife and children in the second movement: "The cry of my children/And the sobs/Of my wife" (24).

Homonymy gives rise to another kind of lexical foregrounding and cohesion, the pun. Puns are often described as involving double or multiple meanings, an intentional ambiguity. What puns usually do is introduce more than one lexical item by means of a single phonological sequence. The multiplicity of possible meanings in the context can create layers of unexpected cohesion. One way writers make puns is by manipulating spelling to suggest multiple lexical items by a single word (homography and homophony). One striking instance of such usage is the reference to *arms* in "the stone floor/Lifts her powerful arms/In cold embrace" (11). The immediate literal meaning of *arms* here is that used in reference to limbs, though it has already been explained that this is an instance of personification. This meaning of *arms* collocates with its use in "see the muscles/Of my arms" (13). But *arms* can refer to weapons and is suggestive of those "powerful guns and rifles" used by the jailers, especially if related to "why do they ram my feet/With the butt/Of their rifles" and "uniformed Brothers" (16). In both instances, the single word *arms* is homophonic (/a:mz/).

Homophony can also give rise to puns in instances in which two words may not be homographic but are pronounced alike. In the first movement the prisoner's description of his loss of blood contains the possibility of punning the word *cheetah* that reminds one of *cheater*. "Youthful blood leaps/Like a cheetah." *Cheetah*, a feline, pronounced /tʃiːtə/, brings to mind the homophonic equivalent cheater (/tʃiːtə/), which means "one who cheats: an officer who collected the fines to be paid into the Exchequer" (in Shakespearean times; *Chambers* 1977: 222). The homophony here could be seen in this second meaning to relate later with the words *caught, find* in 8), where the central issue is "Was I caught cheating?":

8) I was not caught
Dancing stark naked
Around your house.
Did you find me
In bed with your wife
Or raping your mother? (15)

The effect of this second pun is not as direct as the first but is equally a possibility in the context of the poem in which crime, discovery, and punishment are re-echoing themes.

Lexical foregrounding can also be achieved with the aid of reiteration involving the repetition of one lexical item, as is obvious in the stanza below:

9) My head rests
On her flat
Whitewashed breasts.
She kisses
My bosom
My neck
My belly button
My back
My buttocks
And shoots freezing bullets
Through my bones. (11-12)

The first-person singular possessive pronoun *my* is used seven times. This repetition produces a cataloging effect. The deliberate slowness of the rhythm is metrically evocative of the slow and methodical spread of the cold as it virtually "undresses" the prisoner in their "love tangle." The use of enjambment here may make the reader want to produce the lines at a faster rate to reveal the urgency of the "spread." But even then, the end-pauses unmarked by punctuation and the repeated use of *my* at the beginning of each of lines 5-9 slow down the speed. This repetition of *my* may be seen as the prisoner's way of emphasizing the effect of the cold floor—emphasizing the degree of personal knowledge of the suffering involved in this "they-affect-me-so-I-should-know-if-you-doubt-me" stance. This personalization of the experience through the use of *my* ties cohesively with the use of other variants of the first-person singular pronoun ("I," "me," "mine") in all the movements of the poem. Texts 1-3) and 6-9) support this. This usage pervades the song. For instance, in section 2 he pleads insanity ("I plead insanity,/I am/Mad,/Can't you see?" 24) and later contradicts himself ("I am not insane," section 8, 67). In section 4 he blames his father for marrying his mother (36) and threatens to desecrate his father's tomb for it ("I will exhume your bones/And hang you/By the neck," 38). In the same way, he gloats over his cold-blooded murder of the politician ("Yes/I did it/And,/My God,/What a beautiful/Shot!" section 8, 66) and later complains that he was not a "thug" and deserved congratulations (67-68). He still pictures himself as a political hero, despite his disillusionment: "I want to raise my hands/And acknowledge/Their cheers /I want to shake hands," section 10 (77).

V

The kinds of cohesive properties of the lexis discussed above are not the only possibilities in this long poem. But they are significant because they show the deliberate poetic design in the choice of words and their arrangements to produce some of the effects described. This attempt, in the tradition of *interpretative stylistics*, has involved "breaking the poem to pieces" for its different facets of interpretation and interplay of elements. (See Gregory 1974; Handscombe 1970; Leech 1970; and Sinclair 1966.) As. R. J. Handscombe (1970) has observed,

> The means by which a poet creates a feeling or body of feelings in his readers' minds are complex and subtle, sometimes so subtle and complex as to pass unnoticed, for

in these circumstances it is the emotions that are first required to respond and not the intellect. But it is only when we can understand—and, hopefully, explicate—the means that we can make any progress with the meaning. (30)

The discussion here has made it obvious that the violence done by and to the prisoner, the brutality with which he is treated, his general discomfort as he laments his fate in his cell in section one, permeates the lexis of the poem. It is to be seen as an important factor in cohesion in relation to the other movements of the song. Sexual images also pervade the text. These tie in with a strong "libidinal" sexual theme that has been traced, especially in relation to Prisoner's delusive recapture, often very vividly, of the desecration of his matrimonial bed by the "Big Chief" (44) in the fifth movement, and his desire to sleep with French girls, drink cognac, and go on a sexual jamboree (in sections 12 to 15, 89-118; Heywood 1980).

Reiteration is a major cohesive factor in the poem's unity. The reiterative pattern varies, and this variety lends intensity to the poem. For example, the clause pattern "Listen to the footsteps . . ." in the first section is repeated in other movements, but the objects of our attention are varied as the prisoner draws attention to other aspects of the society's ills:

Listen to the Chief's dog (22)
Listen to the Song/Of the flies (52)
Listen to the millipede/Whispering a lullaby . . . (81)
Listen to the sandy tunes (105)
Listen to the wailing tunes (105)
Listen to the orphans (114); and so on.

This structure ties the different movements together grammatically.

This kind of cohesive pattern is also present in the repetitive recurrence of the *I plead* + *direct object* structure first used in section one (12). It is repeated with variation in the third movement ("I plead smallness"; "I plead fear"; "I plead hopelessness"; and so on., 33), which coheres anaphorically to the choral pattern "Do you plead/Guilty/Or/Not guilty?" in the first movement (and in most of the other movements: 21, 30, 32, 44–45), and "I plead hunger," "I plead insanity" (of the second movement, 20) and, cataphorically, to "I plead guilty to pride" of the thirteenth (100). A significant relationship exists between the prisoner's ironic acceptance of being guilty of the various ("hunger," "poverty," and so on.) "misdeeds" that readers realize are not crimes, and the satiric intention of metaphorically drawing attention to his plight and the injustice of the authorities who imprison him for non-crimes (Ofuani 1986).

These kinds of cohesion are responsible for the thematic unity of the poem. According to Adrian Roscoe (1977), the poem's theme of post-colonial disenchantment is not new, for many writers have explored it since the early 1960s; what is new is that "not only is the subject weighty" but that "its treatment tells us so" (54). This treatment is partly achieved through lexical cohesion and is done so perfectly and appropriately so as to give the poem its status of being "Okot's angriest poem," and helps it achieve the "symmetry," the balance that Roscoe has aptly observed exists in the treatment in this work in which Okot p'Bitek "applies all his strength" (54).

UNIVERSITY OF BENIN—NIGERIA

Notes

This paper was presented in an earlier version at the 7th Ibadan International Conference on African Literature, University of Ibadan, August 1982. The author thanks Dr. Niyi Osundare for his suggestions and criticisms.

1. *Song of Prisoner* is here treated as a single unified text. A text, defined as "any passage, spoken or written, of whatever length, that does form a unified whole," is the premise for any useful discussion of the concept of cohesion. See Halliday and Hasan: 1.

2. A complementary relationship should exist between stylistic and literary critical analyzes of texts. For instance, Ayo Banjo (1982: 9) sums their interrelationship by saying that "the stylistician is not in competition with the literary critic but rather offers a solid base on which to anchor our literary criticism." Stylistics is therefore an aid to literary criticism.

3. Heywood (1980: 65-83) has tried to justify Prisoner's rage in this poem. She saw it as an indictment of social abuses and

the pervasive sense of collusive pollution, a rage that is occasioned by the oppression and betrayal of the down-trodden by the elitist bourgeoisie.
4. *Song of Lawino* has 13 sections; *Song of Ocol* has nine; and *Song of Malaya* has seven.
5. The linguistic model used here is Halliday (1961: 241-92). In the grammar, the noun group (phrase) has three main constituents: *Modifier* (m), *Head* (H) and *Qualifier* (q). The *Head* is obligatory; the *modifier* and *qualifier* are optional elements.
6. This reading seems responsible for Blishen's title to the American edition of the Song in which he tries to suggest that the Prisoner was Patrice Lumumba of Congo (Zaire). See Blishen 1971.
7. Such a referent is in the language of case grammar performing the function of "Force" in initiating actions in which it has no volition. See Traugott and Pratt 1980: 192.
8. Chomsky, *Aspects of the Theory of Syntax*. An alternative approach is provided by Angus McIntosh (1961: 325-37), which discusses such "collocational" patterns in terms of the claim that lexical items belong to sets that have certain "ranges," that is, tolerable extensions.

Works Cited

Banjo, Ayo. "The Linguistic Factor in African Literature: A Keynote Address." Unpublished paper, 7th Ibadan International Conference on African Literature, University of Ibadan, August 1982: 9.

Bazell, C. E. et al., eds. *In Memory of J. R. Firth*. London: Longman, 1966.

Blishen, Edward. Introduction to *Song of a Prisoner*. New York: Third Press, Joseph Okpaku Publishing, 1971.

Chambers Twentieth Century Dictionary. New Edition, with Supplement. Ed. A. M. Macdonald. Edinburgh: Chambers, 1977.

Chomsky, Noam. *Aspects of the Theory of Syntax*. Cambridge, Massachusetts: MIT Press, 1965.

Collins, Terence. "Self-Image Through Imagery: Black Arts Poets and and the Politics of Excrement." *Maledicta* 3, 1 (1979): 71-84.

Gathungu, Maina. "Okot p'Bitek: Writer, Singer, or Culturizer." In *Standpoints on African Literature*, ed. Chris L. Wanjala. Nairobi: East African Literature Bureau, 1973: 52-55.

Gregory, Michael. "A Theory for Stylistics Exemplified: Donne's 'Holy Sonnet XIV.' " *Language and Style* VII, 2 (1974): 108-18.

Gutwinski, W. *Cohesion in Literary Texts*. The Hague:Mouton, 1976: 26.

Halliday, M. A. K. "Categories in the Theory of Grammar," *Word*, 17 (1961): 241-92.

___. "Lexis as a Linguistic Level." In Bazell: 148-63.

___ and Ruqaiya Hasan. *Cohesion in English*. London: Longman, 1976.

Handscombe, R. J. "George Herbert's 'The Collar': A Study in Frustration." *Language and Style* III, 1(1970): 29- 37.

Heron, G. A. *The Poetry of Okot p'Bitek*. London: Heinemann, 1976.

Heywood, Annemarie. "Modes of Freedom: The Songs of Okot p'Bitek." *Journal of Commonwealth Literature* XV, 1 (1980): 65-83.

Leech, Geoffrey N. *A Linguistic Guide to English Poetry*. London: Longman, 1969.

___. "'This Bread I Break'—Language and Interpretation." In *Linguistics and Literary Style*. Ed. Donald Freeman. New York: Holt, Rinehart and Winston, 1970): 119-28.

lo Liyong, Taban. "Two Songs by Okot p'Bitek: *Song of Prisoner, Song of Malaya.*" *Dhana: Makerere Arts Festival '71* (1971): 59-61.

Luce, Stanford. "Increment and Excrement: Celine and the Language of Hate." *Maledicta* 1, 1 (1977): 43-48.

Marshment, Margaret. "Reply to Atieno-Odhiambo." *Busara* 4, 1 (1972): 63-70.

MacIntosh, Angus. "Patterns and Ranges." *Language* 37 (1961): 325-37.

Ofuani, Ogo A."Okot p'Bitek: A Checklist of Works and Criticisms." Research in African Literatures, 16, 3 (1985): 370-83.

___. "A Stylistic Analysis of Okot p'Bitek's Poetry." Ph.D. thesis, University of Ibadan, May 1985.

___. "The Form and Function of Repetition in Okot p'Bitek's Poetry." *META:Journal of Translators* 34, 4 (1986): 300-13.

___. "Digressions as Discourse Strategy in Okot p'itek' Dramatic Monologue Texts." *Research in African Literatures* 19, 3 (1988): 312-40.

Ogunyemi, Chikwenye Okonjo. "'The Caged Bird Sings' African

Prison Poetry." *Review of International English Literature* 13, 4 (1982): 65-84.

Ojuka, Aloo. "*Two Songs*: A Discussion, 2." *Standpoints on African Literature*, ed. Wanjala.

p'Bitek, Okot. *Song of Lawino*. Nairobi: E.A.P.H., 1966.

___. *Song of Ocol*. Nairobi: E.A.P.H., 1970.

___. *Song of Prisoner*. In *Two Songs*. Nairobi: East African Publishing House, 1971.

Roscoe, Adrian. *Uhuru's Fire:African Literature, East to South.* Cambridge: Cambridge University Press, 1977.

Sinclair, J. McH. "Beginning the Study of Lexis." In Bazell: 410-32.

___. "Taking a Poem to Pieces." In *Essays on Style and Language*. Ed. Roger Fowler. London: Routledge and Kegan Paul, 1966: 68-81.

Traugott, Elizabeth Closs and Mary Louise Pratt. *Linguistics for Students of Literature*. New York: Harcourt Brace Jovanovich, 1980.

Wanambisi, Monica Nalyaka. *Thought and Technique in the Poetry of Okot p'Bitek*. New York: Vantage Press, 1984.

THE STYLISTIC SIGNIFICANCE OF THE GRAPHOLOGICAL STRUCTURE OF TABAN LO LIYONG'S *ANOTHER NIGGER DEAD*

Ogo A. Ofuani

I

Criticisms of Taban lo Liyong's poetic form, particularly in *Another Nigger Dead*, have tended to disregard totally or to gloss over cursorily the peculiar nature of the typographic/graphological shape of his poems, dismissing it as merely incidental and nonfunctional.[1]

Adrian Roscoe, for instance, sees him as "eccentric" and passes off the use of lowercase letters without punctuation as merely "curious."[2] Roscoe does not consider the possibility of lo Liyong using lowercase letters in *Another Nigger Dead* for significant stylistic effects, especially since earlier, in *Frantz Fanon's Uneven Ribs*, the poet had been more conventional in the use of forms that he now openly and constantly deviates from.[3] In the same vein, Timothy Wangusa says that

> In form and expression he is among the very "freest" verse writers, defying all rules and guides. And yet a central preoccupation of his poetry is that of the very nature of poetry.[4]

Recognizing lo Liyong's "preoccupation" with the nature of poetry is one thing, but realizing that it may be responsible for his own practice of the art—and that he expects his practice to be taken seriously—is another. Wangusa does come close to making an evaluation of the stylistic import of lo Liyong's "free" verse but shies away at the last moment.

In his review of the collection, Eldred Jones not only considers thematic issues but ponders the linguistic significance of the medium. His evaluation, however, is marred by the imprecision that characterizes that of other critics. To Jones, the poet's ideas "sometimes straight, sometimes ironic, serious, parallel, contrasting, are massed together to produce a prickly, jumpy effect" in *Another Nigger Dead*.[5] About lo Liyong's graphological deviation, he observes that "for the eye alone the poetry seems to flow, but for everything else . . . lack of punctuation slows down comprehension."[6] This suggests that lo Liyong's nonuse of punctuation is an unnecessary nuisance.

This paper attempts to trace a relationship between lo Liyong's graphological deviation in *Another Nigger Dead* and his conception of poetic art, particularly the significance he attaches to this process.[7] The frequency of this deviation is not accidental. If *Another Nigger Dead* is compared with the earlier volumes, it becomes clearer that graphological deviations are textually discriminant. It therefore devolves on the critic to unambiguously describe their stylistic importance.[8]

II

In the earlier *Frantz Fanon's Uneven Ribs*, lo Liyong was more conventional as far as the canonical aspects of poetic form are concerned. He used stanzas, verse-lines, capitalization, punctuations, and free verse. Many of the poems in *Frantz Fanon's* conform to conventional patterns, but there are a few that are experimental in that they pre-empt the deviational pattern, a technique which becomes the norm in *Another Nigger Dead*.

In the earlier volume lo Liyong had not yet (as it seems) "found his feet" and therefore was unsure about how much to differ. Because he was obsessed with the issue of the appropriate form for his poetic art, volume had the tone of a manifesto. He says, for instance, in "The Best Poets"

1) Ask not
reader
if this be
poetry
or
not
because it isn't. (36)

He re-echoes this thought in "The Throbbing of a Pregnant Cloud" when he observes

2) Times have changed
Prose is poetry now
Perhaps thoughts are now poetry
And weather prattle
Prose (25)[9]

The experimental nature of *Frantz Fanon's Uneven Ribs* is clear if passages 1) and 2) are compared. The first makes one statement in seven lines. Its first six lines are imperative, issuing instructions to the "reader" while the last line offers a reason for the instruction. The conventional features adopted are the typographical practice of beginning a sentence with a capital letter ("Ask"), and line 7 ends with a period. But there are signs of deviations from poetic norms. A sentence in ordinary prose writing is not the same as a sentence in poetry. The poet here has broken up a single sentence into seven lines. Poetry has its own internal conventions of beginning each line with a capital letter. But in lines 2–6, lo Liyong deviates from this practice. Easy to notice also are the freedom in line length and the unrhymed nature of these lines. Example 2) seems more conventional. It is made up of five lines, each beginning with a capital letter. Though no punctuation marks occur at the end of lines 1 and 2, the declarative structure of their clauses makes the reader observe a mandatory pause at the end of each. We also use our predictive knowledge of the English language to realize that lines 3–5 makes two clauses. Technically, the last line should end with a period, but it does not. This stanza is at the end of a section of the poem, and though the absence of a full-stop creates the impression that the line is enjambed, the syntax provides a clue and we stop at the last line. No two poems could be more different than these two.

Still struggling to find a suitable poetic idiom, lo Liyong dismisses poetry because "nobody speaks" it; its thoughts are arranged unnaturally ("Best Poets"). He also dismisses prose as too wordy and time-consuming for the reader. Instead he will offer something in between that looks like poetry but is not: it is a mosaic made up of single thoughts set out simply, as he makes us understand: "I would be dead/before/poetry rule-full I learn" (38). This excerpt contains signs of the type of coinages that abound in *Another Nigger Dead*, as in the compounding of the noun "rule" and the adjective "full" to evolve an adjectival compound "rule-full" which is post-posed (inverted) to give it a poetic tone. This search for the proper form pervades all the serious poems in *Frantz Fanon's Uneven Ribs*. In section IX of "The Throbbing of a Pregnant Cloud," he even thinks that he is a "poetaster," an experimenter, an apprentice merely poeticizing:

> 3) Don't be mad man
> All this is prose
> Plain plain old prose
> You are not suited to poetry
> Perhaps you are a poetaster
> But really man this is prose stuff
> And prose it is man (25)[10]

Elsewhere in the same collection, lo Liyong talks of his "grand folks" being "eloquent" in "neither prose/nor poetry;/rule-wise," because "story-tell they/in words" (38). If his intention is to emulate this story-telling mode he fails, especially in *Another Nigger Dead*, which lacks a clear story-line and has no consistent narrative pattern. But there is a strong urge for him to speak in his poems, in drawing to close in on the colloquial ranges of the English language. This is obvious in the preponderance of the indexical markers of conversational speech we find in his poems. An examination of examples 1) and 3) above reveals the use of the clipped or enclitic forms ("Don't," "isn't,"

"I've," "that's," and so on.); intimacy signals such as the evocative "man" in lines 1, 6, and 7 of passage 3) and in the very familiar tone adopted. Even signs of the "cultural syncretism" he talks about in *The Last Word* are realized linguistically in this passage.[11] Features of Black (American) English "rap" speech forms are realized in various ways: the repetition of the neutral lexical item "man" even in places where it is not necessary (lines 1, 6, 7); the reduplication of an adjective (for emphasis) in line 3 ("plain plain"); the adjectival qualification of an abstract noun that does not normally take a temporal adjective (as in "old prose" in line 3); the use of the word "stuff" in place of "material" (in line 6); even the use of the coordinators "perhaps," "but," and "and," which gives the passage the hesitant rhythm of the "rap" speech that easily characterizes Black English.[12] These features are not restricted to "Best Poets" but also found in "Uncle Tom's Black Humor," from which example 4) is extracted:

4) AUNT JEMIMA she done teach young master how to
be man yes sir she done it yes maam he gone done it (70)

The example has features we may be tempted to classify as pidgin: in line 1, the use of "done" as verbal auxiliary in its past participial form ("done teach"). But in line 2, we see indexical syntactical markers of Black English in "she done it" and "he gone done it" which are not exactly pidginized forms but typical of Black English, especially its "pre-recent past" tense.[13] We also notice the absence of proper punctuation in these two lines. For instance line 2, after "man," should have contained at least two sentences, graphologically marked out as: "Yes Sir, she done it" and "Yes, Ma'am, he gone done it." One wonders, therefore, whether lo Liyong's quest for a purely authentic and personal, idiosyncratic ("Tabanic") poetic form is responsible for this experimentation, in the "breaking of the rules" in some of his most formally different poems in *Frantz Fanon's Uneven Ribs*.

In "Uncle Tom's Black Humor" and in the first part of "To Susan Sontag, with Love," as too in passage 4) above, personal pronouns, line beginnings, and proper nouns are not capitalized and punctuation marks are left out. The only capital letters used are boldface characters in words which are made to visually stand out as some kind of poetic "shouting voice," for emphasis, in the midst of small letters:

> 5) a. because i laboured hard in the fields (5c) . . .
> now i am the best boxer
> mohammed ali or no mohammed ali
> we keep the championships (67)

> b. and master does all the worrying for us miss sarah
> the children **AUNT** and **UNCLE** the
> undergrowth is too
> good to be left i am a permanent parasite . . . (70)

> c. temperance societies filled donations
> teetotalers get grand ovations
> but not alcohol only intoxicate
> **KNOWLEDGE** does
> homer turned keats on
> elgin marbles broke his heart
> poor sweet nightingale (59).

The shouting-voice boldface forms mentioned earlier are "**AUNT**" and "**UNCLE**" in line 2 of 5b), "**KNOWLEDGE**" in line 4 of 5c), and "**AUNT JEMIMA**" of example 4). These texts from "Uncle Tom's Black Humor" and "To Susan Sontag, with Love" sufficiently illustrate how different lo Liyong was trying to be.[14] The most conventional typographical feature overlooked is the beginning of lines with capital letters. In examples 4) and 5), the first-person singular nominative pronoun "I" is not capitalized; names such as "Mohammed Ali," "Miss Sarah," "Homer," and "Keats" are left in small letters. All other graphological signals such as quotation marks to mark direct speech in 4) and the use of commas and full-stops in both 4) and 5) are avoided. This pattern will form a significant feature of *Another Nigger Dead*. The possibility therefore seems to be that this initial experimentation in canonical deviation in *Frantz Fanon's Uneven Ribs*, as far as the quest for a Tabanic poetic voice and form is concerned, seems settled with some finality of purpose and determination in *Another Nigger Dead*. Hence the poet advises us in "The Best Poets": "Call it/What you may/Digestible/bit by bit/my thoughts I present/read on" (38). But the poet's instruction that we "read on" presents difficulties of interpretation without the use of conventional graphological marks.

III

A discussion of the stylistic significance of graphological deviation in *Another Nigger Dead* hinges on the issue of lo Liyong's quest for an appropriate medium and form. He had in the manifesto-like *Frantz Fanon's Uneven Ribs* ("The Best Poets") let us know that the major influences in his poetry are E. E. Cummings and Ezra Pound, two poets he calls "the best artisans," "with eyes for shape of poetry," its architecture, because

> 6) they write
> marv'lously
> modernly
> like me. (39-40)

Both are modern poets with well-known idiosyncrasies.[15]

The modernity lo Liyong mentions in 6) is in line with his philosophy of cultural syncretism. It seems responsible for the eventual shape of all the poems in *Another Nigger Dead*, which are Cummingsian in form, and on occasions even more innovative than Cummings's. Like Cummings, lo Liyong does not use line-initial capitals. He uses small initial letters, irrespective of whether the initial word marks the beginning of a sentence or not. This pattern pervades the collection, with the exception of the dreamlike prose of "Batsiary in Sanigraland," and poems like "bless the african coups" and "the filed man laughed and said" where capitals are used in the midst of small letters (in groups like "**ANOTHER NIGGER DEAD**" and "**POVERTY**" in the two poems, respectively). The foregrounding effect of such boldface type has been discussed earlier. This practice deviates not only from poetic convention but also from the external norm of ordinary language use, from which poetic language is expected to deviate in the first instance. It is true that lo Liyong goes further and differs from Cummings in his total disregard of every other punctuation mark: commas, full-stops, semicolons, apostrophes, exclamations, and so forth.

He is not, however, as morphologically adventurous as Cummings, whose unusual coinages include words like "unwish," "manunkind," and "unself" in the poem "pity the busy monster, manunkind."[16] Cummings does not start the lines of that poem with capital letters but does use the punctuation marks that lo Liyong avoids. Both poets exhibit about the same degree of eccentricity and this aspect of lo Liyong's poetic form seems to have been responsible for the evolution of what Wanjala has referred to as "the Tabanic genre," a poetic form he dismisses too easily as "undisciplined."[17] But in spite of Wanjala's assessment, we discern some order, some cohesion, in the "disordered" pattern to allow lo Liyong the credit of conscious artistry. This feature of his art is significant because it has certain stylistic effects (to be discussed shortly) despite the fact that the poems, at first glance, look like exercises for punctuation practice:

7) a. free lance critics circumscribe perimeters
   consign to gehenna and posterity
   what an elusive age
   no homer
   prize distributed (21)

8) b. the african coup is an old beast
   insecure under rugs
   youngsters with short memory
   whereas the future (23)
   c. i dont drink with harry
   call me no misanthrope father saw my loneliness
   gave me brothers to keep (44)
   d. not pride but glorification of my maker
   makes me use my talents for what they are worth
   ive clowned enough (44)

These poems exhibit some of lo Liyong's eccentricities, including the nonuse of capital letters for proper nouns and for the first-person-singular pronoun: "gehenna" (Gehenna), "homer" (Homer), "african" (African), "harry" (Harry), and "i" (I); the neglect of periods at the end of lines or sentences; the lack of apostrophe marks in numerous contracted, clipped colloquial forms such as "dont (don't), "ive" (I've), "wheres" (where's), and so forth. Such deviations abound in the collection.

IV

This rejection of graphological conventions in *Another Nigger Dead* reflects lo Liyong's conception of poetic form. He seems to see his poems, though written, to be primarily spoken. Therefore, there is no need to obey poetic conventions. This attempt to reproduce the illusion of speech could be responsible for the ultimate graphological structure of these poems. If the thoughts of conventional poetry are unnaturally arranged and prose is too wordy and time-consuming for the reader, could this new pattern not be lo Liyong's compromise? Does he see the structural patterning of sentences in English as merely formal, unrealizable, abstract, and thereby unnecessary in poetry, the actually realized pattern being utterances, strand so on.hes of sound-meaning relations where punctuation marks are artificial and unimportant?

Lo Liyong does not provide an answer, but our point is that these graphological deviations are not merely cosmetic. If the poet intends his poems "be read as if spoken,"[18] without providing the graphic signals that act as phonological cues for reading, then the options for interpretations are left open to the reader. In some of the poems, the reader can successfully use his intuitive knowledge of the expected patterns of English to predict where the punctuation marks should be put to give a "correct" reading to the poems. Such predictive powers, which can be applied to 4), 5), and 7), for instance, include our recognition of interrogative patterns and the use of the appropriate intonational cues irrespective of lack of punctuation. This is also exemplified by 8):

8) a. then the filed man laughed the last laugh and said
   didn't i tell you my people
   with good advice from the east
   we can triumph over all our difficulties (9)
   b. lets go back to land
   and leave the city to whom (17)
   c. because i have gray hair
   why assume acts of ages
   wisdom of youth should mellow
   in mind or time (29)

In these examples from *Another Nigger Dead*, we can easily predict the interrogative structures in line 2 of 8a) ("didn't i tell you . . . "), line 2 of 8b) ("leave the city to whom"), and line 2 of 8c) ("why assume . . . "). In 8a), for instance, we also notice that the narrator reports the exact speech of "the filed man," but in Free Direct Speech (FDS).19 In spite of the introductory clause "the filed man . . . and said," with the verb of saying in the past, lines 2–4 are that man's exact words. But the quotation marks are missing, and lines 2–4 are not reported because the pronoun in line 2 is still the first-person singular "I" instead of "his," and "we" in line 4 remains in place of "they." The expected pronominal change that accompanies reported speech is missing. A knowledge of the system of the English language aids our predictive ability. But in some poems it may not be so easy to predict, at initial reading, the intended structure, as the poet may have intended to be ambiguous.

One kind of ambiguity caused by the above deviations is lexical. What would normally be interpreted as more than a word may, because of its present homographic shape, be given an equally homophonic reading. The poem "denied the lives of cats" (26) provides a good example:

9) denied the lives of cats
let the many grow through me
am only a weak vessel
cant stand a split

It is possible to give a dual interpretation to the homographic and homophonic "cant" in line 4. It can be interpreted as "can't," the enclitic colloquial form of the negative modal auxiliary "cannot" in which mood (lack of tolerance) is suggested; or as "cant," a lexical verb meaning "to turn on the edge or corner; to lift or toss suddenly," in which case it properly collocates with "vessel" (ship) and "split" in lines 3 and 4: "am only a weak vessel/cant stand a split." This interpretation is likely if we allow that the poet is being equivocal. The second "cant," because it is homophonic with the first, should be taken as a pun. This second reading may require the aid of juncture pauses between "cant" and "stand" and between "stand" and "a split" in line 4.

The poem "there goes my son" (11) provides another good example of the type of ambiguity caused by graphological deviations. A cursory reading may leave the impression that lo Liyong is exhorting bourgeois qualities. But the first four lines of the poem indirectly convey an ironic exhortative tone. It manifests itself not through the tone of the persona but through the contrast between what is expected by the poor, trampled people and what the persona expects:

> 10) there goes my son
> a bright lad doing well at school
> my heart flows with honey when people remark
> hell be as successful as his daddy

There is an unmistakable conspiratorial tone, giving the impression that the persona expects the reader to take his side. But the unpunctuated "hell" in line 4 is ambiguous. The first urge is to read the form visually as "hell" (the biblical inferno, which should collocate with Satan/Devil). But the absurdity of "hell," its dislocation in the context of "successful" (syntagmatically) immediately warns that either there is a misreading or a poetic exploitation of sectional restrictions (as an instance of poetic license). This reading has a further possibility which, though far-fand so on.hed, finds support in the rest of the poem. The poet, without using punctuation, uses direct speech with some lines of the poem as narrative introductory clauses. The line "hell be as successful as his daddy" is clearly what "people remark" (in line 3), but as in 8a) above this is FDS. Since punctuation marks are missing, line 4 could be read as follows (that is, if the marks are added at the level of the whole line): "Hell! Be as successful as his daddy!," where we assume that "hell" is being uttered by the exasperated and unsuccessful "people." The poem also explores the division between the haves and have-nots as a potential source of social strife. The declarative tone of this reconstructed fourth line is borne out in other lines in the poem, each preceded by an introductory clause:

> i) others will say/his father was the best hunter
>   with spears (5-6)
> ii) others will envy/brought up well at home (8-9)

But even if line 4 is read as "he'll" (the contracted form of "he will"), it still registers the contrast between the young man and his father on one side against the adverse situation of those not as successful, the "people," the "others" of the poem who "envy" the youngster for his education and ill-gotten wealth. But that is if the situation is viewed from the perspective of the narrator.

The irony in the poem (and the source of lo Liyong's satire) lies in the fact that the persona himself re-echoes (in his self-righteousness) the criticisms made against his son and his corrupt ways: "but his pens sign fat cheques" (line 7). He refers to the careful process of looting the people's resources with the aid of the "pen" rather than through some overt methods that could be easily detected and punished. The lexico-phonological ambiguity of line 4 is also re-enacted in the last line: "hence my sons an elect." The graphic shape of the line suggests at least two readings. There are no clues to any one appropriate interpretation.

The possible readings are, first, "my sons, an elect"—in which case "sons" is read as plural and the addition of the comma after "sons" suggests that "elect" relates anaphorically to "selection" in the penultimate line such that his sons form an "elect" (a select group). The addition of the comma will, therefore, give the four items (after the narrator's concluding "hence") the status of two noun groups in apposition, with "an elect" postmodifying "sons" (or, alternatively, as an instance of the compression of a declarative clause in which the copula is omitted: "my sons are an elect"). The second reading will be "my son's an elect," in which case one son is involved (and rightly so if we relate this line to the first line where reference is made to a singular "my-son," also called "a bright lad"). The apostrophe mark added to "sons" leaves us with a noun group + verb (equative copula) construction (instead of the plural "sons"), followed immediately by the second noun group acting as subject complement: "my son is an elect." The present simple copula "is" is thus in its contracted form as "my son's an elect."

The interpretation given to "elect" will remain the same in both cases but has greater force if only one son forms "an elect" in the second reading. The difference in effect will therefore be one of degree. The masses are still the worse off for being neglected and exploited. The satiric effect is biting, and the social criticism strong, irrespective of the reading given to the line since "an elect" is significant. It is the phrase that carries the social comment of the poem, and the satire is in the exposure of a situation where the few ("son" or "sons") are elitist "selected" or separated from the many for luxury, education, and wealth. The many suffer; they can only complain. Their complacency is also a point against them. Hence the indifference of the speaker (or lo Liyong?). The question that we ask, and the poet seems to intend that we ask, is "Are the many justified in their envy?," in spite of the levity with which the persona narrates the situation. In the answer lies the comment.

Of significance too is the layout of the poems in stanzas. It is our expectation that the beginnings and ends of lines of poetry do not occur at the margins of the page, but wherever the poet means them to occur, with the result that a poem may have irregular margins. In the same way, breaks in the thematic progress of a poem are indicated not by indentations, but spacing, and one speaks of *stanzas*, not *paragraphs*.[20] In poetry, these patterns are normal, expected, but deviant in the sense that they deviate from the norms of ordinary language typographic practice.

The typographical line of poetry, like the typographical stanza, is "a unit which is not paralleled in non-poetic varieties of English; it is independent of, and capable of interacting with, the standard units of punctuation. This interaction is a special communicative resource of poetry."[21] In this sense, we can say that most of the poems in *Another Nigger Dead* are conventional. They are arranged in stanzas, particularly the longer poems at the beginning and end of the collection. But some internal deviance from this poetic convention is noticed in the regularity and length of these stanzas from one poem to another. The two long poems that begin and end the collection are of irregular lengths and arrangements. The other poems are single stanzas of varying lengths and patterns. But they are all so textually cohesive, especially in the repeated use of the "I" (and all its other variants), that one shares Roscoe's assessment that "every stanza is listed as a poem,"[22] suggesting that the collection is a single poem, a single experience (made up of different stages of meditations), Taban lo Liyong's. In between the two long poems are scattered recollections of the poet on numerous subjects. They come quickly, as if the poet hurriedly set them down on paper before he forgot.[23] This is bolstered by the epigrammatic, proverb-like quality of these single-stanza poems, which makes them easy to remember. The grammatical structure of these short-stanza poems also aids in highlighting this facility. The extraordinary cohesiveness of the syntactic structure—repetition of clauses of the same structure; repetition of noun groups that have equal number of syllables; repetition of verb types, especially in their morphological shapes; the use of the personal pronoun "I" ties the experiences in all the poems to a single personage—makes them so memorable and emphatic that the epigrammatic quality mentioned above is given prominence.

An analysis of the syntactic structure of the four-line poem "building a life philosophy" (36) will suffice as illustration:

11) building a life philosophy
through juggling with words
fashioning home truths
by exploring the obscure

The persona here assumes some exophoric knowledge on the part of the reader. Therefore, he does not supply the grammatical subject(s) of the main verbs in lines 1 and 3. This makes the experience almost universal since the theme of the poem (futility in literary creativity?) may apply equally to both poet-speaker and to the reader. With the omission of the subject, we have two parallel, almost balanced nonfinite participle clauses of the PCA (Predicator, Complement, Adjunct)[24] declarative pattern (the PCA would have been imperative but for the *-ing* form of the verbs). The first two lines make up one clause and the last two lines another. They are paratactic in the sense that unless the deleted subjected is implied, the clauses are left detached, more so as the verbal auxiliary, before the *-ing* participle verbs, is deleted too. At the clause level, the Predicator is made up of verbs of the *-ing* present progressive form ("building," "fashioning"), indicating that the actions are ongoing. The direct complements of the verbs, the C component at initial level of delicacy (clause analysis), are made up of two noun groups of almost the same structure, without qualifiers: "a life philosophy" (m m H), "home truths" (m H).[25] The Adjunct

(A) components are composed of prepositional phrases made up of a preposition acting as a connective ("through," "by") and the completive elements which are rank-shifted clauses of PA and PC structures, respectively ("juggling with words," "exploring the obscure"). At another level of delicacy, the A components contain the same -*ing* participle verbs' ("juggling," "exploring"), while the other parts contain nominals performing different functions.

There is thus a balance in terms of the constituent structure at any one level of delicacy, and this kind of regularity in the repetition of structures characterizes the poems in *Another Nigger Dead*. Consequently, there is a great deal of textual cohesion in these rather simple paratactic structures, not only at the individual poem level but also at the level of all the poems taken as a single text. As I said before, this gives them an easy-to-remember facility.

But generally—and unlike the poems of fellow Ugandans[26] Okot p'Bitek, Joseph Buruga, and Okello Oculi—*Another Nigger Dead* has no sustained narrative line. All we have is a collection of poems that relate what the speaker thinks, remembers, wishes, imagines, fantasizes. The first-person singular ("I," "me," "my," "mine") is used throughout to identify a single voice and a single consciousness. Therefore the tendency is to want to see the collection as a dramatic monologue unified as a psychological continuity that offers itself as one man's consciousness ("i know some who maintain it does not exist;" "didn't i tell you my people;" "there goes my son;" "i was weaned;" and so on). Its point of view is situated within an individual's consciousness, lo Liyong's, and this is textually specified with actual mention of lo Liyong's name: "I am also called Taban/Very near to Caliban . . . " (*Frantz Fanon's Uneven Ribs* [41]); "me i said to myself taban cool it baby . . . " (*Another Nigger Dead* [57]). Taban lo Liyong's poetry therefore differs markedly as a genre from the song tradition of Okot p'Bitek and his followers.[27]

V

Taban lo Liyong deliberately uses graphological deviation to effect phonological and/or semantic ambiguities. In such ambiguities, as we have seen, a combination of phonological, structural, and semantic clues rather than straightforward graphic ones are used as disambiguators. The interpretations we can consequently give to them are not just merely conjectural or speculative, but very likely and plausible. They are intended to be stylistically significant.

The emphasis on the graphological deviation patterns of *Another Nigger Dead* and their total significance is not intended to imply that they are the only significant deviations in this deceptively simple collection of poems. We could highlight lexical collocational deviations in "the filed man laughed and said" (8) that remind one of Dylan Thomas's "a grief ago." Deviant morphology is also poetically exploited in coinages involving unusual uses of the abstract noun suffix *-ness* to derive possible nouns from adjectives (such as "dunderheadedness") or even unlikely ones like "grabiousness" in the poem "i walked among men in america for a year without a human soul to solace me" (54)—another poem that is reminiscent of Cummings' coinages or the style of William Carlos Williams. This discussion does not, however, rule out the fact that a complex interrelationship exists between all of them. The poet's peculiar use of the graphological mode is discussed because it has so often been neglected in typical literary discussions.

Taban lo Liyong's poetic form is not merely "curious" or incidental but deliberate and conscious. Its use of free verse and lowercase letters and its neglect of punctuation marks are intended to be significant; hence, they are foregrounded. His is not deviation for deviation's sake but conscious art intended for the kind of purposes highlighted above, especially the ambiguity in graphic interpretation which the present typographic shape of the poems yields. A "normal" poetic form would have been too normal and would not have yielded the kind of stylistic effect yielded by this apparently deviant form. However, since these deviations have become the rule rather than the exception in *Another Nigger Dead*, it would be appropriate to conclude that they acquire a degree of normalcy which is internal to the collection, a normalcy that puts them in a class of their own as poetry of direct utterance, an escape from the stylized ornamentation and restrictiveness of conventional marks.

UNIVERSITY OF BENIN—NIGERIA

Notes

1. Prominent among them are Eldred E. Jones, "Taban lo Liyong: Review," *African Literature Today* 6 (1973): 176-77; Ismael R. Mbise. "The Struggle for Identity in Selected East African Literature and Art," Diss. University of York, Toronto, 1979; Adrian Roscoe, *Uhuru's Fire: African Literature East to South* (Cambridge: Cambridge University Press, 1977); Satoru Tsuchiya, "Modern East African Literature: Erom Uhuru to Harambee," *World Literature Today* 52.4 (1978): 569-74; Timothy Wangusa, "East African Poetry." *African Literature Today* 6 (1973): 46-53; and Chris L. Wanjala, "The Tabanic Genre," Busara 3.4 (1971): 23-29.
2. Roscoe, 114
3. In this paper, reference will be made to the African Writers Series editions of Taban lo Liyong's texts: *Frantz Fanon's Uneven Ribs* (London: Heinemann, 1971) and *Another Nigger Dead* (London: Heinemann 1972). All page references to these works will be interpolated within the texts.
4. Wangusa, 49.
5. Jones, 177.
6. Jones, 177.
7. Ken L. Goodwin, "Taban lo Liyong," in his *Understanding African Poetry: A Study of Ten Poets* (London: Heinemann Educational Books, 1982): 78-92, discusses lo Liyong's conception of his poetic art but is silent about the experimental nature and poetic significance of the graphological shape of the poems.
8. In his lighthearted discussion of the "basic anatomy" of East African writing, Bernth Lindfors presents a short but very insightful analysis of lo Liyong's poetry. See Lindfors, "A Basic Anatomy of East African Literature," in *Design and Intent in African Literature.* ed. David Dorsey, Phanuel A. Egejuru, and Stephen Arnold (Washington: African Literature Association and Three Continents Press, 1982): 51-57. He notes that lo Liyong "has experimented with various types of fiction, poetry, essay and aphorisms" (52) and, unlike most other critics, concludes that "his message is less important than the medium" (53).
9. "The Throbbing of a Pregnant Cloud" is one of the poems in

Frantz Fanon's in which lo Liyong expresses at length the difficulties he encountered as he struggled for the appropriate language to say what he wants in an effective way.

10. Taban lo Liyong made this point too in his interview with Heinz Freidberger. He pointed out that by training he was a prose writer. See *Cultural Events in Africa* 57 (London: Transcription Center, 1969): I-III.
11. In *The Last Word* (Nairobi: East African Publishing House, 1969), lo Liyong propounds a theory of cultural permutation he calls "cultural syncretism." He wants to create a literary "superman" by mixing traditions and technique. He defines cultural syncretism as "a synthesis and a metamorphosis—the order of things to come. It assimilates and it discriminates, it picks, it grabs, it carries on" (206).
12. See J. A. Harrison. "Negro English," in *Perspectives on Black English*, ed. John Dillard (The Hague: Mouton. 1975): 143-95.
13. Joan G. Fickett, "Ain't, Not, and Don't in Black English," in *Perspectives on Black English*: 86-90.
14. This urge to be different has also been identified in lo Liyong's approach to the short story. See F. Odun Balogun, "Taban lo Liyong's *Fixions*: A Study in the Absurd," *Journal of the Literary Society of Nigeria* 2 (1982): 25-35: and Elizabeth Knight, "Aspects of Taban lo Liyong's Narrative Art," *African Literature Today* 12 (1982): 104-17.
15. One of such idiosyncrasies which lo Liyong has adopted, as is evident from the self-praise in text (6), is that "like Ezra Pound, he unashamedly makes poetry out of his own emotional life" (Goodwin: 90).
16. E. E. Cummings, *Complete Poems*, 1913-1962 (New York: Harcourt, Brace, Jovanovich, 1972), 554.
17. Wanjala, 29.
18. Michael J. Gregory, "Aspects of Varieties Differentiation," *Journal of Linguistics* 3.2 (1967): 177-98.
19. Geoffrey N. Leech and M. H. Short, *Style in Fiction: A Linguistic Introduction to English Fictional Prose* (London and New York: Longman, 1981).
20. For a full discussion of the canonical conventions of poetry, see S. R. Levin, "Internal and External Deviation in Poetry," *Word* 12 (1965): 225-37.
21. Leech, *A Linguistic Guide to English Poetry* (London: Longman,

1969): 47.
22. Roscoe, 130.
23. Lo Liyong talks about the process of his poetic composition in *The Last Word*: I walked to my apartment, threw my suitcase on the bed and sat next to it. I then held my big head between my powerful hands. I squeezed it, and squeezed it hard, till it thought. When thoughts came, they poured like tropical rain: big and fast. I pulled out a pencil and wrote fast, capturing every drop of thought. Quoted by Roscoe (31), who aptly described this style as "a confessional strain, a stream-of-conscious-tell-it-all mode suggesting an honest mind's encounter with a myriad viewpoints" (115).
24. The linguistic model used here is that of Halliday, and the terms *Subject, Predicator, Complement,* and *Adjunct* are as used in his "Categories in the Theory of Grammar," *Word* 17 (1971): 241-92. The terms are represented in linear order as S., P., C., A.
25. In the grammar, the noun is composed of three main constituents: *modifier* (m), *Head* (H) and *qualifier* (q). The *Head* is the obligatory constituent: the *modifier* and *qualifier* are optional.
26. Though lo Liyong was born in Uganda and is a Lwo like Okot p'Bitek, he "now states himself to be Sudanese." See Elizabeth Knight, J. Bardolph, and Angus Calder, "A Bibliography of East African Literature in English, 1964-1981, *Journal of Commonwealth Literature* 17.1 (1982): 182.
27. Four poems in lo Liyong's *Frantz Fanon's* are in the tradition of Okot p'Bitek: the three dramatic monologues "Uncle Tom's Black Humor" (66-71), "The Marriage of Black and White," (96-111), and "Student's Lament" (117-46); and the short conversational narrative "Telephone Conversation Number Two" (72-73). But lo Liyong's poems contain a much wider range of reference and of ideas than p'Bitek's, though lacking his musical quality.

Works Cited

Balogun, F. Odun. "Taban lo Liyong's *Fixions:* A Study in the Absurd," *Journal of the Literary Society of Nigeria* 2 (1982): 25-35.
Cummings, E. E. *Complete Poems,* 1913-1962 (New York: Harcourt,

Brace, Jovanovich, 1972.
Dillard, John (ed.) *Perspectives on Black English*. (The Hague: Mouton. 1975).
Dorsey, David, Panuel A. Egejuru, and Stephen Arnold (eds.) *Design and Intent in African Literature*. Washington: African Literature Association and Three Continents Press, 1982.
Fickett, Joan, G. "Ain't, Not, and Don't in Black English," in Dillard, 86-90.
Freidberger, Heinz. *Cultural Events in Africa* 57 (London: Transcription Center, 1969): I-III.
Goodwin, Ken L. "Taban lo Liyong," in his *Understanding African Poetry: A Study of Ten Poets* (London: Heinemann Educational Books, 1982): 78-92.18.
Gregory, Michael J. "Aspects of Varieties Differentiation," *Journal of Linguistics* 3.2 (1967): 177-98.
Harrison. J. A. "Negro English," in *Dillard*, 143-195.
Jones, Eldred E. "Taban lo Liyong: Review," *African Literature Today* 6 (1973): 176-77.
Knight, Elizabeth. "Aspects of Taban lo Liyong's Narrative Art," *African Literature Today* 12 (1982): 104-17.
Leech, Geoffrey N. *A Linguistic Guide to English Poetry* (London: Longman, 1969): 47.
—, and M. H. Short, *Style in Fiction: A Linguistic Introduction to English Fictional Prose* (London and New York: Longman, 1981).
Levin, S.R. "Internal and External Deviation in Poetry," *Word* 12 (1965): 225-37.
Lindfors, Bernth. "A Basic Anatomy of East African Literature," in Dorsey et al.
Liyong, Taban lo. *Frantz Fanon's Uneven Ribs*. The African Writers Series. (London:Heinemann, 1971).
—, *Another Nigger Dead*. The African Writers Series editions (London: Heinemann, 1972).
Mbise, Ismael R. "The Struggle for Identity in Selected East African Literature and Art." Diss. York University, Toronto, 1979.
Roscoe, Adrian. *Uhuru's Fire: African Literature East to South* (Cambridge: Cambridge University Press, 1977).
Tsuchiya, Satoru ."Modern East African Literature: Erom Uhuru to Harambee," *World Literature Today* 52.4 (1978): 569-74.
Wangusa, Timothy. "East African Poetry." *African Literature Today* 6

(1973): 46-53.
Wanjala, Chris L. "The Tabanic Genre," *Busara* 3.4 (1971): 23-29.

TABAN LO LIYONG'S *THE UNIFORMED MAN*:
A RECONSTRUCTIVIST AND METAFICTIONAL PARODY OF MODERNISM

F. Odun Balogun

The iconclastic postmodernist experimentations in Taban lo Liyong's short-story collection *The Uniformed Man* (1971) can easily upset the reader who prefers the realistic mode of writing. Taban lo Liyong disturbs and disorients this class of readers with his confident assertive ego; his frank treatment of subject matter; his irreverence toward traditional religious beliefs, philosophies, literary luminaries, critics and the establishment; his parodies of ostentatious modernist erudition; and the liberty he takes with his intrusive and digressive narrative technique, which produces fragments and collages rather than smooth chronological narrations.

Taban, a graduate of the University of Iowa Writers Workshop, admits to the charge that his works are "arbitrary or nonconformist," but he asks:

> So what? Isn't each writer an arbitrary maker, ordering or reordering the world? Isn't each reader a naturalized subject who submits to each author's dictatorship at his own peril and continues the relationship as long as it is mutually beneficial? (lo Liyong 1969:8)

Moreover, he believes that "writers are to be more knowledgeable than the readers and should be ahead in intellectual leadership" (79). A reading of Taban's books of essays, poetry collections, and prose works will convince even the most biased reader that he is either a genius or one who has worked exceptionally hard to maintain intellectual leadership of his audience. His erudition infuses his writings with a confident, proud ego that one of his most hostile critics agrees is "an egoism of the enlightened individual" (Nazareth 1978:38).

A disturbing frankness is the hallmark of *The Uniformed Man*. This frankness is evident in his treatment of sex, but even when he describes the sex act with graphic vividness, such as in the following passage, he is casual and ironic, not pornographic:

> I went in, found her behind the door and as soon as I was in, the door closed, she opened her thighs wide, my middle was trapped between them, and four minutes passed for me in patty-cake, patty-cake, patty-cake ... and a crowning oblivion. (lo Liyong 1971:13)

The frankness, casualness, and irony with which Taban describes his experience as a young boy trapped by a sexually starved older girl in the village, would not surprise readers familiar with the treatment of sex in modernist and post-modernist Western fiction. In Ronald Sukenick's "The Death of the Novel," (1969), for example, sex is not only casually and frankly discussed, but presented in a mood of cynicism and artistic self-conscious exhibitionism critical of public taste:

> Meanwhile my chief concern is whether I'm going to be able to sell this unprecedented example of formlessness. How can you sell a current in a river? Maybe I better put my editor into it, he's a terrific editor, maybe that'll do the trick. A few more plugs like that and he won't be able to afford not to publish it. Or how about a little sex, that's the ticket. That's what this needs. A little sex. Okay, a little sex. (49)

And true to his promise, there was more than enough sex in the rest of the story.

There is good reason to compare Taban with contemporary Western avant-garde writers. It is not simply because he studied at the University of Iowa's Writers Workshop in the 1960s, but because he consciously promotes a philosophy of "Synthesism":

> John Pepper Clark is simply adopting a Greek technique for use on a work in hand. There is no harm in that. In fact, we need more Greek, English, and so on., ways of doing things adopted by Africans.... It is ridiculous to bar an African from adopting foreign techniques.... It is not so much the technique as the personal style the artist has, his personal mark with which he stamps his works which is important. (lo Liyong 1969:53; see also 79, 132)

In defending Clark, Taban is indirectly defending himself, for his works reveal a consciousness of the techniques of avant-garde experimentations in Western fiction. These techniques, however, are distinctly stamped with Taban's synthesizing personal mark in *The Uniformed Man*. Taban has moved far ahead of Raymond Federman's proposal that new fiction be "deliberately illogical, irrational, unrealistic, non sequitur, and incoherent" into what Thomas LeClair describes as "the next stage forward, synthesizing experimental forms, employing technical innovations to defamiliarize the materials of realistic fiction and not just the literary text" (Le Clair 1982:260). LeClair might equally have been describing the method and objective of Taban's fiction when he defines the style of American reconstructivist "avant-garde of mastery" whose "intent is transformation—of the work and of the reader, who is solicited, confuted, and released into a new system of ideas" (262).

Like the reconstructivists, Taban keeps "disorienting and reorienting" his reader in order "to first disturb, then revise the reader's notion of his culture" (265). For instance, Taban is anxious for the African to get rid of his negritudist misconception of innate humanity, and hence he shows in The Uniformed Man that all human beings are essentially violent and inhumane in nature. The only way Africans can come to grips with the violence of slavery, colonialism, and neocolonialism is to understand it. The African must also be freed from his slavish attachment to what Taban calls African "medieval past" (1973: 80), as well as from acquired Western philosophies, beliefs, and myths, if he is to compete successfully in the world of advanced technology. It is for this reason that The Uniformed Man is full of irreverence toward especially European classical philosophers and major characters in Christian mythology. To begin with, he insists in The Uniformed Man that "the gods were imaginary, in the first place" and "have remained imaginary ever since" (58). The myth of the immaculate conception is ridiculed (55), Jesus is presented as an impotent (22) bastard (53), and Christ's famous sayings are twisted around: "Dirty hands do not harm us as much as what comes from inside a man" (43); and in *Thirteen Offensives* (1973) he says, "Blessed are the poor if they work hard to get rich" (91).

Taban's attitude to Christianity is the iconoclastic posture of a messiah and not the impiety of an irreverent nature, for he tells us that once "when I toured Europe I saw the spires, I saw massive crosses and other symbols in front and inside the churches. These cried out for my spiritual responses, stimulated me, and I gave of whatever piety I had" (lo Liyong 1969:51). His attitude is ideologically and politically motivated for he also says that "the good news Jesus of Nazareth brought had been used by his priests to trample down on the black man" (lo Liyong 1973:118). Earlier he had explained:

> Christianity is "the servants" religion, as Friedrich Nietzsche spent all his life telling the world. When it was introduced into Africa, the bulk of the population was serving one king or one war-leader or another; so Christianity was quickly embraced because it sang the same humility, the same self-negation, the same lack of ambition for things that really matter because they were difficult to attain; it is the religion of despair, the special diet of the week. (2:81-82)

Taban sums up the ideological impulse for his Christian impiety this way: "Whoever gives man dignity is called Messiah. In that context Nkrumah, our Redeemer, our Osagyefo, is greater than Christ"(lo Liyong 1971:13). Thus, Taban is not merely making a gratuitous modernist exhibitionist gesture by his irreverence but is seriously engaged in reassessing religious and philosophical beliefs and in subjecting his readers whom he rough handles to the same process of reassessment.

Thus, Taban lo Liyong is not only a reconstructivist but also a philosophically concerned metafictionist.[1] This is evident on the pages of *The Uniformed Man*, where he is constantly holding conversation with, and taking to task, Plato, Aristotle,

Socrates, Locke, Buddha, Christ, and others. His witty aphorisms and epigrams reflect his philosophical turn of mind and reveal his spirited, ongoing argument with past philosophers:

> Nature withstands patiently; man rushes, slips and falls.
> Ubi Sunt? (lo Liyong 1971:24)

If you want to have conscience, learn a lot of prohibitive things which are contrary to the ways of nature. Sure enough you will find yourself following nature and being remonstrated by previous "learning" for your waywardness. That is what they call conscience—learning the unnatural and the impossible and failing as surely as could be predicted, then blaming yourself for the failure. (28)

> The truth is: nobody is a failure if he does not regret. (33)
> You are no sooner born than you are approaching death. (41)
> An alcoholic and a prostitute travel fast in the path of pleasures, so says Aristotle. Add to that a rider: the prostitute will derive catharsis and a purgation of the over-riding emotions.... (64)

The impact of these quotations is fully comprehended only in their integrated context. The last quotation, for instance, continues an argument about the nature of art involving Horace, Castelvetro, Sir Philip Sidney, Wilde, Plato, Shakespeare, and Teiresias.

A critic complains that Taban's "literary echoes do not reverberate with meaning" as those of other writers such as T. S. Eliot (Nazareth 1978:39). What the critic fails to observe is that while Taban delights in the use of modernist and postmodernist techniques, he is usually parodying these same techniques.

In *The Uniformed Man* Taban reveals his ironic attitude to the techniques he uses in at least two ways. First of all, he overuses these techniques and beats them to death. This is the case with the myriad appearances of literary, philosophical, and political allusions used in parody of the ostentatious erudition of the modernists. It is also the case with the overfrequent use of parenthetical and direct digressions, some of which are epical in their extensiveness. Here also is the reason for the superfluity in the use of the collage technique. No story in the collection is narrated in a chronological, uninterrupted manner. A typical story no sooner begins than it is interrupted by a seemingly unrelated digression that is followed by many more seemingly unrelated digressions. In the end, however, the story turns out a united whole with every one of the digressive fragments playing a vital role in advancing the central thesis of the story.

If we understand, for example, that "Prescription for Idleness" is about different levels of violence and how people cope with them, then we can appreciate the relevance of the digressive fragment that relates the love story of the Hare and the Cock for Miss Gazelle, which is recounted by Brother Tortoise. The zoo and prison are obvious symbols of violence; and while some like the robber who breaks jail resist violence through physical action, others cope with it intellectually as does Brother Tortoise with his escapist love story; while yet a third group is like the despicable Cock who not only accepts the violence visited on him from the outside but also perpetrates self-inflicted violence out of stupidity and greed and because of the deceit and selfishness of society.

There is, however, a subtle problem here: critics such as Elizabeth Knight (1982:104-07), who fail to perceive the relevance of the fragments to the main plot, believe that lo Liyong has lost control over his story. However, when we do recognize the unity between the story and the fragments, we are apt to forget that the overwhelming use of the digressive fragments is a parody of the modernist technique of the collage.

The second way we know that lo Liyong is parodying his modernist technique is his use of footnotes, N.B.s, and explanatory parenthetical digressions that confuse rather than shed light. A typical example is the footnote on "Mount Abora" on page 21. Other times, as in the paragraph of penultimate "Herolette," we are given a summing-up that is in fact the beginning of a new digression from the story. This method has been canonized in *Fixions* in the story titled "Tombe 'Gworong's Own Story" (see Balogun 1984). Also the technique of the "minimal story" is reduced to absurdity in the do-it-yourself story, "Project X," where we have only the skeletal plan for a story rather than the story itself. This is an over-extension of the modernist practice of involving the reader in the creative process. Here is all that is contained in the tantalizing story, which reveals perhaps the farthest a writer can possibly go in inviting readers' participation in the process of writing:

> Project X
> Two enemies meet on the street. They pass each other going in opposite directions.
> The various changing shapes of their faces.
> The plot for the next encounter.
> You may also use: a boy and a beautiful girl;
>   a criminal and a policeman;
>   a would-be robber and a banker
>   lugging a sack of gold. (36)

Taban's relationship with his reader reveals an instance of the convergence and synthesis of two different literary sources. He avails himself of the advantage of the rapport between audience and raconteur typical of oral performance by establishing familiarity with his reader, whom he often addresses directly as "Madam" and "Sir" in "A Prescription for Idleness." He frequently interrupts his story to address the reader with asides such as these:

> I will research into that. (17)
> I wonder if some critics will be so unfair to me as the barbarous *Quarterly* was to Keats.... It would be good to find
>   out. (23)
> Unlike other authors, I show you where my sympathies
>   lie. (43)
> (We don't know many curses, if you know any choice ones,
>   indulge yourself). (56)

Sometimes Taban moves from respectful author-reader familiarity to a parody of modernist disrespectful overfamiliarity. Such is the case when he uses expletives (35, 64) or when he commands the reader, saying: "Do this for me, will you? Say A aloud now say B..." (41). He is purposely taunting, trying the reader's patience, when in the last story he devotes a lot of space (60-61) to describing the familiar mechanism of bicycles. Until the reader realizes he is being called upon by this seemingly insulting description to draw similarities between the inhuman mechanism of the bicycle and the robotism of the protagonist who is a soldier, the reader feels his intelligence is being insulted. Also, very often Taban carries on self-editing in the process of telling his story and, understandably, this is not agreeable to some readers who feel they are being taken for a ride: "The trucks were many; I have already said that" (9); "Then there was, there were, those vying sisters—Martha and Mary" (22); "It was good he lost it—the sight—I mean, afterwards" (64). Taban's self-consciousness as an artist is also a product of both his modernist consciousness and attachment to folklore. To the extent that he is conscious of the creative process and wants to deliver his text as effectively as possible, he is like the self-conscious oral raconteur. When, however, Taban purposely reveals his technique as narrator, he is being modernist.

Peter Nazareth (1978) says that "Taban the folklorist is genuinely creative" (45; also 35). In the effort to achieve a beautiful narration, Taban borrows heavily from folklore. Knight has correctly observed that Taban does not only borrow from folklore and give his fables modern setting, but also parodies the folklore-borrowed techniques (104-05, 108). Taban's fables usually exhibit a folkloric mixture of reality and fantasy and often have morals that are pointed and obvious in *Fixions* but less so in *The Uniformed Man*. As in *Fixions*, the poetic beauty of *The Uniformed Man* has a largely folkloric origin. The use of a song-like poetic refrain is partly what makes "Asu the Great" such a pleasing story. The refrain also serves as motif for the chase and escape from violence. The folkloric formula that Taban calls the "progression-and-repetition motif" (lo Liyong 1973:114; lo Liyong 1969:74) which Nazareth defines as "call-and- response, chanting pattern"(45) and Knight describes as "one line of advancement of the story followed by one line of recapitulation" (105), is frequently used to achieve a beautiful poetic rhythm. It is, however, not as elaborately employed in *The Uniformed Man* as in *Fixions*.

Taban's rhythmic prose is also a result of the use of the traditional poetic devices of repetition, alliteration, imagery, and phrasing. None, for instance, can remain impassive to the beauty of the following, irony notwithstanding: "But changed into an angel, his thoughts would have been full only of nectar, ambrosia and glory unimaginable." (7) Brother Tortoise, we are told, "shares scales with snakes and crocodiles; legs with lizards and cats; shells with armadillos and snails." (2) And here is how the stone-rolling episode is described: "We rushed to the road and rolled it away. Then he would get it, carry it to the road. We took it out. He did it again, we repeated ours. He did; we did. Did, did" (12). Here is another example: "The Lord is good. He permitted Asuban to do his deeds. He did the deeds; he died by the deeds" (49). In the following sentences the meaning in a text is metaphorically called "food" and the printed text "plates": "I have reached a point of knowing certain things so thoroughly that when I read or re-read the same article, I derive no meaning from it. . . . I have already eaten the food and derived nourishment from it. The plates are of no value now" (32).

Although one cannot deny the beauty of phrases such as the above, it is also obvious that Taban is using them in parody of the seriously conceived poetic prose. Every occurrence of poetry is attended by some deflationary detail that invariably induces a mood of ironic humor. The poetic romanticism of the first quotation is undercut by the improbability of its hyperbolic fantasy. The incongruity in the association between some of the animals in the second example undermines the rhythmic parallelism of the captivating phrase built on the repetitive use of the preposition "with" in combination with the conjunction "and." A mood of childish playfulness pervades the poetic cadence of the third example just as there is an obvious deflationary irony in the descent from "intellect" to "emotions," thence to "glands" and finally to "physiologies" in the following passage that humorously echoes church litanies:

> From the scourge of these imagined gods, human intellect, save us. From the dogmatisms of short-sighted Platoes, human emotions, save us. From enslavement to all myths, our glands, save us. From all the unknown social woes, our physiologies, save us. (60)

Taban's love for word-play, already remarked by critics, like Knight and Nazareth, is evident in *The Uniformed Man,* in which there are also neologisms through Acholization and Swahilization. Latin and French are incorporated into the text. Colloquial speech is also mixed with standard English usage, sometimes to the extent of incomprehensibility, as in some pages in "Asu the Great." If we consider all of what Taban manages to say in a story, we will begin to appreciate the amazing brevity of his style. Thoughts rush one after another and the speed is often reflected in the fast tempo of his sentences, which are sometimes left uncompleted. Some of the quotations above well illustrate this.

Once again, however, the frivolity of the puns, the estranging effect of the neologisms and foreign phrases, the absurdity of the incomprehensible colloquialisms, the suffocating crowding of information into the text and the mad pace of rushing thoughts are all evidence of the author's parodic intent.

It is inconceivable how any critic could believe, as did Nazareth (48,49), that Taban is ideologically irrelevant as a spokesman for the Third World peoples and that he is an artistic failure. We may dislike Taban's ego, which sometimes leads him to making himself his own subject matter, as in "The Education of Taban lo Liyong" and partially in "Herolette," "Asu the Great" and "The Uniformed Man," but we must remember that there is nothing strange in autobiographical fiction. Moreover, in the late 1960s and early 1970s when *The Uniformed Man* was written, it was the habit among avant-garde artists to "take themselves directly as their major characters and work their own interiors—in confessions, analysis, fantasy—as subject matter" (Hicks 1981:7).

Taban does not flatter the people of the Third World, just as he does not condone the weakness of the people of the developed nations. Rather, he uses his art to challenge the former to match the achievements of the latter. Taban believes in the unity of all men, "in the final analysis," he says, "society is also one" (lo Liyong 1971:xv) and he sees the differences in human beings as only a matter of "difference in degree," for, as he points out, "A reliable balance sheet of innate qualities of the Blacks and the Whites and the Yellows has not yet been drawn up. For all practical purposes, there are no differences in them" (lo Liyong 1973:82). This is why Taban applies the same rule to all and believes the Third World has the capacity to catch up with the developed nations.

Taban is thus relevant, but he may be difficult to read. He believes a work of literature should engage the reader intellectually, an engagement that should be uniquely pleasurable provided the reader is patient and the writer has done his homework (lo Liyong 1971:xiii-xiv). As readers, our homework in understanding Taban consists in realizing how his synthesis of the techniques of folklore and postmodernist reconstructivist metafiction on a canvass of parody produces a strangely realistic fiction, for the achievement of Taban is that he has defictionalized fiction and, by so doing, renewed it. Reading *The Uniformed Man*, everything looks so simple, so ordinary that one wonders if this is fiction. But it is fiction in which there is a great deal of art and a distinct Taban stamp. An arbitrary stamp, perhaps, but "art is arbitrary" as Taban points out:"Anybody can begin his own style. Having begun it arbitrarily, if he persists to produce in that particular mode, he can enlarge and elevate it to something permanent, to something other artists will come to learn and copy, to something the critics will catch up with and appreciate" (lo Liyong 1969:163).
UNIVERSITY OF BENIN—NIGERIA

Notes

1. Jack Hicks defines philosophical metafiction in these terms *In the Singer's Temple* (Chapel Hill: North Carolina University Press, 1981), 18-19: "With Borges's *Labyrinths*, we can fix the beginning of interest in short, highly self-conscious, philosophically concerned fiction, a strain of writing termed metafiction by William Gass and Robert Scholes. . . . They are metafictions in a dual sense: as metaphysical fiction, the prime interest of which is in a world of ideas; and metafiction, a literature extended beyond its former possibilities, transcending an essentially mimetic status. Borges provided early instances, but he is simply one expression of a broad international impulse."
2. Elizabeth Knight, "Taban lo Liyong's Narrative Art," *African Literature Today*, 12 (1982):104-17.

3. See my analysis in "Characteristics of Absurdist African Literature: Taban lo Liyong's *Fixions*—A Study in the Absurd," *African Studies Review*, Vol 27, 1 (March 1984):52-3.

Works Cited

Balogun, F. Odun. "Characteristics of Absurdist African Literature: Tabon lo Liyong's *Fixions*—A Study in the Absurd." *African Studies Review* 27.1 (March 1984):52-53.

Hicks, Jack. *In the Singer's Temple*. Chspel Hill: North Carolina Univ. Press, 1981.

Knight, Elizabeth. "Taban lo Liyong's Narrative Art." *African Literature Today* 12(1982):104-107.

LeClair, Thomas. "Avant-garde Mastery," *TriQuarterly*, 53 (Winter 1982):260.

lo Liyong, Taban, *The Last Word* (Nairobi: East African Publishing House, 1969), 8.

____. *Thirteen Offensives Against Our Enemies* (Nairobi: East African Literature Bureau, 1973), 80.

____. *The Uniformed Man* (Nairobi: East African Literature Bureau, 1971.

Nazareth, Peter, "Bibliography, or Six Tabans in Search of an Author," *English Studies in Africa*, Vol 21.1 (1978):38.

Sukenick, Ronald, "The Death of the Novel," in *The Death of the Novel and Other Stories*. (NY: Dial Press, 1969):49.

SOUTH AFRICAN LITERATURE

REGISTER AS A FUNCTION OF CONTEXTUALIZATION:
A SURVEY OF THE SOUTHERN AFRICAN VARIETY OF ENGLISH

✶

Benjamin J. Magura

The uses of a variety of a particular language may depend on a number of factors which we may loosely refer to as *contextual*. Such a contextual situation, as a theoretical construct, has factors which "systematically determine the form, the appropriateness, or the meaning" (Lyons 1978: 572) of a language or variety-event. It is language variation in terms of these factors that makes the language varieties distinct. For, the appropriateness of a speech event within its 'province' (Crystal and Davy 1969: 71) or 'domain' (Fishman 1978: 68) may be explained in terms of the concept of *register*. Halliday, McIntosh and Strevens (1964:77) explain that "the category of 'register' is needed when we want to account for what people do with their language." Leech (1966:68) defines 'register' in terms of systematic variation as "use in relation to social context."

This means that when we look at the variations of language in its different contexts and situations, what we see are various 'registers.' Likewise, Strang (1968:21) considers 'register' as a "dimension of variation (that) depends not on the user but on the use." What all these definitions tell us is that registers can be viewed as a special kind of language use in a special social situation. DeStefano (1973:189) clearly explains this by saying:

> Language use varies with the social circumstances the speaker is in; he switches from one register (or 'style' as Labov

calls it) to another depending on who he is talking to, the topic, or other social variables.

Variations within Black English in Southern Africa may be explained in terms of 'register' according to the "context of situation." Lyons (1978:607) explains the idea of context of situation by pointing out that "every utterance occurs in a culturally determined context of situation; and the meaning of the utterance is the totality of its contribution to the maintenance of what Firth refers to as "the patterns of life in society in which the speaker lives and to the affirmation of the speaker's role and personality within the society." What then, we may ask, are the various registers in African English? Alternatively, how are various registers manifested in African English while still retaining an African identity linguistically?

Sociolects in African English

It may be useful at this point to start the discussion of stylistic features by briefly examining the various sociolects in the African variety of English.

What Joos (1967:1962) provides us in his classification of styles is taxonomically appealing. However, it is not very easy to delimit all style as it relates to social dialects, we might want to use a framework that rests upon categorization of sociolects. Other forms of analysis seem to have run into some problems of clarity. For example, Labov's original delimitation of style (see Labov 1972: 100-11) into "careful" and "casual" speech was found inadequate when other linguists tried to use this method. The use of sociolects as a basis of classification of styles presumes that linguistic features that bear social significance will also show parallel behavior along a social-class continuum from less formal to more formal. In practice what this means is that if a feature is more common in a lower social class than in an upper class, it will also be more common in less formal styles than in more formal styles, or vice-versa. With this approach, we are, therefore, combining the notion of social class with that of style.

The Acrolect in African English

The acrolect in African English is the prestige subvariety used by the educated speakers of the African English speech community. It is the subvariety used in formal situations. The acrolect in the African English variety is very much like the standard form in the native varieties. The slight difference between the two lies in syntax, lexicalization, and in the discoursal strategies.

(i) *Syntax*. The syntax in the acrolect, while deceptively similar to the syntax of native variety on the surface, shows a deviation in meaning in certain expressions. Such deviation should, I think, be attributed to the idiomatic nature of the local languages. Consider the following examples:

1. How is she *keeping*? (African cf. *The Island*, 57) vs. How is she *doing*? (American)
2. *Give* me the news. (*The Island*, 56) vs. *Tell* me the news.
3. I cannot understand how some people can own large houses while others do not have even a place to *hide their heads* (sleep or live). *Staffrider*, Sept./Oct. 1980.
4. "Then you are only a woman. *You have no mouth.*" (You cannot say anything). (Mungoshi: 16).
5. I have *killed many moons* in that hut. (I have spent many months in that hut.) (Okara: 54)
6. *To eat other's ear.* (To have a private talk.)
7. "Aren't we neighbours and hasn't he *grown up in my eyes?*
8. "Every year *when the rain is in the nose* either my wife or I am taken ill. (The rainy season is close by.) (Mungoshi: 22)
9. Non-white is a terrible word to use *for a description of us.* (For describing us.) (*Drum* 6.2.72)
10. "Mr. Styles, take the *card* please!" (picture) (*Sizwe*

Bansi is Dead, 13).

11. Meet our Best Dressed Men

    For the man in the evening: 'A roll-up collar jacket—my favourite colour is royal blue—a turn-up-less pair of trousers and other essentials. (*World* 1968)

12. "*Straight!*" said Noah bluntly .... (clear!)
    "Ek verstaan, Captain. I know *straight* what you mean to do." (clearly) *A Ride on the Whirlwind* (Sepamula 1981:24)

13. "How do you feel about Mandla coming along with us?" "*I am* easy. I am your hands, not your brains." (Sepamula 1981: 28)

14. Aniko: I am alright my child, I am alright. How are you?
    Mrie: *Carrying on* Mama. Trying *to carry on.*
    Aniko: Yes, these are hard times, but we must carry on. (Athol Fugard: *Coat*, 10-11)

15. Laurenti: Where is that husband going to come back to if you leave the house? And if you do leave it you know they'll most probably *endorse you out* and back into the Reserves.

(ii) *Lexicalization*: For the most part, lexicalization in the acrolect is very close to the forms in standard variety. But because of the desire to use much ornamentation in the use of English a lot of overgeneralization of some word forms found in the standard varieties is evident. Consider the following overgeneralization of the *-er* formative nouns:

Night-lifers as in: Soweto's *night-lifers*. (Those who go out for a nice time or for functions at night)
' This will be one big week-end for *nite-lifers* in Johannesburg' (*World*, March 6, 1968)
chief-mourner (the bereaved at a funeral, the very next of kin to the deceased)
'Mrs. Florence Sithole was chief-mourner at the graveside' (*World*, March 21, 1968)
Race-goer (one who frequents horse-racing)

Wood-seller (a person who moves around selling firewood)

Church-goer (not just one who goes to church, but a devout Christian)

'I am divorced and I appeal to you to get me a wife. She should be a *church-goer*' (World, July 5, 1968)

drinker (drunkard)

'Alcohol draws the water out of the tissues of the body and hardens them. This makes the *drinker* still feel thirsty' (*World*, Jan. 15, 1968)

go-getters (hustlers)

'An organization called Olympia promotions led by Allastair Jacob is proving to be a music-promoting body of real *go-getters*.' (*World*, March 15, 1968)

picnickers

'A Soweto gunman on a bus terrorized and shot at a group of *picnickers* who were returning home from Haartespoort Dam.' (*World*, Jan. 11, 1968)

knifer (a knife-using fighter)

'*Knifer* runs riot in Rockville shebeen' (*World*, July 5, 1968)

manager-trainer (manager as well as trainer of a soccer team) also *patron-manager*

trainer-coach (one who is both a trainer and a coach)

place-seekers (young students looking for places into secondary school)

'The government is pushing semi-illiterates and *place-seekers* into its Bantu Territorial Authorities.' (World, Jan. 3, 1963)

pennywhistler (one who goes after loose women)

traffic-stopper (a traffic police officer)

grudge-killer (one who terrorizes other people because of a grudge he might have against them)

'Police have launched an intensive search in townships here for a *grudge-killer*' (*World*, Feb. 13, 1963)

ticket-jumpers (people who avoid going through the usual train station gates and jump over the railway fences to avoid paying for the ticket) *staff-riders* or *staffers* (people who board and alight from the train while it is in motion)

child-stealer
'She spat at me as if I was a *child-stealer*'
(Themba 1972: 25)

Most if not all of these formations could be found in varieties of native English. What makes them so prominent in the African variety of English is the frequency with which they are used. Part of the explanation for this frequency would be the users' desire to come up with a highly colourful and ornamented language. There is pride that the users get from such a flowery language. This feature in the style of the African variety of English may be a carry-over from the idiomatic nature of the users' own African languages. The colourful language is not only evident in -er formative nouns. It can also be found in other expressions. Consider the following article about an impending soccer match between the "Black Birds" and the "Black Pirates."

Pretoria Black Birds *Are Flying High*

Pretoria's Black Birds are determined to overwhelm the Black Pirates on Saturday at Orlando Stadium. They have phoned Mr. D. Matsamai the Black Pirates' *patron-manager* to say that *their Black wings will poke into the gleaming eyes of their opponents. They are going to snatch the whip from the Black Pirates and give them a sound leathering!* (World, Jan. 3, 1963)

Sometimes such an aspiration for a highly ornamented language and style may lead to incorrect use of adverbs as in:

Now it is up to the Birds and Bucs to play the game *cleanly* and *sportingly*. (*World,* Jan. 19, 1968)

On other occasions this is carried too far and results in some awkward but creative collocations as in *crying shame:*

It is a *crying shame* that this should be the case even with such high class teams. (*World,* Jan. 19, 1968)

The colorful nature of the style in the acrolect of the African English variety may take various forms. Sometimes it appears in quite vivid, but comical analogies such as the description of a professional boxer who fell in love with a girl and got 'knocked down' to the point of engagement. This is expressed as follows:

> Robert Dikobe, a professional boxer, was *knocked out when he met Miss Miriam Tsetla and the prize he had to pay was an expensive diamond ring and an engagement party.* Many boxers and socialites attended. (*World*, Nov. 18, 1968)

Sometimes the analogies are taken from characters in English literature, showing the exposure the users of this variety have to masterpieces of English literature. Consider the following description of a beautiful singer who was beaten during a brawl.

> One of the people who get the lion's share of the mean punch was Abigail Kubhek, *that Cleopatra of song and stage* and winner of last year's festival. (*World*, Nov. 18, 1968)

The acrolect in this variety shows some Latinate expressions in its lexicalization. Such use of Latinity (cf. Kachru 1977: 39, 224) is intended to be a mark of high education. Consider the following examples in sentences:

> The sergeant behind the counter told her to take it easy, to wait until the criminals were so well-asleep that they might be caught *flagrante delicto.* But Baby was dancing with impatience at 'the law's delay.' (Themba 1972: 7)

> He paid the lobola—that hard-dying custom of paying bride-price— getting some of his friends and home-boys to stand for him in *loco parents.* (Themba 1972: 16)

One of the most interesting forms of lexicalization in the acrolect of the African variety of English is the creative, but expressive collocational device. Such a device is used to capture, as succinctly as possible, the meaning intended. Consider the following examples that are found even in creative literature: *the tin bird* (aeroplane; Mungoshi 1975: 30); *now-now girls* (modern girls; Mungoshi 1975: 62); *my own-own niece* (my very close niece; Mphahlele 1967: 196); *daughter-of-the-people* (a native *woman*; Mphahlele 1967: 191).

The Mesolect in African English

The mesolect in the African variety of English is a subvariety often used by African people with some education that is not advanced enough to have acquired the acrolect. In some cases, educated people who would otherwise normally use the acrolect, may switch to this subvariety in semiformal situations. Thus, if we took users of the African variety of English as a speech community, these users could then be visualized along an imaginary line, a speech continuum, according to their speech patterns. The users of the most prestigious variety would be at the top of that continuum with the users of the least prestigious, the basilect, at the bottom. Somewhere in between this continuum lies the mesolect.

The mesolect differs from the acrolect in the extent to which these subvarieties deviate from the standard variety. While the mesolect is much closer to the standard variety, it is further removed from it in style. This subvariety can be identified by its lexical, phonological, and syntactic features.

(i) *Lexicalization*: The idiomatic nature of the African variety of English is perhaps best seen in this subvariety. Whether it be for ornamentation or for expressive creative collocations, this isolect has some interesting expressions such as: *cop-shop* (police station) (*World*, March 8, 1963); *magistrate's tears* (any hot beverage—tea/coffee) (*World*, March 15, 1968); *Sheila's Day* (Thursday, the day on which most women in domestic services are off duty) (*World*, June 5, 1968); *snatch-boys* (pickpockets) (*World*, Feb. 13, 1968); *Spinach* (cheap clothing material sold to lower-class people) (Mphahlele 1967: 5); *queen's tears* (strong liquor, usually spirits); *land-eater* (vehicle—especially land-owner's); You must be *wake-up wake-up* (alert) (*Staffrider*, Vol. 5, No. 2 1983); *drumstick* (revolver); *cow-in-the-tin* (condensed milk).

Hybridization is a very productive linguistic process in this subvariety. The process is also frequently used in the acrolect. This process involves two or more linguistic elements, one of which is from the local languages. Like the straight loan words, this device is useful in its being more precise in description. Consider, for example, the following: *dagga-boy* (a helping hand whose duties are to prepare and mix several mixtures for building, e.g., concrete); *multi-man* (a man who practices the use of herbs); love-muti (a charm to entice people into love); *panga-killer* (one who uses a sharp knife for homicide); *impi-line* (a line of a Zulu regiment).

Another productive process in this subvariety is the *semantic innovations* whereby English words have acquired a completely different meaning in African English usage. As such, these linguistic items identify Black usage, for example: *paraffin* (gin); *the boys* (African guerrilla fighters); *sweet potato* (landmine); *witch's hour* (dawn); *ex-islander* (prisoner freed from Robben Island).

Sometimes lexicalization shows collocationally deviant forms which demonstrate semantic shifts such as *skin-teaser* (a dancer who shakes his/her body in a very funny but entertaining manner); *ticket-jumper* (one who avoids following the ticket line and hence illegally boards the train or enters a show without paying); *roaring silence* (dead silence); *bachelor quarters* (barracks in urban African townships for migrant laborers); *wolf-whistle* (signal sound by whistling made to a girl by men); *smeller-out* (African witchdoctor)'

Deculturation of English in this variety is quite evident in the non-translated loan words. These are words taken directly from Bantu languages and are used profusely in English. They are useful in being more expressive of what the user wants to mean. Consider the following examples: *maiza* (African beer brewed from maize); *idhlozi* (ancestral spirits); *malombo* (jazz idiom combining tribal rhythm with urban jazz); *mai-mai* or *ai-ai* (absolute alcohol used to lace drinks); *kwela-kwela* (police pick-up van); *sangoma* (a person claiming supernatural powers of divination).

Some lexical items are culture-specific linguistic expressions. These expressions are derived from certain culture-specific milieu. They are, therefore, best understood in the context of the African culture. Take for example: *circumcision* or *initiation school* (an initiation period during which young men locally known as *abakwetha* are circumcised according to tribal custom and then admitted to the rights of manhood); *circumcision dance* (a ceremony after circumcision where young initiates dance as part of the initiation school); *coming-out-party* (a ceremony to commemorate the permission given to a baby to be taken out of the house after a certain period of confinement following its birth); *rain-queen* (a tribal medium in charge of asking for rain from the ancestral gods); *sangoma dance* (a ceremony to invoke spirit mediums).

ii) *Phonological Features*: The range of verbal repertoire in users in African English, as in other bilinguals, may be identified in terms of the variety's formal features and their functional domains. One of such features is *foregrounding* (Kachru 1982: 28). It is the deliberate use of certain phonological, grammatical, and lexical devices for the sake of attracting attention. In the mesolect, the use of foregrounding may be deliberate or may result from inability to pronounce the linguistic item in the proper way. Take for example, *drown de sorry* for 'drown the sorrow'; *uscuse-me* or *ooscuse-me* for 'excuse me' (now a term of contempt applied to an educated African of the professional or white-collar middle class, usually used in derision); *ketshi* for 'cash'; *ooclever* or *uclever* 'towns-folk'; *ivups* 'wide turn-up trousers without any turn-up—'flappers'; *oomac* or *uMac* (term used to address older men among townsfolk); *ooMackazi* or *uMackazi* (the woman counterpart of *uMac*); *scuse-me activities* (middle-class activities); *scuse-me people* (middle-class people); *idance* (ballroom dance).

Many prefixes and suffixes from Bantu languages, are attached to basically English items. Such hybridization results in the interesting examples we have seen above. A breakdown of the hybrid elements can be shown as follows:

u—(ex) scuse-me; *u*—clever; *i* dance; *u*—Mac;
u—Mac—*kazi*. (elements from Bantu language in italic)

(iii) *Syntactic Features*: A number of typical syntactic deviations are similar to what has been identified in Nigerian, Ghanaian, and Kenyan English (see Kirk-Greene 1971; Sey 1973; Chenebauh 1976; Angogo and Hancock 1980; and Zuengler 1982). For example, we also find omission of function words in this variety. Consider the following examples in Bokamba (80):

i) Let strong football team be organized.
ii) He won by overwhelming majority.
iii) He gave me tough time.
iv) I am going to cinema.
v) I am going to post office.

Similar examples in South African Black English are found in examples such as:
   a) He fought and boxed like a champion of old. (*World*, March 18, 1968)
   b) David Shuping, most wanted criminal in South Africa was arrested on farm few miles from the border *dorp* of Mafeking. (*World*, Dec. 6, 1968)
   c) I was awakened by noise of people fighting in my yard, when I peeped through window, I realized that it was my *house* (husband) fighting his son. (*World*, Jan. 11, 1968)
   d) If we could get rid of present "Papa mentality" there are three things we could strive for
      - compulsory education up to age of 21
      - better housing
      - relaxation of influx control
      (*World*, Jan. 17, 1968)
   e) The East Rand has terrific social beat this week-end. It will be time of gaiety all round .... parties, parties, parties thrown by married couples and even the law. (*World*, March 11, 1968)

Another common syntactic feature is the unnecessary pluralization of certain nouns. In other varieties, such as those referred to in Bokamba (82), this phenomenon is described as redundant *pluralization*. Examples from Nigerian and Ghanaian English include the following taken from Bokamba's text:
   a) I lost all my *furnitures* and many valuable *properties*.
   b) There were thunderous *noises* of laughter and *chats*.
   c) She walked in such *paces* that combined her college *learnings* of how to behave.
   d) The teachers will be given the *respects* they deserve.
   e) But in modern warfare ... the *damages* caused are great.
   f) I was in charge of all *correspondences*.

South African Black English shows similar tendencies, as is demonstrated by the following examples:
   1) We want *brains* on the authority not blue blood

(kith and kin or nepotism). (*World,* Jan. 3, 1963)
2) About two thousand people turned up to give their last *respects* to Mr. Alfred Marokwane, well-known socialite businessman. (*World,* March 18, 1963)
3) It should be acknowledged that the forces of resistance by the people are causing panic in the *corridors* of power in Pretoria. (*Sowetan,* Oct. 3, 1983)
4) He does not have any interest in a new state and the right to vote if this only makes a few of his people leaders and gives them *big monies,* houses, and *motors* (motor cars). (*World,* Jan. 3, 1963)
5) I think I will try to look for some *jobs* in the garden. (Fugard, *Sizwe Bansi is Dead,* 259)

Many other syntactic deviations noted for other varieties also appear in varying degrees in the South African variety. However, a much more interesting type of syntactic deviation is syntactico-semantic in nature, involving sentences that are grammatically acceptable, but logically unsound to a native speaker of English. Examples in this category show a very strong bias toward the culture of the users. The medium is English, but the meaning and mode of expression is culture-bound or even "culture-specific." Consider the following examples:

1) Her calculated silence preaches volumes. (Mungoshi: 8)
2) Leave them be. [or] Let her be. (Mungoshi: 12)
3) The Earth takes back its own. (Mungoshi: 18).
4) Thank the soil that he can still tell the difference between bottled morality and our proud tradition. (Mungoshi: 115)

Structurally, sentences such as the five examples given above, are reminiscent of Joseph Heller's famous line on the fate of the rebel Dunbar in *Catch 22*: "They disappeared him." The difference here would be that the sentence may easily be construed ungrammatical, but semantically sound. The situation in the five examples is just the opposite. They are grammatically acceptable, but semantically—at least to one not familiar with African culture—deviant. The anomaly in these sentences is unlike what we find in the famous Chomskyian sentence

Colorless green ideas sleep furiously. For in this sentence there is no semantic explanation of this string of syntactically well-formed words. All of the sentence 1-5 can be explained semantically by either the metaphorical expressions of the Bantu languages or the belief system of the African people. In sentence (1) Her calculated silence preaches volumes, this is a translation of a Bantu saying into the English language. In Shona, for example, a similar and common saying is *Kunyarara kwakwe kunoreva zvakawanda*, which means "His/her silence means (says) much." It is fairly safe for us to conclude that since the author is a Shona speaker, this is the meaning he had in mind. Otherwise *silence* cannot preach.

Sentence (2) seems to be a literal translation from Shona. The word order is exactly the same as we would find in the Shona equivalent of that English sentence: *Rega va-/a-kadaro*. The *va-* marks a plural prefix, and the a- is the prefixal element for singular reference. Again, this is a common Bantu saying which has been transcreated into this variety of English.

Sentences (3) through (4) are more interesting because of their obvious rootedness in African culture. Even if we try to apply the Katz-Postal integrated theory of linguistic descriptions (Katz-Postal: 30-67), criticized as it has been, the projection rules will fail to map out the intended meaning of these sentences. The dictionary meanings that we find provided for *earth* and *soil* would not be +*human*. Consequently, it would not make much sense to talk of *earth taking something*, or even of *soil telling*.... In their attempt to put forward a theory for linguistic descriptions, Katz and Fodor (1964x:19) purported that

the syntactic structure of a sentence, by providing the formal relations between the lexical items, determines what possible combinations of meanings there are in the sentence. Thus the characterization of the syntactic structure given by SD from the syntactic component determines, in part, how the semantic information from the dictionary entries associated with the lexical items is combined by the projection rules.

Such a semantic theory does not seem to work for these sentences. What would help in the understanding of these sentences is some knowledge of the African traditional philosophy. In the African belief system, the ancestors (also vicariously known as *shades, abadhala, the old ones,* and so on, in SABLE) are metaphorically referred to as *the earth, the soil.* It is in this sense, then, that these lexical items take on a +human selection restriction.

The Basilect in Sable

The basilect in the Southern African English is attitudinally the lowest subvariety in the speech continuum of this Black English variety. It forms the main speech pattern of those with little or no formal education. Although this is not the focus of the analysis of this variety, suffice it to say that it is perhaps used by the majority of the African people in this region. Creative writers have exploited the basilect by using it to depict the social level of their characters. Consider how Mphahlele (1967: 124-25) imitates this subvariety in a letter written by Marta, mistress of a murdered man. She writes to the wife of that man and says,

> Dear Missis Molamo, I am dropping this few lines for to hoping that you are living good now i want to teling you my hart is sore sore. i hold myselfe bad on the day of youre mans funeral my hart was ful of pane too mauch and i see myselfe already o Missis Molamo already doing mad doings i think the goods are beatting me now for holding myselfe as wyle animall forgeef forgeef i pray with all my hart child of the people. now i must tel you something you must noe quik quik thees that i can see that when you come to my hause and then whenn you see me kriing neer the grafe i can see you think I am sweet chokolet of your man i can see you think in your hart my man love that wooman no no i want to tel you that he neva love me nevaneva he livd same haus my femily rented in Fitas and i lovd him mad i tel you i lovd him mad i wanted him with red eyes he was nise leetl bit nise to me but i see he sham for me as i have got no big ejucashin he got too much book i make nise tea and cake for him and he like my muther and he is so nise ia ma shoor he come to meet me in toun even new se are 2 merryd people bicos he remember me and muther looked aftar him like bruther for me he was stil nise to me but al wooman can see whenn there is no loveness in a man and they can see lovfulness. now

he is gonn i feel I want to rite with my al ten fingas becos i hav too muche to say aboute your sorriness and my sorriness i will help you to kry you help me to kry and leev that man in peas with his gods, so i stop press here my deer i beg to pen off the gods look aftar us

I remain your sinserity

missis Marta Shuping.

In spite of the more pronounced deviation from the native variety of English, this basilect does show some of the deviations that get carried over to the other higher-lects. For example, we find in this text repetitions such as *sore sore; forgeef forgeef; quik quik; nevaneva*. This is a productive process that we also find in both the mesolect and acrolect. Consider, for example, the following similar process:

never-never. The music of the old timers made the people remember the city of *never-never.*

I had managed to touch Mrs. Moraise's son, Alf, who runs a fish and chips shop in Newclare, for a packet of the same on the *never-never. (World,* June 21, 1968)

big big. Whale of a sight on view this week: *the big big* affair. (*World,* June 23, 1968)

wake-up wake-up. You must be *wake-up, wake-up.* (*Staffrider*)

We worked and worked. (*Staffrider*)

What Mawasha (31-33) refers to as 'errors' in the English of Form II Northern Sotho students are actually a mixture of mistakes and deviations along the same lines as those in Marta Shuping's letter. These mistakes and deviations can be broken down into three categories:

a) those caused by poor or inadequate control of the syntactic system of English

b) interference of the L_1 idiom with the L_2 (English) idiom

c) poor control of the phonological system of the
English language, showing a tendency to fall back to
a much more familiar L_1 system

Problems under (a)—those caused by poor or inadequate control of the syntactic system of English—were really syntactic mistakes, as was the case with Mawasha's examples (31):

1) *The teachers gives...
2) *.... this two kings...
3) *Our school have...
4) *We does not have...
5) *We sings...
6) *There is many...
7) *He are a strict man.
8) *He don't want...
9) *When someone approach...
10) *Things which is...
11) *We writes a test...
12) *We has many flowers...
13) *There are no telephone in the school.
14) *The school are surrounded by a fence.
15) *We looks like European children.

These mistakes involve number agreement or what is traditionally referred to as subject and predicate agreement in English. This could be characterized as follows:

16) i) NP-PRON VP ART MODIFIER NP
 (singular)
ii) NO-PRON VP MODIFIER NP
 (plural)
 (subj) (cop) (obj)

In most Bantu languages, particularly Northern Sotho and Shona in this case, the syntactic situation is different. In these languages the equivalent of 16 (i) and 16 (ii) is mapped by 17 (i) and 17 (ii), respectively.

17) i) COP. NP REL. PARTICLE MODIFIER
 (subj.) (sing.)
ii) COP. NP REL. PARTICLE MODIFIER
 (subj.) (plural)

A contrastive analysis of English, Shona, and Northern Sotho on the basis of this characterization bears this out in such sentences as:

> English: We write a test.
> *Ti- nonyora vhunzo*
> Shona: *Tinonyora vhunzo*
> N. Sotho: *Re ngwala moleko*
> English: He writes a test.
> *u- nonyora vhunzo*
> Shona: *Unonyora vhunzo.*
> N. Sotho: *O ngwala moleko*

Much more interesting cases are those resulting from the interference of the vernacular idiom with that of the English language. Consider the following example:

> 18) **Lebowa* of beasts and men.
> [*Lbowa la kgomo le motho*)
> (Where "Lebowa" refers to an area in the Northern Transvaal)

The word-for-word (lexis-bound) translation of the Northern Sotho idiom fails to alter the sociocultural nature of the expression. But in spite of the fact that the medium is English, a native speaker of English would make no sense whatsoever of this saying. It has a 'context-specific' meaning alien to the English socio-cultural background.

Other errors—those in category (b), consisting of interference of the L_1 idiom with the L_2 (English) idiom arise from an attempt at matching the syntactic system of the L_1 (Northern Sotho) with the syntactic system of L_2 (English). Consider the following ungrammatical English sentences compared to their perfectly grammatical Northern Sotho equivalents. (These sentences were written by Form II [Grade 9] students.)

> 19) *Where they wash with education
> [mo ba hlapang ka thuto
> *Mo bahlapang ka thuto.*
> 20) *The teachers whom they are teaching us . . .
> [barutsi bao ba rutang rena]
> *Barutsi bao ba rutago rena . . .*

21) *The school it is shaped like 0
   [sekolo sona se agilwe bjalo ka 0]
   Sekolo sona se agilwe bjalo ka 0.

22) *The students are always listen to the principal.
   [barutwana ba hlogo theeletsa ke mehla yohle]
   Barutwana ba theeletsa hlogo ke mehla yohle.

23) *We undress our shoes
   [re apola tsa rona dieta]
   Re pola dieta tsa rona.

24) *Our school is too education
   [sa geso sekolo se kudu/gabotse ruta]
   Sekolo sa geso se ruta kudu/gabotse.

25) *Teachers learn us different subjects.
   [Barutsi ba ruta re tse fapaneng dithuto]
   Barutsi ba re ruta dithuto tse fapaneng.

The confusion between *teach* and *learn* which we see as the error in (25) is a common one. The local languages do not have a lexical item that makes the distinction between the two. A similar confusion is found in other verbs, too, e.g., *borrow* vs. *lend*. Occasionally one hears sentences like 'Can you borrow me some money?' or 'Will you borrow me your pen?'

The non-standard pronunciation and incorrect spelling created in Mphahlele's letter quoted earlier demonstrate the problems that arise from the English phonological system—poor control of the phonological system of the English language, with the speakers showing a tendency to fall back to a much more familiar L_1 system. Users of English in the basilect may have corresponding sounds with those they mispronounce and consequently misspell. Errors resulting from such poor control of the English phonological system can be classified into roughly four areas:

26) Vowels:
   *injoy (enjoy)
   *drealing (drilling)
   *encluding (including)

27) Consonants:
   *byong (beyond)
   *juniform (uniform)

28) Voiced vs. Voiceless
   *depate (debate)
   *hart (hard)
29) *1 o'tlok (1 o'clock)
   *winmill (windmill)
   *fillims (films)

These characterizations confirm that the Black variety of English transfers much of the L1 features into an L2 situation.

Stylistic Characteristics

In this section I shall discuss certain stylistic tendencies common in the South African Black English. These characteristics are singled out on the basis of the frequency with which they appear in the African use of English.

Crystal and Davy (1969:90) give a broad definition of stylistics as "the description of the linguistic characteristics of all situationally-restricted uses of language." This broad definition suggests the broad co-variation of linguistic items and features. Ullmann (9), on the other hand, see stylistics as concerned "with the expressive and evocative values of language." This view of stylistics is similar to the Chomskyian view that there is a distinction between stylistic and non-stylistic variation. Riffaterre (25) describes stylistics as a discipline that "studies those features of linguistic utterances that are utilized to impose the encoder's way of thinking on the decoder." Osgood (1960:360) defines style as the "individual's deviations from the norm for the situation in which he is encoding." What seems to define stylistics in the discourse of African texts is the patterning of social markers and cultural tendencies with the theme of the text. In this context, it is the cultural component of discourse which carries meaning and is imposed on the decoder as the encoder's way of thinking.

Some stylistic features that are common tendencies in this variety were touched on under "style as a function of register." Here emphasis is being made of those features that were not stressed under that discussion. Discussion of these stylistic features will be divided into contextually transferred units and stylistic features depicting flamboyance in the use of English.

Modes of Address

Modes of address in African English fall within what Kachru (1983: 102) refers to as the "socially determined speech-functions." A pragmatic view of the African variety of English accommodates the pragmatic devices of this non-native variety. In their use of English, it is very difficult for the Africans to drop completely certain culturally fixed exponents of their culture. Modes of address are some such exponents. Since these exponents are not found in English, there is a transfer of these units from an L1 situation to L2 Consider the following examples: *chief* 'sir'; *home-boy/home-girl* 'someone close to you, who also comes from the same *area as you; son-of-Africa; chum; son of my daughter; mother of John; father of John.*

In the Zulu tradition, these modes of address may be praise names or 'eulogies.' Consider how Plaatje exploits them in *Mhudi*: "Hail, *Great Lion! Monarch of the woods and glades*, and *ruler of the hills and vales!*" (Plaatje 1978: 177). Or "Silence, silence, *warriors of the Matebele, guardians of the safety of the Great One, he who is Terror of the breadth of the world*... (Plaatje 1978: 101; cf. Shakespearean plays).

These modes of address may also come as curse terms or forms of swearing. Take for example the following:

"*By the great dead Barolong,* and *the dead mother who gave me life*, I wish I had a beard like that.
"*By the high-born of the Great One.*"
Curse words: *these Khonkhobes, these sons of women!*

The Grand Style

Under grand or flamboyant style I shall discuss those linguistic items that have been described as depicting *verbosity* or *preciosity* (see Sey 1973: 124ff, or Goffin's reference to *Latinity* with respect to the Indian style of English). In the African variety of English there is also a dimension of impressionistic generalizations in some of the stylistic items.

Flamboyance can be seen in the coining of certain items on the basis of some form of creativity. Consider the blending of Biblical connotations with the formation of an adverb in

Nicodemously. "The birth-right of most Xhosa was Nicodemously signed away in Umtata." (Sowetan, Sept. 29, 1983). Flamboyant creativity is also seen in coinages such as ex-islander for 'an ex-prisoner' at Robben Island; eight-percenters for the 8% population that voted for the New South African tricameral parliament; *bunga assemblies* for 'the derided parliaments of the Bantustans.' Flamboyance in the over-generalizations of certain items may be exemplified by lexical items such as: *discobatics* "The funny dancer is Sam, the local heart-throb when it comes to *discobatics*" (*Sowetan*, Oct. 6, 1983); or *legalbatics*: "Bob Loyora is the main speaker who bubbles and foams . . . . We get an impromptu lesson in *legalbatics*." (*Sowetan*, Oct. 6, 1983).

An excessive craving for verbose and long expressions is a common characteristic of the African variety. See how the authors of the following passages cannot help but throw in words like *credulity* and *longevity*.

A careful tracking of hints, off-the-record conversations, and material published in scientific journals will indicate when the doctor is ready to make an announcement, it will certainly shake the *credulity* of laymen . . .

The importance of this project to human health and *longevity* is almost beyond calculation. It would bring mankind to the threshold of a new era of freedom and death. (*World*, March 29, 1983).

Mention was also made earlier about the *-ite* formative nouns. It may also be added here that although most of these nouns are found in L_1 usage, the frequency with which they occur in the Black English variety is rather curious. What is more, the formation of these nouns has advanced to some very interesting generalizations, for we also find expressions such as: *congressite* (for a member of the African National Congress—ANC); *socialite school teacher*, or even *socialite husband* (*World*, Feb. 11, 1963). This kind of generalization is spreading to other formatives. A jazz fanatic is referred to as a *jazzophile*.

There is also a noticeable increase in the use of certain expressive phrases. It is not fully known at this stage whether they are actually a result of direct translation from L_1 or whether they are just stylistic coinages. Whatever they are, they seem to be very expressive. A few of these are: *up-and-up*: "jazzwise,

Pietersburg is on the *up-and-up*" (*World,* Feb. 23, 1968); *up-and-coming*: "I warn other clubs to watch out for these *up-and-coming* lads." or "the *up-and-coming* Thembisa Swallows." Sometimes the coinage is obviously a deviation from the common English idiom. See how *far* or *much better* is replaced by *miles better* in the following sentences: "The Johannesburg Non-European General Hospital which had the busiest Christmas among the hospitals is reported to have been fairly busy, but *miles better* than . . ." (*World,* Jan. 21, 1963).

Conclusion

Emphasis on the contextual units has been made to show the effects of the context of culture on the style and meaning of the African variety of English. It needs to be realized that a language variety is usually maintained by social pressures within its own group of speakers or users, although they will seldom be aware that they are maintaining it. In many cases, subconscious pressures maintain the variety while the user's every conscious effort is to change to another. Group identity is perhaps the strongest of such pressures.

The greatest risk and misconception in dealing with language varieties which reflect some ethnic behaviour patterns, including speech patterns, is that some people will erroneously conclude that the patterns are genetic. To speak of an African variety of English is to risk having people think of either a sub-standard variety or a non-educated variety. Yet what should be emphasized are the social factors that determine the variety patterns. Such is the case this paper has tried to address.

UNIVERSITY OF BOTSWANA—GABORONE

Works Cited

Angogo, R. and I. Hancock, "English in Africa: emerging standards of diverging regionalisms?" *English World-Wide: A Journal of Varieties of English* 1.1 (1980): 67-96.

Chinebuah, I. K., "Grammatical deviance and first language interference." *West African Journal of Modern Languages* 1:(1976) 67-78.

Crystal, David and Derek Davy, *Investigating English Style.*

Bloomington: Indiana University Press, 1969.
DeStefano, Johanna S., ed., *Language Society and Education: a profile of Black English*. Worthington: Jones Publishing Company, 1973.
Firth, John R., "Personality and Language in Society." *The Sociological Review* 42.2 (1950) 37-52.
─── "Modes of Meaning." *Essays and Studies of the English Association*. N.S. 4(1951): 118-49.
Fishman, Joshua A., ed., *Advances in the Study of Societal Multilingualism*. The Hague: Mouton, 1978.
Fugard, Athol, *The Coat*. Cape Town: A. A. Balkema, 1971.
─── *Boesman and Lena*. New York: Samuel French, 1971.
─── *Sizwe Bansi is Dead* and *The Island*. New York: Viking Press, 1976.
Halliday, M. A. K., Angus McIntosh, and Peter Strevens, *The Sciences and Language Teaching*. London: Longman, 1964.
Joos, Martin, *The Five Clocks*. New York: Harcourt, Brace and World, 1967.
Kachru, Braj B., "Models of English for the Third World: White man's linguistic burden or language pragmatics?" *TESOL Quarterly* 10.2 (1976) 221-39.
─── "The New Englishes and Old Models." *English Language Forum* (July, 1977) 29-35.
─── *The Other Tongue: English Across Cultures*. Urbana: University of Illinois Press, 1982.
Katz, J. J. *An Integrated Theory of Linguistic Description*. Cambridge: MIT Press, 1964.
Katz, J. J. and J. A. Fodor, eds., *The Structure of Language*. Englewood Cliffs, NJ:Prentice Hall, 1964a.
─── "The Structure of a Semantic Theory." *Language* 39 (2) 170-210, 1964b.
Kirk-Green, Anthony, "The Influence of West African Languages on English" in Spencer, John (ed), *The English Language in Africa*. London: Longman, 1971.
Labov, William, *Language in the Inner City: Studies in the Black English Vernacular*. Philadelphia: University of Pennsylvania Press, 1972.
Leech, G. N., *English in Advertising:A Linguistic Study of Advertising in Great Britain*. London: Longman, 1966.
Lyons, John, *Semantics I and II*. Cambridge: Cambridge Univ. Press,

1978.

Mawasha, Abram L., 1982. "A Study of Common Errors in Written English with Special Reference to North Sotho- Speaking- Children." *Elite Reporter* 7.2 (June 1982).

Mphahlele, Ezekiel, *In Corner b. Short Stories.* Nairobi: East African Institute, 1967.

Mungoshi, Charles L., 1975. *Waiting for the Rain.* London: Heinemann.

Okara, Gabriel, 1963. "African speech, English words." *Transition* 4.10 (1963): 15-16.

Osgood, Charles, "Some effects of motivation on style of decoding." In Sebeok, T. A. (ed.) *Style in Language.* Cambridge, Mass: MIT Press, 1960.

Plaatje, Sol, *Mhudi.* Washington: Three Continents, 1930.

Riffaterre, Michael. *Essais de Stylistique structurale.* Paris: Flammarion, 1971.

Sepamula, Sipho, *Third Generation.* Braamfontein: Skotaville Publishers, 1986.

Sey, K. A., *Ghanaian English.* London: Macmillan, 1973.

Strang, B. M. H., *Modern English Structure.* London: Arnold, 1968.

Themba, Can, *The Will to Die.* London: Oxford Universoity Press, 1972.

Ullmann, S., *Semantics.* Oxford: Blackwell, 1962.

CONTRUBUTORS

Edmund L. Epstein is professor of English at Queens College and the Graduate Center—City University of New York. He is the author of several books on linguistics and on modern literature, among them *Language and Style,* and *Linguistics and English Prosody* (with T. F. Hawkes), and has been editor of *Language and Style: An International Journal* for almost thirty years.

Robert Kole is an instructor of English at Queens College/City University of New York and a PhD candidate in English at the City University of New York Graduate School. He is a Shakespearean scholar who specializes in textual issues as they relate to the staging of plays. A frequent contributor of theater reviews to *Shakespeare Bulletin,* he has been assistant editor of *Language and Style: An International Journal* for eight years.

Efurosibina Adegbija is a Professor in the English Department at the University of Ilorin, Nigeria.

Oluwole Adejare is a Professor of English at the University of Ife, Nigeria.

Tony E. Afejuku is a Senior Lecturer in English at the University of Benin, Nigeria. He specializes in Autobiography/Biography and a collection of his poetry is forthcoming.

Gabriel A. Ajadi is a Professor in the Department of Modern European Languages at the University of Ilorin, Nigeria.

F. Odun Balogun is a Professor of English at the University of Benin, Nigeria.

Michael Cosser is a lecturer in the Academic Staff Development Centre at the University of Witwatersrand, South Africa.

Benjamin J. Magura is a Senior Lecturer in English at the University of Botswana. His book, *The Sociology of English in Southern Africa,* is forthcoming, as well as a novel.

Ogo A. Ofuani is a Professor of English Language and Literature at the University of Benin, Nigeria. His specialty is the language of African literary texts, particularly East African poetry. His book, *Understanding Okot p'Bitek: His Life and Works,* is forthcoming.

Bertram A. Okolo is a Senior Lecturer in the Department of Linguistics and African Languages, University of Benin, Nigeria.

Taiwo Oloruntoba-Oju is a Professor in the Department of Modern Languages, University of Ilorin, Nigeria.

James O. Omole is a Professor in the Department of English and Literary Studies, University of Abuja, Nigeria.

Mabel Osakwe is a Professor in the English Department at Delta State University, Nigeria.

INDEX

Abiku, 81ff
Abrahams, Peter, 3, 16
ACE (American Colloquial English), 116
Achebe, Chinua, 41, 55, 149
   Arrow of God., 19, 30, 37, 42, 149
   Man of the People, A, 149
   No Longer at Ease, 149
Ackley, Donald, 72
Adejare, Oluwole, 19-20, 22, 24, 26, 28, 30, 32, 34, 36, 38, 149
Adewoye, Sam, 55
Adler, Max K., 149
Afejuku, Tony E., 3-4, 6, 8, 10, 12, 14, 16
Afolayan, A., 37
Ajadi, Gabriel A., 185-186, 188, 190, 192, 194, 196, 198, 200, 202
Ajeigbe, Olapade, 42, 55
Aldridge, M.V., 149
Aluko, T.M., 37
   One Man, One Wife, 20, 37
Amankulor, James Nduka, 149
American Colloquial English (ACE), 116
American English, 60, 62-63, 116, 128, 147, 233
Angogo, R., 286
Another Nigger Dead (lo Liyong), 229-230, 237, 243

Aristotle, 185-186, 188, 191, 254-255
Armah, A.K., 31, 37
Arnold, Stephen, 245, 248
Arrow of God. (Achebe), 37
Austin, John, 44, 55
Awonoor, K.
   This Earth, My Brother, 20, 37

Baba Sala (Moses Olaiya), 32
Bach, Kent, 55
Balogun, F. Odun, 246-247, 251-252, 254, 256, 258, 260, 262
Bamgbose, Ayo, 149, 202
Bantu (languages), 273-274, 277, 280
Barbag-Stoll, Anna, 149
base language, 122, 125-126
Bazell, C. E., 226
Beckett, Samuel, 146, 149, 152
   Waiting for Godot, 149
Beier, Ulli, 149, 202
Bell, Roger T., 150
Bergson, H., 167
Berry, M., 37
Bishop, M., 167
Black, Edwin, 202
Black English, 128, 233, 246, 248, 266, 275, 278, 283, 285, 287
Black English, South African, 275, 283
Blishen, Edward, 210, 226
Bowen, T.J., 150

Brown, Gillian, 150
Brown, H.D., 184
Buddha, 255
Buruga, Joseph, 243
C. C. T. A..(Symposium on Multilingualism), 150
Campbell, George., 185, 202
Castelvetro, 255
Catch 22 (Heller), 276
Catford, J.C., 37
Chatman, S., 111

Chinebuah, I. K., 286
Chinese, 114
Chinese, Cantonese, 114
Chinese, Mandarin, 114
Chinweizu, Jemine, 100
Chomsky, Noam, 226
Christ, Jesus, 93, 142
Clark, J. P., 81-82, 88, 100, 150
   Casualties, 90, 100
   Dirge, 90, 98, 100, 119-120, 137, 148
   Example of Shakespeare, The, 150
   Reed in the Tide, A, 82, 88, 100
Clark, John Pepper, 253
Cluett, R., 167
Coat, The (Fugard), 287
Cole, P., 168, 183
Collins, Terence, 226
Combat, The (Omotoso), 37
Conklin, Groff, 202
Conrad, Joseph, 59
   Under Western Eyes, 59
Corbett, Edward P. J, 202
Cosser, Michael, 113-114, 116, 118, 120, 122, 124, 126, 128, 130, 132, 134, 136, 138, 140, 142, 144, 146, 148, 150, 152
Crystal, David, 111, 150, 286
Cummings, E. E., 235, 246-247

Dahomey, 118
Dance of the Forests, A (Soyinka), 119, 152
Danish, 114
Dathorne, O.R., 55
Davidson, Alice, 183
Davidson, Basil, 150
Davison, Alice, 55
DeCamp, David, 150
Defoe, Daniel, 150
Dennis, Jamie, 150
DeStefano, Johanna S, 287
Deutsch, Babette, 150
Dillard, John, 246, 248
Dingome, Jeanne, 150
Dore, J., 183
Dorsey, David, 245, 248
Double Yoke (Emecheta), 30
Dukore, B.F., 167

Edet, R.N.., 150
Egejuru, Panuel A., 248
Egudu, Romanus, 16
Eliot, T.S. *Four Quartets*, 150
Ellis, Rod, 150
Emecheta, Buchi, 42, 55
   Double Yoke, 30
   Second Class Citizen, 30
Emenyonu, Ernest, 55
English, 11, 19-21, 23-27, 30, 32-38, 41-42, 45, 48-51, 54-69, 81, 86, 88, 94-95, 98, 100-101, 107, 110-111, 113, 115-117, 120, 123-126, 128-

129, 131-133, 135, 141, 146-152, 159-160, 168, 202, 208, 227-228, 231-233, 237-238, 241, 246-248, 253, 260, 262, 265-288
English, American, 60, 62-63, 116, 128, 147, 233
English, American Colloquial (ACE), 116
English, Black, 128, 233, 246, 248, 266, 275, 278, 283, 285, 287
English, Ghanaian, 274-275, 288
English, Kenyan, 274
English, Liturgical (LE), 115
English, Nigerian, 41-42, 45, 48-51, 54-56, 120, 124, 126, 129, 131-133, 141, 146-147, 149, 274-275
English, nonstandard, 58, 60-61, 125
English, Pidgin, 58, 60-61, 64-65, 117, 120, 124, 126, 129, 131-133, 141, 146-147, 149, 151
English, Simplified (SIME), 117
English, South African Black, 275, 283
English, Standard, 33-34, 60-61, 65, 98, 115, 260
English, West African Pidgin, 58, 60
Enkvist, Nils Erik, 111
Enright, D.J., 202
Esu, 96, 137
Example of Shakespeare, The (Clark, J.P.), 150

Fagbure, G., 150
Fagunwa, D.O., 185, 187, 189, 191, 193, 195, 197, 199, 201-202
 Ogboju, 185, 187-188, 194-197, 200-201
Fanagalo (pidgin), 148
Federman, Raymond, 253
Fickett, Joan G., 246, 248
Firth, John R., 287
Fixions (lo Liyong), 246-247, 262
Fodor, J.A., 287
Forest of Thousand Demons, The: A Hunter's Saga (Fagunwa), 202
Four Quartets. (T.S.Eliot), 150
Fowler, Roger, 55, 111, 150, 228
Frantz Fanon's Uneven Ribs (lo Liyong), 230, 245, 248
Freeman, Donald, 227
Freidberger, Heinz, 246, 248
French, Middle, 132
Fugard, Athol, 268, 287
 Boesman and Lena, 287
 Coat, The, 66, 287
 Island, The, 267, 285, 287
 Sizwe Bansi is Dead, 276, 287

Gatheru, R. Mugo, 3, 15, 17
Gathungu, Maina, 227
Ghanaian English, 274-275, 288
German, 61-62, 70, 72
Gibbs, James, 150
Gilliatt, Penelope, 150
Givón, T., 183
Gods are Not to Blame, The (Rotimi), 38
Goodwin, Ken L., 245, 248
Gordon, D., 184
Greenbaum, Sidney, 111
Gregory, Michael, 88, 227, 246,

248
Grice, H.P., 55, 168, 184
Gumperz, John, 72
Gurr, Andrew, 150
Gutwinski, W., 227

Hall, Robert A., Jr., 151
Halliday, M. A. K, 55, 88, 100-101, 111, 227, 287
Hancock, Ian F., 151
Handscombe, R. J., 223, 227
Harnish, Robert M., 55
Harrison. J. A., 246, 248
Haugen, Einar, 58, 72
Heine, Bernd, 151
Heller, Joseph, 276
    Catch 22, 276
Heringer, J., 55, 184
Hernandez, Edward, 72
Heron, G. A., 227
Heywood, Annemarie, 227
Heywood, Christopher, 202
Hill, Trevor, 151
Hodge, Bob, 150
Holmes, J., 152
Homer, 193, 234, 236
Horace, 255
Hymes, Dell, 151

Idanre (hills), 96, 104-105
"Idanre" and Other Poems
    (Soyinka), 84, 88, 101, 111
Igbo (language), 171
Igbo Olodumare *(The Forest of God)*, 198-199, 202
IL (interlanguage), 123
Ilorin (province), 118
In Corner b. Short Stories.
    (Mphahlele), 288
interlanguage (IL), 123

Interpreters, The (Soyinka), 57-59, 61, 63, 65, 67, 69, 71-73, 75, 77, 79
Irele, Abiola, 185, 202
Izevbaye, D.S., 151

Jakobson, Roman, 151
Jesus Christ, 93, 142
Jeyifo, Biodun, 55
Johnson, Samuel, 201-202
Jones, Eldred E., 245, 248
Joos, Martin, 287
"Journey" (Soyinka), 92
Judd, P., 151

Kachru, Braj B., 287
Kampeas, R, 167
Katrak, K, 151
Katz, J.J., 287
Kempson, R., 168
Kenyan English, 274
Kikuyu, 14
King, Adele, 16-17
Kirk-Green, Anthony, 287
Kleinecke, David, 151
Knight, Elizabeth, 246-248, 256, 261-262
Kongi's Harvest, 20, 30, 38
Kress, Gunther., 150
Kwa (languages), 21

Labov, William, 55, 151, 287
Labyrinths (Okigbo), 37
Lagos, 30, 37, 62, 70, 118, 125, 150, 202
Lakoff, G., 184
Lakoff, R., 184
Lance, Donald M., 72
language, base, 122, 125-126
language, target (TL), 123

INDEX | 295

Larsen, Stephan, 151
Larson, Charles, 31
Last Word, The (lo Liyong), 262
Late Latin, 132
Latin, 129, 132, 260
Latin, Late, 132
Lawrence, D.H., 59, 72
   Plumed Serpent, The, 59, 72
Laye, Camara, 3, 15-17
LeClair, Thomas, 253, 262
Leech, Geoffrey N., 227, 246, 248
Lerner, A.J., 151
   My Fair Lady, 135, 151
Levin, S.R., 246, 248
Levinson, S. C., 184
Lindfors, Bernth, 55, 245, 248
Lion and the Jewel, The, 19-20, 38
Liyong, Taban lo, 227, 229, 241, 243-248, 251, 253-255, 257, 259-262
Lodge, D., 168
   Small World, 162, 168
lo Liyong, Taban lo, 227, 229, 241, 243-248, 251, 253-255, 257, 259-262
   Another Nigger Dead, 229-235, 237-239, 241, 243-245, 247-249
   Fixions, 246-247, 256, 258, 262
   Frantz Fanon's Uneven Ribs, 229-235, 243, 245, 248
   Last Word, The, 91, 233, 246-247, 262
   Thirteen Offensives Against Our Enemies, 262
   Uniformed Man, The, 251-255, 257-262
Longinus, 8, 16-17

Loreto, Todd, 152
Luce, Stanford, 227
Lyons, John, 287

Macdonald, A.M., 226
MacIntosh, Angus, 227
Madmen and Specialists (Soyinka), 41, 49, 56
Mafeni, Bernard, 151
Magura, Benjamin, 265-266, 268, 270, 272, 274, 276, 278, 280, 282, 284, 286, 288
Marshment, Margaret, 227
Mawasha, Abram L., 288
Mbise, Ismael R., 245, 248
McDermott, R.P., 183
Middle French, 132
Molete, 104
Molière, 162
Moore, Gerald, 16-17, 151
Mphahlele, Ezekiel, 3, 15, 17, 288
   In Corner b. Short Stories, 288
Mühlhäusler, Peter, 151
Mungoshi, Charles L., 288
   Waiting for the Rain, 288
My Fair Lady (A.J.Lerner), 151

Nash, Ogden, 159
Nazareth, Peter, 258, 262
Nemser, W., 151
Nigeria, 15, 27, 30, 37, 41, 53-54, 61, 64-65, 67, 69, 78, 87, 100, 110, 118, 134, 144-145, 149, 157, 167, 183, 202, 225, 244, 246-247, 261
Nigeria, Western, 118
Nigerian English, 41-42, 45, 48-

51, 54-56, 120, 124, 126, 129, 131-133, 141, 146-147, 149, 274-275
Nigerian Pidgin English (NPE), 120, 133, 147
No Longer at Ease (Achebe), 149
Norwegian, 72, 114
NPE (Nigerian Pidgin English), 120, 147

Obalende, 64-65
Obatala (creation god), 96
Obiechina, Emmanuel, 16-17
Obilade, Tony, 151
Ochs, E., 183
Ofuani, Ogo A., 205-206, 208, 210, 212, 214, 216, 218, 220, 222, 224, 226-230, 232, 234, 236, 238, 240, 242, 244, 246, 248
Ogboju (Fagunwa), 185, 188, 195
Ogun (myth), 96
Ogunbiyi, Yemi, 202
Ogunbowale, P.O, 151
Ogunyemi, Chikwenye Okonjo, 227
Ojuka, Aloo, 228
Okigbo, C. *Labyrinths,* 37
Okolo, Bertram, 169-170, 172, 174, 176, 178, 180, 182, 184
Olabimitan, Afolabi, 202
Olatunji, O., 101
Omole, James O., 57-58, 60, 62, 64, 66, 68, 70, 72-74, 76, 78-79
One Man, One Wife (Aluko), 37
Omotosho, Kola, 55
  Combat, The, 19-20, 37
Orton, Joe, 116

Osa, 62, 64
Osakwe, Mabel, 81-82, 84, 86, 88-90, 92, 94, 96, 98, 100, 103-104, 106, 108, 110
Osgood, Charles, 288
Osundare, Niyi, 16-17, 73, 79, 225
Ọ̄yọ̄ (dialect), 118

Palm-Wine Drinkard, The (Tutuola), 38
p'Bitek, Okot, 205, 210, 225, 227-228, 243, 247
  Song of Lawino, 37, 208, 226, 228
  Song of Malaya, 211, 226-227
  Song of Ocol, 208, 226, 228
  Song of Prisoner, 205, 207-211, 213, 215, 217, 219, 221, 223, 225-228
  Two Songs, 210, 227-228
PE (Pidgin English), 117
pidgin, 44, 58, 60-61, 64-65, 117, 120-124, 126, 129, 131-134, 141, 146-151, 233
Pidgin English, 58, 60-61, 64-65, 117, 120, 124, 126, 129, 131-133, 141, 146-147, 149, 151
Pidgin, West African, 58, 60
Plaatje, Sol, 288
Plato, 254-255
Plumed Serpent, The (D.H. Lawrence), 72
Poe, Edgar Allan, 202
Portuguese, 123, 125, 132
Pratt, M. L., 72
Pratt, William., 202
Pride, J.B., 152

Probyn, Clive T, 152

Quirk, Randolph, 111

Rayfield, Joan R., 72
Received Pronunciation (RP), 71
Reed in the Tide, A (J.P.Clark), 82, 88, 100
Ride on the Whirlwind, A (Sepamula), 268
Riffaterre, Michael, 288
Road, The (Soyinka), 113, 115, 117-119, 121, 123, 125, 127, 129, 131-133, 135, 137, 139, 141, 143-145, 147, 149-151
Robin, L.D, 168
Roscoe, Adrian, 225, 228-229, 245, 248
Ross, A.S.C., 152
Rotimi, O., 38
    Gods are Not to Blame, The, 20, 38
RP (Received Pronunciation), 71
Russian, 59

Sadock, J. M., 184
Sala, Baba (Olaiya, Moses), 32
Schieffelin, B., 183
Scott, Jerrie, 150
SE (Standard English), 115
Searle, J. R., 184
Sebeok, T., 152, 288
Second Class Citizen (Emecheta), 30
Sekoni, 'Ropo, 152
Selinker, L., 152
Sepamula, Sipho, 288

Ride on the Whirlwind, A, 268
    Third Generation, 288
Sewall, Samuel, 161
Sey, K. A., 288
Shona (language), 277
Short, M. H., 72, 246, 248
Sidney, Sir Philip, 255
Silverman, K., 168
SIME (Simplified English), 117
Simplified English (SIME), 117
Sinclair, J. McH., 228
Sizwe Bansi is Dead (Fugard), 276
Small World (Lodge), 162, 168
Socrates, 255
Solarin, T, 152
Song of Lawino (p'Bitek, Okot), 228
Song of Malaya (p'Bitek, Okot), 227
Song of Prisoner (p'Bitek, Okot), 205, 227
Sotho, Northern, 279-281
South African Black English, 275, 283
Soyinka, Wole, 3, 15-16, 49, 56-57, 72-73, 79, 81, 84, 98, 111, 113-114, 146, 150-152, 158, 185, 202
    Collected Plays I., 147, 152
    Dance of the Forests, A, 119, 148, 152
    "Idanre" and Other Poems, 84, 88, 101, 111
    Interpreters, The, 19-20, 25, 38, 57-61, 63, 65, 67, 69, 71-75, 77, 79
    Madmen and Specialists, 41, 49, 51-53, 56
    Road, The, 92-93, 110, 113-

121, 123-127, 129-139, 141-152, 259
Shuttle in the Crypt, A, 101
Three Short Plays, 152
Trials of Brother Jero, The, 20, 38, 113
Spencer, John, 88, 111, 152, 287
Stampe, D. T., 184
Standard English (SE), 115
Strang, B. M. H., 288
Strevens, Peter, 287
Styan, J.L., 168
Svartvik, Jan, 111
Sukenick, Ronald, 252, 262
Swedish, 58, 114
target language (TL), 123

Teiresias, 255
Themba, Can, 288
   Will to Die, The., 196, 288
Third Generation (Sepamula), 288
Thomas, Dylan, 106, 244
TL (target language), 123
Traugott, Elizabeth Closs, 228
Trew, Tony, 150
Tsuchiya, Satoru, 245, 248
Tutuola, Amos, 37, 60, 72, 202
   Palm-Wine Drinkard, The, 19, 38
Two Songs (p'Bitek, Okot), 227

Udoeyop, No, 111
Ullmann, S., 288
Under Western Eyes (Conrad), 59
Uniformed Man, The (lo Liyong), 251, 253, 255, 257, 259, 261
Unoh, S.O., 56
Vanel, A., 184

Voice, The (Okara), 37
Waiting for Godot (Beckett), 149

Waiting for the Rain (Mungoshi), 288
Wangusa, Timothy, 229, 245, 248
Wanjala, Chris L., 227, 245, 249
Wardhaugh, R., 184
Warren, Austin, 16-17
Welsh, 113
Will to Die, The (Themba), 288
Wilson, John, 152
Wright, L.B., 168

Yankowitz, Susan, 152
Yiddish, 58
YOR (Yoruba), 117
Yoruba, 21-22, 24-26, 28, 32-35, 58, 60-63, 65-69, 74, 83, 85, 94, 96-97, 99, 101, 115, 117-119, 124, 137-138, 140, 144, 146-151, 157, 159, 185-187, 190-192, 197-198, 201-202
Young, P., 38, 88

Zulu, 273, 284